Hong Kong in Revolt

Hong Kong in Revolt

The Protest Movement and the Future of China

Au Loong-Yu

First published 2020 by Pluto Press
345 Archway Road, London N6 5AA

www.plutobooks.com

British Library Cataloguing in Publication Data
A catalogue record for this book is available from the British Library

ISBN   978 0 7453 4145 3   Hardback
ISBN   978 0 7453 4146 0   Paperback
ISBN   978 1 7868 0677 2   PDF eBook
ISBN   978 1 7868 0679 6   Kindle eBook
ISBN   978 1 7868 0678 9   EPUB eBook

This book is printed on paper suitable for recycling and made from fully managed and sustained forest sources. Logging, pulping and manufacturing processes are expected to conform to the environmental standards of the country of origin.

Typeset by Stanford DTP Services, Northampton, England

Simultaneously printed in the United Kingdom and United States of America

Contents

Acknowledgements

I would like to express my deep gratitude to Rachel Page, who read the whole manuscript and gave valuable advice. I would also like to thank Promise Li, Wong Hon Tung, and 'C.N.' for reading part of the manuscript and helping to improve it. Last but not least, I would like to thank the '1997 generation', who had both the sensitivity and the courage to stand up for the Hong Kong people and to claim back what is owed to them.

Preface

At the last stage of copy-editing this book, Beijing made another offensive against Hong Kong by tabling a draft bill intended to impose its will on the national security law of Hong Kong. This is no less than a statement pronouncing the death of Hong Kong's autonomy. This action has raised the already brewing China–US global contest to a new level. Upon advice from the editors, I have added a section on this issue in the final chapter. While I was writing it, a huge protest wave, in solidarity with George Floyd who was killed by the police, was sweeping across the US. The issue is much debated in both Hong Kong and mainland China. With all these new events breaking out one after the other, like it or not, the world will never be the same.

Au Loong-yu
5 June 2020
Hong Kong

Introduction

As I write these lines, the Chinese government in Beijing has launched a new round of offensives against Hong Kong's autonomy. On 17 April 2020, both Beijing's Hong Kong Liaison Office and Hong Kong and Macau Affairs Office (HKMAO) reinterpreted the Basic Law of Hong Kong and argued that they have the right to exercise supervision over Hong Kong's affairs, despite Article 22 of the Basic Law, which states the opposite. This is not just a war of words. The Liaison Office said what it did because it had already mounted a forceful attack on Dennis Kwok, the pan-democrat lawmaker, for obstructing the tabling of a bill criminalising disrespect of the Chinese national anthem. Kwok reminded Beijing that it is bound by Article 22. The two offices openly replied, 'no, we aren't'. On top of this, the Hong Kong government is widely believed to have acted under instruction from Beijing when it arrested fifteen of the most well-known pan-democrat politicians for 'illegal assembly' on 18 April 2020. Although the pan-democrat parties did not lead the 2019 Hong Kong Revolt – no party did – Beijing still considers them to be culprits in light of their sympathy with the protests. In general, these are acts of revenge for this revolt – the biggest ever in Hong Kong. Two million protesters took to the streets, a great political general strike took place, masked protesters repeatedly and intensively fought with the police, and eventually the Hong Kong and Beijing governments were humiliated and forced to withdraw the hated extradition bill (see Chapter 1).

In October 2019, when I first began seriously thinking about how to write this book, the movement had reached a critical juncture as the second and third general strike calls had failed to mobilise workers. Beijing and the Cathay Pacific airline had retaliated against the most militant sector of strikers, the aviation industry workers, by firing dozens of them. At that time, I wrote that it was unlikely that the next strike would be successful and that the movement might enter into decline after a period of stalemate. I did not expect that the failure to achieve another strike would be overcome by the brave young generation, who took on the government with even more intensive street fighting, culminating in the occupation of two major universities in Hong Kong, and followed by heavy clashes between occupiers and the riot police. The youth could not bear the pain of only having yet achieved one of their 'five demands', and so they continued to fight. They were eventually defeated. Yet this setback was again overcome by the overwhelming victory of the opposition in the ensuing District Council elections, followed by another million protesters taking to the streets for the New Year's Day march in 2020. This was the second time that Hong Kongers had successfully defeated Beijing's attempt to table a bill aimed at destroying their liberties and civil rights, after the 2003 protests that obviated the introduction of the National Security (Legislative Provisions) Bill by Beijing. Hong Kong is no longer just 'a goose that lays golden eggs'. For the first time its people have made the whole world listen, not as a goose, or what protesters themselves jokingly called *gong zyu* ('Hong Kong pigs', who only focus on making money and have no interest in participating in public affairs), but as millions of living, kicking human beings who aspire to freedom.

The local people called their protest the 'anti-China extradition bill movement'. Some considered the movement to be practically anti-China, or even anti-Chinese, while others thought that it was just anti-Chinese Communist Party (CCP). But let us not forget that the five demands, which include the demand for universal suffrage, were what unified millions of people in this great revolt. This is not to say that there were no anti-CCP or anti-China elements in the movement. My aim with this book is to reflect as much as possible on the hugely diverse and multi-faceted nature of this movement that lasted for seven months. I am not a neutral observer. I participated in the movement, yelling slogans and joining in civil disobedience, as I did in the 2014 Umbrella Movement. But I have tried to understand the different groups and currents without regard for my own position, because only in this way can one grasp the real dynamics of a movement and ask the right questions about it.

With the outbreak of the Covid-19 pandemic in Wuhan, and its spread to Hong Kong, the writing of this book became more difficult. I had to spend a great deal of time cleaning and stocking up on supplies. I had no idea that soon half of the world would be in the same predicament. With this outbreak, resentment against the Chinese government, or the

Chinese, or both, has become stronger, and has quickly gone beyond the city's limits. There is a similar logic behind both Beijing's attack on Hong Kong's autonomy and the regime's handling of the Covid-19 pandemic. It first manifested itself in the regime's contempt for the laws they themselves had made. In the first case it practically ignored the Basic Law of Hong Kong, in the second case the Wuhan authorities simply ignored the Law on the Prevention and Control of Infectious Diseases, which contributed to the spreading of the disease. Behind both important events one can identify the same logic of the Chinese bureaucracy, which combines in its hands state coercive power and the power of capital above all other classes, a bureaucracy which is simultaneously committed to industrialisation but also carries strong elements of premodern absolutism. It is a bureaucracy which learned a lot from its Western counterparts in terms of public administration, but it is also one which is permeated with the residues of a premodern political culture, the culture of imperial China. It was no accident that President Xi Jinping, in his report to the Nineteenth Party Congress, stressed 'passing on our red genes' in the great endeavour of making China's military strong.

These features give the CCP an incredible amount of power, but this necessarily entails all the evils of bureaucracy (with Chinese characteristics): rampant corruption, arrogance, bureaucratic red tape, dysfunction, the formation of cliques, and factional in-fighting, all of which promote tendencies like plundering public wealth, institutionalising degeneration, unnecessarily creating enemies, magnifying problems instead of solving them, keeping officials overloaded with entirely useless work, and making subordinate officials act in counterproductive ways. Both the revolt and the pandemic were necessary products of this monolithic party-state. Both proved that while this half-premodern but all-powerful bureaucracy could industrialise the country at lightning speed it was also increasingly difficult for it to face the challenges of the modernisation that it had created, not to mention those of highly integrated global capitalism. A brief discussion of this topic allows us to see through this apparently monolithic machinery and identify its internal divisions and contradictions, its strengths and its weaknesses.

With this perspective in mind, the 2019 revolt is even more significant. Beijing has always been deeply frustrated by the fact that Hong Kong is the sole city within its rule that remains politically defiant.

Whatever weaknesses the revolt displayed, it was nevertheless a great democratic movement of which common people were the heroes. Who taught these former *gong zyu* the value of democracy? It was none other than Beijing itself. With the pandemic, Beijing is also teaching its people the value of transparency and democracy as well. After the death of the doctor and whistleblower Li Wenliang, hundreds of thousands mourned him online and posted greetings to him. One Wuhan resident even dared to say the following:

> I hope people understand that . . . what they need is a government which protects the ultimate interest of each and every citizen. This ultimate interest is not just about property, but also about lives! If I am fortunate enough to live, I will no longer be concerned with the bullshit about the great revival of our nation! Nor about the dogs' fart of the Belt and Road [Initiative]! I won't even care . . . if Taiwan is independent or unified! In this crisis I just wish I could have rice to eat and clothes to wear . . . I am above all an individual, a living person! Sorry, I can't afford to love a government and a country which just allows me to rot in a moment of crisis![1]

SUMMARY

Chapter 1 provides an overview of the revolt by first explaining the extradition bill, followed by summarising the events of 2019 by dividing them into four major stages, so as to understand their dynamics. It then goes further to explore the three main components of the movement and its diversity in terms of political inclination.

Chapter 2 tries to present the main 'actors' who either helped to provoke the outbreak of the revolt or who were actual players within the movement, and how they, each in their own way, contributed to the protests. Through available surveys and analysis this chapter also traces the rise of what I called the '1997 generation', which constituted the backbone of the revolt.

Chapter 3 describes in more detail the most important protest or strike events, so that readers can have a glimpse of what happened on the ground, of what the protesters said and did, of how they sweated, bled, yelled, and fought.

Chapter 4 goes on to discuss the issues about the movement that I think are the most important. Some see it as a movement for freedom; others see it as right wing and racist, or as a movement of silly people manipulated by foreign imperialists. A lot of people, for instance, have found the waving of US flags and the posting of the 'alt-right' icon Pepe the Frog distasteful to say the least. But how did the protesters themselves, in their hundreds of thousands, interpret these aspects of the movement?

The final chapter sums up the themes of the previous chapters. Hong Kongers had been overly moderate for decades. They largely tacitly accepted their role as a goose that lays golden eggs, with no rights to universal suffrage, as long as London or Beijing treated them well by giving them free range, and not caging them. Yet a paranoid Beijing dragon so feared losing control of its goose that it began to harass it repeatedly, eventually leading it to resist. Where does Beijing's fear come from? Why did it act this way? Why has Beijing, since 2012, felt the need to change its policy over Hong Kong? Studying how the CCP bureaucracy reacted to both the revolt and the outbreak of the pandemic in Wuhan not only gives us some clues to the above questions, it also exposes the weakness of this mighty party-state.

Lastly, a word about *pin-yin*. Readers are familiar with Putonghua *pin-yin*, but not Cantonese. Since this was and is a Hong Kongers' revolt, all the slogans and language used are rendered in Cantonese. This book therefore carries a lot of Cantonese *pin-yin* as well. To differentiate the two, Putonghua is put within quotation marks, and Cantonese will be put in italics.

1

An Overview

One may say that the 2014 Umbrella Movement was a prelude to the 2019 revolt.[1] Not only because the former preceded the latter, but also for the fact that most of the elements of the former would have their full expression in the latter. Having a rough picture of the former thus is essential for understanding the latter.

One Country, Two Capitalist Systems

Hong Kong was once described as China's golden-egg-laying goose. When Deng Xiaoping met Margaret Thatcher in 1984 for the signing of the Sino-British Joint Declaration, which outlined the conditions of Hong Kong's handover to China, he said that Hong Kong's capitalist system would be preserved for fifty years because, with the help of Hong Kong, 'China hoped to approach the economic level of advanced countries by the end of that time'.[2]

The Joint Declaration was first and foremost a trade-off between the two countries: in exchange for the UK giving up Hong Kong to China, the UK (and the West in general) insisted that Hong Kong would continue to be treated as a separate customs territory in relation to China, and that under the 'one country, two systems' principle Western economic interests in Hong Kong would also be fully protected. Beijing's plan, on the other hand, was to strike a compromise for the moment but stage a counter-attack later.

Beijing has always insisted that mainland China remains 'socialist', while only Hong Kong is 'capitalist'. In essence, both are capitalist, although in ways that are quite different from each other. The former is a kind of state capitalism, while the latter is a form of laissez-faire capitalism. The two capitalisms complimented each other for a while:

while state capitalism protected China from predatorial global capitalism, Hong Kong's free port status allowed China's capitalism to 'walk on two legs' and gave Beijing a 'window' to the global market. With the help of Hong Kong (and Taiwan), Beijing has been hugely successful in engineering China's rise. Yet the asymmetry in size between the two sides determined that Hong Kong would gradually be integrated into 'Greater China'. Since the turn of the twenty-first century, China's supporters have been telling us that Hong Kong's importance to Beijing has been diminishing. This has the appearance of being true. Whereas in 1983 Hong Kong's GDP was 13.1 percent of China's, in 2013 it had fallen to 3 percent.[3] In light of this, Beijing's supporters have concluded that Hong Kong's usefulness to China is finished, and that the 'Hong Kong goose' should behave itself. Gradually Beijing began to impose an ever more hard-line policy in Hong Kong. It wants to keep Hong Kong's capitalism but not its autonomy and its political liberties.

That is why, when Beijing designed the Basic Law in 1990, it included Article 23 on national security, which aims at restricting the city's political liberties and requires the HKSAR (Hong Kong Special Administrative Region) government to enact local laws accordingly. In 2003, Beijing tried to push through a bill on Article 23 (whose purpose was to 'prohibit any act of treason, secession, sedition, or subversion against the Central People's Government, and to prohibit local organisations from establishing ties with foreign political organisations'), but was defeated by a big protest in which 500,000 people took to the streets.

The Basic Law did vaguely promise that universal suffrage would be implemented step by step after 1997, but with no explicit timeline. Furthermore, it only stipulated the arrangements for the elections of both the chief executive (CE) and the Legislative Council (LegCo) in the first ten years after the handover. Hence, after 2007, the arrangements for the CE and LegCo 'elections' have had to be promulgated by Beijing anew.

The local liberals (not to be confused with the Liberal Party, a business-class party), also known as the 'pan-democrats', have benefited from this partial form of direct election. Their agenda has always been to work within the constraints of the Basic Law to achieve the expansion of direct elections. We shall see how the liberals' plan has been shattered to pieces since 2012, when Xi Jinping took power in China.

The Rise of a New Generation

Ten years before the Umbrella Movement in 2014 there were already signs of a new generation in Hong Kong with very different perspectives and expectations – social and political – when compared to previous generations. It was the collision between Beijing's policies and Hong Kong's new generation which gave rise to the Umbrella Movement.

In general, Hong Kongers, including the young, have tended to be apolitical and conservative. The 1997–8 Asian economic crisis marked the beginning of a new period, when thousands of civil servants came out to the street to protest privatisation. The protests coinciding with the 2005 World Trade Organization Ministerial Meeting in Hong Kong, especially the radical actions of a group of South Korean farmers, inspired many young people. From then on, one witnessed a continuous radicalisation of the youth. The founding of the League of Social Democrats (LSD) in 2006 drew support from a thin layer of young Hong Kongers. This was followed by the 2007 Defence of the Queen's Pier campaign, a conservationist movement, which drew hundreds of young activists. In 2009 the Hong Kong government approved the Vibrant Express high-speed rail project to promote even closer integration between Guangdong and Hong Kong; this was followed by the Moral and National Education Project designed to promote 'patriotism' in education in Hong Kong. These developments were met with immediate resistance from young Hong Kongers, first in 2010 and then in 2012. The 2012 protests were more of a success because of a greater level of civil disobedience, signalling that a young, radical generation had finally arrived on the scene and were prepared to take over leadership from the pan-democrats for a new round of struggle.

Meanwhile, Beijing began to target the culture and language of Hong Kong. Prior to this, Hong Kongers had never made an issue of their mother tongue. Beginning in 2008, the Hong Kong government began to promote the replacement of Cantonese with Putonghua as a teaching medium in the city. This angered local people, especially since they had witnessed what had happened to the people of nearby Guangzhou city in China. For more than two decades the CCP has been pushing a campaign to 'promote Putonghua and abolish Cantonese' in Guangzhou, not only in schools but also in radio and television broadcasting, resulting in the young generation no longer being able to speak their mother tongue.

Eventually this triggered a 'defend Cantonese movement' in Hong Kong and a protest on 25 July 2010.[4] It died out with the increasing repression since 2012. Hong Kong people saw their future in this case and therefore resisted the policy of replacing Cantonese with Putonghua. Forced assimilation over language is always a sign of colonisation. But even the British colonial government never attempted to eliminate Cantonese from schools, let alone the media.

Occupy Central

In 2014, Beijing began to roll out a package of reforms targeting the upcoming 2017 CE election. In exchange for granting universal suffrage in the election, Beijing would retain complete control over the nomination of candidates, to the extent that even moderate liberals would stand no chance of election. This so-called '31 August 2014 decision' was met with widespread discontent in Hong Kong, to the extent that it antagonised even the pan-democrat parties. But it first and foremost angered the youth. The stage was set for a confrontation between Beijing and a young generation of Hong Kongers. The HKFS (Hong Kong Federation of Students) and Scholarism were the two main student organisations which took bold actions that triggered off the Umbrella Movement in September 2014.

There was a prequel to the Umbrella Movement. In March 2013, two well-known academics, Dr Benny Tai and Dr Chan Kin-man, along with Reverend Chu Yiu-ming (whom I collectively call the 'occupation trio') proposed the Occupy Central with Love and Peace (OCLP) movement, whose main purpose was to conduct a civil disobedience action the following year to demand genuine universal suffrage.

It was the occupation trio, not the pan-democrats, which initiated the occupation appeal, showing the latter's increasing irrelevance as a force for social change. After years of participation in elections for a semi-legitimate representative government in Hong Kong, the pan-democrats had become increasingly conservative. They usually won one-third of the seats on the LegCo through winning 55–60 percent of the vote in the direct elections. This should not lead us to believe that they ever possessed organisational strength, however (though this weakness on the part of political parties is also shared by civil society in general, for instance the trade unions). Fragmented into pieces, even the largest party, the Democratic Party, claimed to have only seven hundred members, and even fewer active members.[5] The liberals believed Beijing's promise of universal suffrage for so long that they were among the last to realise that it was wishful thinking.

But the occupation trio's credibility quickly eroded due to their unwillingness to go ahead with their plan for the occupation. This compelled the HKFS to go ahead with their own plan to occupy the downtown Central district of Hong Kong Island on 2 July 2014, during which 511 protesters were arrested but not charged. The occupation trio and the pan-democrats refused to take part in this event and were deeply discredited as a result. Angered by Beijing's 31 August decision, the occupation trio did later plan to hold a three-day occupation starting on the National Day of the PRC, 1 October.[6] But the students were sceptical of their call to action. Again, it was the HKFS who took the initiative and launched a one-week class boycott on 22 September. The movement began to gather momentum.

During the class boycott, the HKFS and Scholarism decided to stage a rally on 26 September, outside of Civic Square, where the Hong Kong government headquarters is located. During the night, they suddenly occupied the square with around one hundred supporters. They were arrested the next day. Yet when the news spread, more than 50,000 citizens came to the scene to protest the arrest. They were met with tear gas, but they refused to give up the streets to the police. It was named the Umbrella Movement because the protesters held up umbrellas to protect themselves from the tear gas. On 28 September hundreds of thousands of protesters came back again. Many joined for the first time because they were angry at the arrests of students and for the firing of tear gas at the protesters the previous afternoon. At this time, the movement moved beyond the range of the students, and evolved into a movement of the middle and lower classes. The occupation even far exceeded the imagination of the HKFS. Similar occupations occurred in the areas of Mong Kok and Causeway Bay as well.

The Failed Strike

On the day of the class boycott on 22 September, twenty-five trade unions and civil society groups issued a joint statement accusing the existing political system of 'repressing the demands of grassroots labour and making the potential to improve people's livelihoods more difficult'. The statement not only called for universal suffrage but the implementation of standard working hours and a universal pension as well.[7] Then, after 28 September, the Hong Kong Confederation of Trade Unions (HKCTU) called a general strike (social workers had already gone on strike earlier in September). The result was that only one and a half unions – the Swire Beverage Employees General Union and the Hong Kong Professional Teachers' Union (HKPTU) – responded to the call (by 'half' I mean that the HKPTU was only half-hearted in its support of a general strike). It was a pity that although a large number of workers came out and took part in the occupation, the majority were not prepared to go on strike.

The Xenophobic 'Localists'

Soon after the Umbrella Movement began, some 'localists' began to mount attacks on the so-called 'left pricks'. Eventually the localists would emerge as the major beneficiaries of the Umbrella Movement.

The Western media tends to view the Hong Kong localists in a positive way, as democratic fighters against Beijing. Yet the picture is far more complicated. Before the Chinese term 'localism' entered into use among social activists and academics there had already been a visible new trend toward localism since the turn of the century, with the rise of conservationists chiefly concerned with preserving old architecture and streets. Eventually this unfolded into the above-mentioned Defence of the Queen's Pier campaign in 2007. Although defeated, the campaign greatly promoted the idea of localism, which reflected at least two distinct discourses: 1) resisting government redevelopment plans, which were seen as destructive to local culture and collective memory; 2) resisting cross-border infrastructure projects involving mainland China so as to protect local autonomy, for instance the 2009–10 protests against the high-speed train project. However, it was the right wing of these very mixed localist discourses which eventually grew bigger. While the term 'localist' refers to a broad current in Hong Kong society which emphasises local values, terms like 'nativist' and 'xenophobic localists' were also used to describe a more specific group of clearly right-wing and anti-immigrant localists. Their spokespersons were Raymond Wong and the scholar Chin Wan-kan (or Chin Wan). Together with

Raymond Wong's apprentice, Wong Yeung-tat, they constituted a 'xenophobic trio', and were nicknamed 'two Wong and one Chin'. Each had their own organisations, however. Their followers' actions in the occupation area included:

- Silencing the voices of other democrats
- Inciting the masses to achieve their goals
- Making use of violence or the threat of violence
- Making racist statements about Chinese people, calling them 'locusts' which should be ousted
- Attacking mainland Chinese immigrants in Hong Kong, accusing them of stealing welfare from the government

The nativists put out stickers with the words *mat seon zo gaau, tai fong saan seoi* ('don't trust the left pricks, be vigilant against any call of disbandment'), which mainly targeted the HKFS and well-known activists who took part in the occupation, and who were allegedly guilty of empty talk while secretly wanting to disband the occupation. Yet the attack itself was nonsense. Their slander aimed to discredit the democratic forces within the movement by hinting that they were somehow associated with Beijing.

They also attacked organisations which hoisted flags or hosted open street forums; followed by harassing picketers from these organisations. On 12 October, on the call of Chin Wan, the nativists went to Mong Kok to disrupt the HKFS street forum.

The xenophobic trio's agitation against the democratic forces was packaged in terms of their being more radical than them. Their slogan was 'the HKFS does not represent us'. Their line of argument was that 'since the Hong Kong government does not represent us neither does the HKFS, or anyone else', and accordingly they opposed all signs and symbols of leadership or political representation: stages, flags, speakers, an assembly, voting, and so on; summed up in the slogan of *caak daai toi*, or 'dismantle the big stage'. They put this into practice whenever the HKFS held a discussion forum with a stage. Their accusation against the HKFS was surely nonsense. The HKFS never claimed to represent everyone, and the forums that they organised did not reject pluralism.

The xenophobic trio could not mobilise more than a hundred people at its height, while the democratic parties and social movement organisations were far larger in number. The xenophobic trio was successful only because the democratic forces were totally unprepared.

The occupation of three main streets, with one of them adjacent to the government headquarters, lasted for 79 days. The movement was eventually defeated and this was followed by a period of reaction. Yet it is still memorable because it was simultaneously: 1) the first radical movement of civil disobedience in the thirty years of the Hong Kong democratic movement; 2) daring enough to stand up to Beijing to demand more political rights than the Hong Kong liberals dared to ask for, and more than Beijing was prepared to give; 3) a locally initiated democratic movement with massive support.

FIVE YEARS OF REACTION

Hong Kong emerged from the Umbrella Movement as a deeply divided city. The divide encompasses two main camps: the yellow camp, who are pro-Umbrella Movement, and the blue camp, who oppose it.

On top of this was that Beijing, through the Hong Kong government, now took frontal attack on Hong Kong's autonomy and its opposition parties by:

- Prosecuting the student leaders of the HKFS and the occupation trio
- Disqualifying eight pan-democrat and localist lawmakers
- Enacting direct intervention on every level of elections in Hong Kong, especially the CE election
- Abducting Hong Kong-based publishers who put out books on China, and specifically on Xi Jinping's private life (the 'Causeway Bay Books disappearances' case)

Making things worse was that the nativists now continued their offensive not against Beijing but against the HKFS. The small groups of xenophobic localist students in different universities immediately initiated a *teoi lyun*, a campaign to call for the withdrawal of their respective students' unions from the HKFS through a student referendum. To justify their attack on the HKFS they now put all the blame for the failure of the Umbrella Movement on the latter. Eventually the four most important students' unions withdrew and dealt a heavy blow to the HKFS. The once passionate youth now descended into passivity. If Beijing had not tried to table the extradition bill there might not have been the 2019 revolt.

THE BILL THAT TARGETS EVERYONE

In early 2018, Chan Tong-kai, a young Hong Kong resident, killed his girlfriend Poon Hiu-wing in Taiwan, before returning to Hong Kong. There is no extradition agreement between Hong Kong and Taiwan, and the pro-Beijing parties pushed for a change to the extradition law in early 2019 so as 'to bring justice to Poon'. This was unconvincing from the start: local legal experts have repeatedly stressed that the extradition of Chan to Taiwan would not require a bill which includes an extradition agreement with mainland China.

On 12 February 2019, the Hong Kong government tabled the Fugitive Offenders and Mutual Legal Assistance in Criminal Matters Legislation (Amendment) Bill 2019 – commonly known as the extradition bill. Hong Kong has extradition agreements with twenty countries, including the UK and the US, but not with mainland China. The pro-Beijing camp, in Hong Kong and overseas, argued that since Hong Kong has extradition agreements with the West, why could it not have an agreement with mainland China? The issue is with the Chinese legal system. China is not only disdainful of the basic due process of law but also of judicial independence. China's court system has a near-100 percent conviction rate, while Hong Kong conviction rates in 2017 were 53.4 percent in Magistrates' Court, 69.2 percent in District Court, and 65.3 percent in The Court of First Instance.[8] This reflects the non-independent nature of the judiciary in China. When the extradition bill was first tabled, the pro-Beijing camp fiercely defended it. The opposing camp responded by half-jokingly suggesting that the bill would allow those faced with extradition the choice to be tried either by the Hong Kong courts under British common law or by the mainland courts under Chinese law. Despite their patriotic rhetoric, even the pro-Beijing parties would not opt to be tried by the Chinese courts. This distrust of the Chinese legal system is tacitly recognised by Beijing and codified in Article 8 of the Basic Law, which stipulates that 'the laws previously in force in Hong Kong . . . shall be maintained', which means that Hong Kong is insulated from China's legal system. Without this insulation there is no such thing as Hong Kong autonomy or 'one country, two systems'. If China's legal system improved significantly then it would be possible to discuss an extradition agreement with China. But in reality it has gone from bad to worse.

There are people within and outside of China who have argued that the bill's sole purpose was to send wealthy mainland Chinese who are wanted for corruption back to the mainland to be prosecuted. If this was the case, then the bill should have targeted only mainland Chinese (although that is not what this author would argue for). Since the wording of the bill was that 'anyone' in Hong Kong would be subject to extradition, not just corrupt, rich mainland people, it implied that the bill could also target both Hong Kong citizens and foreigners alike. It was a bill which potentially targeted everyone, which is why it was met with great hostility at home and abroad. Actually, one pro-Beijing newspaper in Hong Kong reported on a certain mainland authority's interpretation – commonly believed to be the vice-premier, Han Zheng – which explicitly included 'Hong Kong residents' and 'foreigners' as the groups targeted by the bill.[9] When confronted by Hong Kong lawmakers as to whether the bill could also target foreign visitors who happened to be in Hong Kong, Secretary for Security John Lee Ka-chiu simply evaded the question.[10] It is a reasonable assumption that Beijing's actions were meant to retaliate against the US for the latter's pressuring of Canada to arrest Meng Wanzhou, CFO of Huawei. The US Department of State and the European Parliament released statements criticising the bill on 10 June and 18 July, respectively. Germany had already warned that the bill was concerning to the German business community who invested in Hong Kong, and that this might prompt Germany to nullify the extradition agreement between Germany and Hong Kong.[11]

The most ironic aspect of the issue was that it was the local business class who felt betrayed by Beijing. *Mingpao* reported that the business class worried about the bill as much as the pan-democrats did, because many of the early transactions which earned them their first buckets of gold in mainland China were 'shady deals' and could become easy targets for Chinese prosecutors.[12] Their representatives successfully lobbied Beijing to water down the bill by exempting nine categories of commercial crimes from extradition. This was not very satisfying to the business class, because Beijing could still extradite any of them using other pretexts. But their political representatives dared not push further, until the democratic camp, with young people as its radical wing, began to rally over a million people to the streets. Now the stage was set for a great revolt. Only at this moment did the former head of the Liberal Party, James Tien, feel emboldened enough to call for his party to support the shelving of the bill.

THE FOUR STAGES OF THE MOVEMENT

While the Umbrella Movement was an offensive movement because it demanded universal suffrage, the 2019 revolt began with a defensive aim: demanding that the government withdraw the extradition bill. Indeed, the movement was first called the anti-extradition bill movement. We can roughly divide the movement into four stages, and through this we will see how it evolved far beyond its original target and became a major revolt.

1. The Prelude (February to May)

On 12 February, Chief Executive Carrie Lam's administration first proposed the extradition bill. Pan-democrat legislators were quick to voice their opposition to it. On 31 March, the Civil Human Rights Front (a front of more than fifty organisations, most of them civil associations and trade unions, hereafter, the 'Civil Front') hosted its first rally, claiming 12,000 participants. After a month of education and agitation, the next rally on 28 April increased tenfold in size. Without this preparation it would not have been possible to wake up the yellow camp or the young generation – they were still largely demoralised after the defeat in 2014. This is to the credit of the pan-democrats and the Civil Front who came out to oppose the bill, but it was also obvious that they were not optimistic about their fight.

2. Taking Off (June and July)

On 6 June more than two thousand lawyers and legal professionals took to the streets in silent protest against the bill. Little were they aware that in three days, on 9 June, one million people would heed the call of the Civil Front and take to the streets. Equally important, the day also brought back the youth. The number of participants came close to that of the movement that had emerged in solidarity with China's democratic struggle in 1989. The Centre for Communication and Public Opinion Survey (CCPOS) found that on 9 June protesters under 29 years old accounted for 42.8 percent of the total.[13] The young protesters were coming back en masse. The unexpected turnout encouraged everyone, first and foremost the young. The latter came back to the stage again on 12 June to besiege the LegCo building to stop the tabling of the bill (although by then the speaker had already postponed the meeting). This time it was chiefly their show. The same CCPOS survey showed that 68.4 percent of the siege participants were below 29 years old (see below). They tried to charge through the police barricades but were driven back with tear gas and rubber bullets, one of which blinded a teacher. Commonly, the yellow camp had never been supporters of physical clashes with police. Carrie Lam probably counted on this. The next day, however, it was obvious that the public was on the protesters' side. Many people were angry about the police violence and the official characterisation of the '6.12' action as a 'riot'. This was also the time when the movement began to raise its second demand: to stop labelling protesters as 'rioters'.

Carrie Lam felt the heat of the furious public and on 15 June she conceded by announcing that the extradition bill would be temporarily suspended. The next day two million people took to the streets, in effect telling Lam they wanted the bill gone for good, and that they were ready to tolerate low-intensity violence from the radical youth. Their reasoning went as follows: now that both Lam and her police force had become the puppets of Beijing and had violently cracked down on the people, wasn't it logical and worth supporting when the young people, on their behalf, hit back at them? This strong sympathy again reasserted itself very soon after, when the radical youth broke into the LegCo building on 1 July and as Lam continued to refuse to have dialogue with the protesters. The 'Yuen Long incident' on 21 July, where members of organised crime syndicates, with the tacit consent of the police, attacked train passengers whom they believed to be protesters, hardened the yellow camp's support for radical actions against the government. Now they thought that the young people were right from the very beginning when they repeatedly sent out warnings that Hong Kong was dying and that drastic measures had to be taken.

On the night of 21 June, radical youths went to the Liaison Office to spray graffiti on its wall. Some painted the derogative term for Chinese,

Zi-naa, which Beijing would make use of in depicting the whole movement as anti-Chinese.

Lam had become the most hated person in the city, but the people's consciousness now rose to a level where they were no longer satisfied with the pan-democrats' call for her resignation. Having subsided after the defeat of the Umbrella Movement, the call for universal suffrage was increasingly raised again. From that moment onwards, the movement evolved from being defensive to one which was more offensive. When July ended, the movement had evolved far beyond its two demands of early June, adding another three to make up its 'five demands':

- Withdraw the extradition bill
- Stop labelling protesters as 'rioters'
- Drop charges against protesters
- Conduct an independent inquiry into police behaviour
- Implement genuine universal suffrage for both the LegCo and the CE elections

It was these five demands, not the call for independence, as Beijing claimed, which united millions of people. In fact, a random telephone survey in October 2019 showed that only 11 percent of the population was for independence from China while 83 percent opposed it.[14] In contrast the five demands had won the support of the vast majority of the population by the end of 2019.[15]

With the advance of the movement, even Carrie Lam's 'sincere apology' on 18 June and her further announcement that 'the bill is dead' on 2 July could no longer satisfy the protesters.

3. The Climax (August and September)

These two months saw the greatest number of big protests. A report by the Hong Kong Public Opinion Research Institute found that there were only 4 and 7 protests involving more than ten thousand people in June and July, respectively, while there were 22 and 9 in August and September, respectively. In terms of protests involving between 100 and 10,000 people, while in June and July these only numbered in the single digits, in August there were 19 and in September there were 46.[16] (The report only recorded data until 22 October, but judging from other sources it is unlikely that the number of protests between October and December exceeded those during August and September.)

On top of these statistics, there was also one single event which defined this period: the political strike. Back in the middle of June, the young had already called for *saam baa* ('three suspensions') – a strike, a class boycott, and a shut-down of shops. This had however been unsuccessful.

On 5 August, for the first time in many decades, there was a successful political and general strike. The HKCTU estimated that 350,000 workers took part in the strike, and mass meetings were convened in seven districts. One sector of the Hong Kong economy defined the strike movement: the airport and airline industry employees, which half-paralysed the city's international flights. On 12 August, there were huge occupations of the airport.

The last week of August was busy with preparations for the class boycott and general strike on 2 September. On 31 August, a Saturday, there were protests in Kowloon as usual, and some went to the Prince Edward station of the Hong Kong Mass Transit Railway (MTR). The police followed and attacked passengers inside without announcing what crime had been committed. A lot of people were severely injured. Hearsay began to spread that the police had killed someone. The fact that the police had sealed off the station after their action and that the MTR Corporation refused to release all the video records made many people believe that this story was true. This would become one of the watershed moments in stimulating more anger from the yellow camp. Meanwhile, it was enough to encourage further radicalisation on the last day of August, and protesters agitated for another round of 'three suspension' when September arrived.

The airport was occupied again on 1 September and was paralysed. The next day schools started again but both university and high school students decided to greet their new semester with a class boycott. All ten universities and more than two hundred high schools had students on the streets. Seeing no sign of the movement receding, Carrie Lam finally announced her decision to withdraw the bill on 4 September. It was too late. This failed to appease the protesters. Instead the latter began to revise their five demands to 'five demands, not one less'. From that moment onward, the movement also evolved from being an 'anti-extradition bill' movement into the 'great battle to defend Hong Kong's autonomy'.

The 2 and 3 September strike call was not very successful, however, as working people and the unions feared retaliation from Beijing. The latter had already shown its claws after the 5 August strike by first forcing the resignation of Cathay Pacific's chief executive officer, followed by its chairman, John Slosar. The new management soon fired the chairperson of its employees' union and more than thirty employees. Both the students and the unions could find no way to protect strikers from dismissal. Also because of the police ban on demonstrations, there was less of a chance that the so-called *cin wong* ('light yellow') camp would come out to the streets in great numbers. This was to some extent compensated by the high tide of the student movement, heartily supported by hundreds of thousands of *sam wong* ('dark yellow') supporters. (These two terms had been in use since the movement started. While 'light yellow' protesters were likely to be non-violent, the 'dark yellow' protesters were either tolerant of, or practitioners of, physical resistance to police violence.)

Even if the September strike was not very successful, two new developments, for the moment at least, compensated for the unfavourable situation of the strikers. The early-September class boycott was very successful. Along with college students, even high school students organised and boycotted classes. The latter had come out to the streets in the preceding months, but the summer holiday had made their organising impossible. It only became possible when schools restarted in September, and from then on high school students constituted one of the most important components of the movement.

The second new development was that the movement was broadening to the community level. There were community actions in the first stage, and the core activity was the making of the 'Lennon Walls' – first invented during the Umbrella Movement (and probably inspired by the original in Prague). People posted colourful notes to express their aspirations for the democratic change that was under way. In July this spread like wildfire. Following the great strike, polarisation between the blue and yellow camps now reached a red-hot level. Not only did the police tear down posters which targeted them, but the blue camp also now confronted the yellow camp and sometimes assaulted them around the Lennon Walls in different districts. This escalating confrontation led to the broadening of the movement to the community level, as the yellow neighbourhoods would always be on guard to protect the young people. According to one college student activist, 'C.N', in all eighteen districts of Hong Kong, there were corresponding Telegram channels for exchange of information among yellow neighbourhoods. The group around the channels for Tin Shui Wai and Wong Tai Sin were the strongest; 'if any young guy was being harassed by police within five minutes there would be two hundred neighbours coming down to the street to help'.[17]

A second issue was that since September the police were less and less likely to approve demonstrations in busy areas. As a result, many more local-level actions took place. When the police came and teargassed the demonstrators this always affected the neighbourhood as well, and so the angry residents would come out to confront the police; and when the police tried to break into residential buildings without a warrant, they rushed out to try to stop them. Many 'light blue' people evolved into being neutral or even 'light yellow' because of this (see below).

4. A Stalemate (October to December)

From October onwards, the movement entered its fourth stage, which I will describe as a deadlock situation. On the one hand, while the government was able to suppress protest actions, it was unable to suppress the movement as a whole. On the other hand, the movement was in a bottleneck as it found it hard to mobilise a labour strike again, and in the face of the government continuing to resort to banning demonstrations altogether the movement increasingly found it difficult to draw the same numbers of protesters again after the big illegal march on 20 October. Although whenever there was a chance for legal marches the masses' enthusiasm was still high, as was shown by the 800,000 marchers that took to the streets on 8 December.

On 11 November there was another strike call, but it was once again unsuccessful. The class boycott was more successful, and this evolved into fighting between the students and the police between 11 and 14 November at the Chinese University of Hong Kong (CUHK), drawing thousands of young people to come to occupy the campus and its surrounding main roads and railway. This was because many students from other universities or other members of the public also flocked there to help and made the resistance to the police attack on the night of 12 November possible.

However, the lack of organisation and coordinating bodies within the occupation magnified the differences over tactics between CUHK students and those from outside the campus. The former were angry over some outside students' reckless behaviour (destroying facilities). Eventually, the management of the university closed the whole campus down on 15 November, and the occupation ended. Yet just when the big show at CUHK was over, the students at Hong Kong Polytechnic University (PolyU) took over their campus, and on 16 November they practically stopped all traffic in a nearby tunnel which connects Hong Kong Island and Kowloon. The police then besieged the campus for twelve days until most of the occupants either ran away, were arrested, or surrendered themselves.

During the two great actions at the universities there was a third strike call, but it was not very successful either. It was true that many people could not get to work, but this was not because they were striking but because the students, through occupying campuses and the surrounding main roads and railways, practically paralysed half of Hong Kong's busiest area. But these were actions that common folks with a job could not join or were not ready to join. Increasingly there was now a danger of the narrowing of the mass base for radical actions.

Although the radical youth still enjoyed popular support, most of the yellow camp were still reluctant to either go on strike or to fight with the police. If that had happened, then a revolutionary situation might have set in. Increasingly it was clear that this was not happening. The common protesters should not be blamed for a lack of bravery; the asymmetry of forces between Hong Kong and the Chinese state would make any sensible person rethink the idea of a revolution within one city. Hong Kong could only win if mainland China was also ready for a mass upheaval. Yet, this was not in sight.

On the other hand, there were also signs that the support for the five demands of the movement was broadening as well. The defeat of the occupation at the two universities was soon compensated by the landslide victory of the opposition in the 24 November District Council elections. The people's voice was a clear and loud 'no' to Beijing's hardline policy.

In general, the party-political opposition to Beijing in Hong Kong (consisting of the pan-democrats and the 'localists' or 'radical democrats') has enjoyed 55–60 percent support in the LegCo elections, but in District Council elections this had previously dropped to 40 percent. However, in the 2019 elections the opposition garnered 57 percent of the vote (or 1.67 million votes) as opposed to the pro-Beijing parties' 41 percent. This was surely a big victory. In terms of seats, it was an even bigger victory. The opposition won 388 seats in total, an increase of 263 seats, while pro-Beijing parties lost 240 seats and were only able to retain 59 seats. The popularity of the yellow camp, despite the record of violence on their side, was already evident in a November poll before the election: 83 percent of the population laid the blame for violence at the door of the government, while only 40 percent thought that it was also the protesters' responsibility (the two questions were asked separately and were not exclusive of each other).[18] In relation to the three main demands of the movement, a late-September survey showed that they had the support of 80 percent of the interviewees.[19] There was fluctuation over the support rate between June and December, but different surveys showed that the movement's main demands had the support of 70–80 percent of the interviewees. In contrast, after the end of the Umbrella Movement, 33.9 percent of interviewees supported the occupation.[20] In terms of mass base, the 2019 revolt had witnessed a great advance.

The District Council elections were a second major victory, on top of the first, when Carrie Lam withdrew the extradition bill. With these, the great revolt will go down in history as a major achievement for the people, even if it was only a partial victory. In contrast to the defeat of the Umbrella Movement in 2014, which resulted in a long demoralisation, the 2019 revolt will surely continue to encourage activism, even if there will certainly be ups and downs.

Meanwhile, there have been more and more young activists who have realised the importance of labour struggle and who are now calling for joining unions or forming new ones. This was also a response to the traditional unions which were slow in reacting in such a period of turmoil, although credit is due to the CTU for their support for the 5 August strike. Without this strike, it would not have been possible to prove to Hong Kongers the relevance of labour, and to attract a new generation of labour supporters. At the end of December, forty new unions were being formed. At the top of the list is the Hospital Authority Employee Alliance (HAEA), which claims to have recruited one-quarter of the total employees of the Hong Kong Hospital Authority. Thus the 2019 revolt began with great spontaneity, but when it was close to its end its participants became more and more active in organising unions. What a great change indeed.

By December it was clear that neither side of this great contest between the government and the people could decisively win. With more than seven thousand people arrested, a great blow was dealt to the vanguard of the youth, the 'braves' (see below and Chapter 2), and the intensity of radical actions was greatly reduced. Among activists a growing consensus was that the struggle for the five demands was going to be a long-term one.

Also noticeable was that, following the intensification of the social conflict, the slogan at the beginning of the movement, *Hoeng gong jan gaa jau!* ('Hong Kongers, hang in there!'), soon evolved into *Hoeng gong jan faan kong!* ('Hong Kongers, resist!') after Carrie Lam introduced the anti-mask law on 4 October, and further escalated to *Hoeng gong jan bou sau!* ('Hong Kongers, revenge!') after the death of the student Chow Tsz-lok (resulting from his mysterious fall from a height during a protest on 8 November). This anger explained why, even when 2019 drew to an end and radical actions declined significantly, a survey showed that among the 800,000 peaceful protesters on New Year's Day 2020, 55.6 percent still expected an escalation of their actions in the coming period.[21] And towards early December there was a lot of hearsay about certain radical protesters making bombs and buying guns from overseas. Some of them, so it was said, had access to dynamite from the movie-making community. Within a few weeks, the police had made numerous arrests of these 'terrorists'.

About this time, at the end of 2019, the earlier idea of a 'yellow economic circle' began to gather momentum. This was essentially a consumer campaign which encouraged supporters of the yellow camp to buy from 'yellow' shops while continuing to boycott Chinese capital and the MTR (which is mainly owned by the Hong Kong government).

Beijing felt deeply humiliated and began to vent its anger on its own incompetent bureaucrats. Between 4 January and 13 February 2020, Wang Zhiwen, the head of the Liaison Office and Zhang Xiaoming, the head of the HKMAO, were demoted. This was considered as a sign of a power struggle among the Chinese leadership.

With 2019 having receded into history, one may say that the New Year's Day march of 2020 was the finale of the great 2019 drama. With the onset of the Covid-19 pandemic since January 2020, the new union movement of 2019 proved its strength when the HAEA went on a five-day strike and mobilised seven thousand members to pressure a paralysed government to act.

AN INITIAL ASSESSMENT OF THE MOVEMENT

Three Layers Within the Yellow Camp

On 16 June, two million people marched on Hong Kong Island. This gives us a clue as to the rough size of the yellow camp. Yet within the yellow camp there were at least two categories. If the 'light yellows' are moderate because they are more likely to be law-abiding, it is reasonable to assume that they may vote and go to peaceful demonstrations. The 'dark yellows' are staunch democratic supporters whom I will define as more ready to participate in banned demonstrations and non-violent civil disobedience and are also more tolerant or even supportive of certain levels of violence from protesters. The first illegal demonstration broke out in Yuen Long on 27 July, with 280,000 on the streets, an angry response to the Yuen Long incident one week prior. The banned march turned into street fighting again after a police attack. From then on this became the norm. On 20 October another illegal march – this time riskier than the first one – in Tsim Sha Tsui drew 350,000 people. No later illegal marches could compare with this. Those who dared to participate in this banned march were more likely to be 'dark yellow', and the march can be used as a base for a rough estimate of the size of this group.

Another category relates to the means the protesters use: *jung mou paai* (the 'braves') versus *wo lei fei* (the 'non-violent current'). The former were those who dared to fight the police with bricks and later Molotov cocktails. The latter is often seen as synonymous with the term 'pan-democrat supporters'. The former consists of those that advocate and make use of force, from throwing bricks to Molotov cocktails, which the latter abstain from doing so. The 'braves' first became known when

a clandestine group described itself as such and allegedly was associated with a small explosion outside the LegCo building on 9 December
2014. The 2019 'braves' did not necessarily have organisational continuity with the 2014 version; still, the latter might claim the former's legacy.
How large were the 'braves'? No one knows for sure because of their
clandestine nature, but they were much smaller than the 'dark yellow'
current, although they have made recruits from the latter. Some have
estimated their size as being between five and ten thousand, or slightly
more (for more see 'The 1997 Generation' section in Chapter 2).

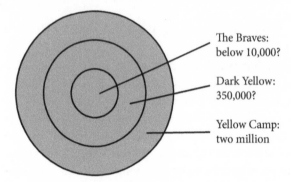

The Braves:
below 10,000?

Dark Yellow:
350,000?

Yellow Camp:
two million

Figure 1   Breakdown of the protest participants

Political Inclination of the Protesters

The yellow camp itself is differentiated by competitive political inclinations. The CCPOS differentiated between seven categories of political
inclination in its October 2019 across-the-board survey (i.e. including
the pro-Beijing parties). For our discussion about the yellow camp we
choose four of them, as below:[22]

Table 1.1   Political inclinations of protesters, 2014–2019

	September 2014	*October 2019*
Moderate democrats	37.9%	40.0%
Radical democrats	3.9%	6.2%
Localists	n/a	14.1%
Centre/no political inclination	48.6%	33.5%

In 2014 there had not been any survey about the localists yet, as it was a new phenomenon. To understand the picture of the localists' mass base before 2019, we can refer to another study which showed that by March 2016 the localists accounted for 8.4 percent amongst all categories of political inclination.[23] The above surveys show the strength of the localists and how fewer people were neutral in 2019 than in 2014. The 'radical democrats' also experienced a significant increase while the pan-democrats' growth was the least impressive.

Another survey showed the political inclinations of protesters at different protests:[24]

Table 1.2   Political inclinations of protesters, June–July 2019

	9 June*	12 June	16 June*	21 June	27 July*
Moderate democrats	43.2%	29.5%	41.1%	29.8%	34.9%
Radical democrats	3.2%	2.1%	3.4%	7.8%	8.5%
Localists	27%	25.4%	18.0%	28.6%	37.4%
Centre/no political inclination	21.1%	38.9%	21.3%	21.1%	8.9%

* These three protests were the largest, while the remaining two were much smaller, but more radical.

One can see that, at the protests surveyed in Table 1.2, there was a higher share of 'localists' than in the city-wide survey in Table 1.1. Neither survey must lead us into believing that the relevant political parties were necessarily as strong (or as weak) as the survey might suggest. Firstly, it is debatable how much these political categories can actually tell us. While the term 'pan-democrat' had a clearer meaning – those who worked within the Basic Law and were in general law-abiding and therefore non-violent – the term 'localist' is quite confusing. 'Localists' range from simply 'loving Hong Kong', and thinking that Hong Kongers' identity must be respected, to outright hatred against mainland Chinese people (for the latter category see Chapter 2). It was not clear how the many thousands of *sou jan*, or first-time activists, interpreted this term. The term 'radical democrats' is also a puzzle. One may argue that this lack of clarity is a reflection of the belated development of party politics in general in Hong Kong, and also of the legacy of colonialism.

Secondly, we should briefly discuss the underdevelopment and organisational weakness of all political parties in Hong Kong. Therefore, when people identified themselves as being from a certain 'current' this did not necessarily imply that they identified with a particular party. When two million people took to the streets on 16 June, the vast majority of them did not belong to any party at all. Also, the high proportion of people identifying as 'centre/no political inclination' might suggest the proportion of people whose political inclinations remained fluid and could change relatively easily. For the many thousands of *sou jan* this was their first or second time that they had joined any protest, waved any flag, or clashed with the police.

Tactics

In terms of political objectives, there is continuity between the Umbrella Movement and the 2019 revolt in that both were pursuing universal suffrage. It is this which partly allowed the latter to continue its mobilisation even after Carrie Lam announced the withdrawal of the extradition bill. On the other hand, in terms of tactics, the 2014 movement was very different from the 2019 revolt. While the former's main tactic was to occupy the main thoroughfares of Hong Kong Island and Kowloon, the latter consciously avoided this tactic from the very beginning. Once the 9 June demonstration had proven the enthusiasm of the people, online agitation chose the 'be like water' tactic instead, which meant demonstrating and confronting the police in a mobile way. The term can be traced to online discussion quoting the words of the kung-fu master Bruce Lee:

Empty your mind, be formless, shapeless, like water. Put water into a cup. It becomes the cup. Put water into a teapot. It becomes the teapot. Water can flow or creep or drip or crash. Be water my friend.

Protests that obtained a license in advance usually had a start and an end point and so were less likely to 'be like water'. 'Illegal' protests, especially towards the later period when the police became even more ferocious, had to 'be like water' to avoid arrests. In this period, most legal marches were also likely to end up 'like water' because they were not able to march to the planned end point, as the police used all kinds of excuses to break up the marches, forcing protesters to disperse into small batches in every direction.

What is interesting to note is that the two biggest confrontations in November, namely the occupation of CUHK and PolyU, were in opposition to the 'be like water' tactic. Rather, they looked more like 'a war of position' than 'a war of movement'.

2

Actors

Although the Umbrella Movement carried a strong spontaneous element, it still had publicly recognised leaders such as the occupation trio and the HKFS. In contrast, the 2019 revolt was largely spontaneous. It was also clear that the youth were the practical leaders of the movement, although they were following instincts and intuition rather than organisations or leaders. In this sense, we may say that the revolt was a leaderless movement. This does not make it a movement without actors, however. As in the previous chapter on the Umbrella Movement, by 'actors' we not only mean those who were directly involved in the movement, but also the oppressing governments in Beijing and in Hong Kong.

BEIJING AND ITS HONG KONG PUPPETS

During and after the Umbrella Movement one already witnessed a new phenomenon, namely that Beijing had even started to target its business allies in Hong Kong. It repeatedly attacked Li Ka-shing, the most well-known tycoon in Hong Kong. The more noticeable change was over the CE election. The Basic Law stipulates that the CE is 'elected' (or 'selected', as Beijing has the final say) by a 1,200-member election committee, itself 'elected' by a number of 'functional constituencies' (representing an economic, social, or professional interest group) mainly composed of representatives of the business sector. In reality, the Liaison Office openly intervenes to make sure the pro-Beijing parties follow its voting instructions. In 2012 it turned even uglier.

The local tycoons have always considered themselves the natural candidates for high government posts, especially the CE position. It was widely believed that Henry Tang, the former leader of the Liberal Party whose father had close connections to Jiang Zemin and his inner circle, had the latter's blessing for the CE job in 2012. He unexpectedly met a challenge from C. Y. Leung, however, a man who was not considered a local business leader. Just before the election campaign started, leaked reports suddenly filled the pages of the media suggesting that Tang had illegally enlarged his mansion when he renovated it. This sealed his fate. Tang unexpectedly lost the election in 2012, allowing Leung to get the job. There were contradictory rumours about the patron behind Leung, some said it was the former president Hu Jintao, others that it was Zhang Dejiang, the former head of the Central Coordination Group for Hong Kong and Macau Affairs of the CCP. Regardless of the rumours, since then the Liberal Party has been less enthusiastic about being a ringleader for Beijing.

The events in 2012 showed that Beijing was not only committed to asserting control over the CE election itself, but also to using the election as an arena for playing out factional struggles within the party. This was even more visible in the 2017 CE election. C. Y. Leung expressed his intention to seek a second term long before the election. In August 2016, the pro-Beijing *Sing Pao* newspaper started a sudden and fierce attack on Leung, accusing him and a mainland power group centred on the Liaison Office of masterminding the Hong Kong independence movement to legitimise their consolidation of power. In September, *Sing Pao* accused the nativist organisation Youngspiration of being Chinese agents and alleged that, contrary to what they claimed, they never took part in the Umbrella Movement, and that some of their members came from an organisation called *Hoeng gong se keoi mong lok* (Hong Kong Community Network) which was led by the well-known pro-Beijing politician Lau Nai-keung. The report hinted that Lau too had the backing of the Liaison Office and had been colluding with C. Y. Leung throughout the protests.[1] This was followed by a more escalated attack, eventually targeting Zhang Dejiang – then one of the seven members of the Standing Committee of the Politburo and head of the CCP's Central Coordination Group for Hong Kong and Macau Affairs – as the head of the power group at the Liaison Office. *Sing Pao* held all three of them responsible for manufacturing the pro-independence movement to effect a power-grab in Hong Kong.[2] Eventually the newspaper named the former Chinese leader and rival of Xi Jinping, Jiang Zemin, as the ultimate patron of the C.Y. Leung–Liaison Office faction.

Sing Pao is a long-time daily newspaper in Hong Kong and was formerly owned by a local family before it was sold to the Chinese merchant Gu Zhuoheng. After Gu started the attack, there were counter-attacks on Gu from the other side, but they were very weak. C. Y. Leung was completely silent over this vicious personal attack. It was widely believed that Gu was acting in accordance with Xi Jinping's faction although it could not be proved. Regardless, C. Y. Leung eventually announced that he would not run again, which showed that *Sing Pao*'s attack might have carried some weight.

Eventually the 2017 CE election became a contest between two candidates, Carrie Lam and John Tsang, both long-time top bureaucrats in Hong Kong. Each probably had his or her own patron in the CCP, as was hinted by many within the pro-Beijing camp. The election itself was much more boring than the prequel, except that the pan-democrats were led to believe that Tsang would be the chosen candidate and threw their support behind him, but it was Lam who would win the contest.[3] She would become the most hard-line CE local people had ever seen.

From the start, no serious person believed Beijing's story that the idea of the extradition bill came from Carrie Lam, and that Beijing played only a supportive role. Events between late August and early September helped confirm the public's suspicion. First there was a Reuters report, which was followed by the leaking of a taped conversation of Carrie Lam and finally her own press conference on the matter. Putting these pieces together revealed the whole picture: Beijing had dictated that Lam table the bill, and when this caused huge protests, she had asked Beijing to let her withdraw it, but Beijing refused. She then attempted to resign, but her resignation was rejected. She admitted to a group of businessmen that 'her hands are tied'.[4] When asked by reporters again and again about the constraints she faced and if Hong Kong autonomy was finished, she just evaded the questions.[5] From that moment onwards, the Hong Kong government had effectively lost its jurisdiction over Hong Kong.

Carrie Lam, in her closed-door confession with the pro-Beijing parties at the height of the movement, remarked that all she was left with was the 30,000-strong Hong Kong Police Force to maintain law and order. According to a British former officer of the Hong Kong police, the police force had always operated under a kind of 'paramilitary internal security mode', not a 'community policing model', which he thought was more suitable to a wealthy and sophisticated international city.[6] Beijing and Lam happily inherited all the repressive aspects of colonial rule, including this 'paramilitary internal security mode'.

If there was some continuity in policing in Hong Kong after the end of colonial rule, there was also a break. Under the colonial government, London sent its own officers to Hong Kong to lead the police force. With the Basic Law in place since 1997, Beijing could not do the same. Yet, since the start of the 2019 Revolt there were rumours about mainland police mixing with Hong Kong police. The French daily *Figaro* quoted Jean-Pierre Cabestan, a professor at Hong Kong Baptist University, as saying that 'the Beijing government has covertly added two thousand mainland Chinese policemen into the Hong Kong police'.[7] Another Reuters report in March 2020 said that, according to a senior foreign diplomat, four thousand People's Armed Police had joined the Hong Kong police on the frontlines to observe the protests.[8] The Hong Kong police denied the allegations.

Beijing also tightened control over the mainland media and internet, so as to discredit protesters as anti-Chinese. In August, departmental guidelines from an unnamed regional propaganda department in China were circulated online; they are worth quoting:

> Positively reporting on any demand about democracy and liberty from Hong Kong citizens shall be strictly forbidden. Accordingly, the event should be characterised as 'three struggles':
> the struggle between patriotic people and those calling for independence;
> the struggle between peace and violence;
> the struggle between rule by law and rioting.[9]

By September it was obvious that this hard-line approach was only driving more Hong Kongers, and others around the world, to oppose Beijing's bill. Beijing was also seeing discontent among its own civil servants (see below). On 4 September, Carrie Lam withdrew the bill, but by then it was too late.

Beijing did succeed in dividing Hong Kongers from mainlanders, thanks also to the Hong Kong nativists' stigmatisation of mainland Chinese, especially evident when, instead of using the word 'China', they used the word *Zi-naa*, the Cantonese version of the Japanese word '*Shina*' (which is very derogatory to Chinese people) in their attack on the Liaison Office on 21 July. Many mainland visitors might have felt hostility from certain Hong Kongers since then. Although some mainland Chinese people supported the Hong Kong protests, it was also obvious that many did not. To be fair, Beijing's censorship and propaganda, driven by its powerful state machinery, played a decisive role in shaping 'public opinion' in mainland China, while the Hong Kong nativists only played second fiddle. Nevertheless, at every crucial moment at which Beijing needed photos and videos showing that 'Hong Kongers discriminate against Chinese' it was the nativists who lent Beijing a hand.

Yet as 2019 drew to an end, Beijing's miscalculation led first to their defeat over the extradition bill, followed by another defeat in the District Council elections. Beijing had already fallen into an unfavourable situation after losing ground in the trade war with the US, would these setbacks trigger further factional fighting at the highest levels of the regime? The Chinese state is like a black hole, invisible to outsiders. Still, we can guess something about the possible situation inside this black hole by observing how surrounding objects are being pulled towards it and how it releases radiation. Further examination of the question 'if the extradition bill came from Beijing, which department or leaders were responsible?' might be helpful.

According to a Reuters report, the idea for the bill came from the Central Commission for Discipline Inspection (CCDI), the CCP's anti-corruption body, who pressed the officials in charge of Hong Kong affairs to make Carrie Lam table the bill, although this is something that she has denied.[10]

This Reuters report, even if it is true, should not lead to the conclusion that the CCDI was the sole Chinese department responsible for the bill. The current head of CCDI is Zhao Leji, who is also a Politburo Standing Committee member. Alongside him is his colleague Han Zheng, the leader of the CCP's Central Coordination Group for Hong Kong and Macao Affairs (CCGHKMA), the highest body overseeing Hong Kong and Macau affairs. It is unlikely that Zhao Leji and his CCDI could make Carrie Lam table the bill without first seeking approval from Han Zheng. It is also widely known that Han Zheng visited Shenzhen multiple times during the upheaval around the bill in Hong Kong to coordinate actions between Carrie Lam and the pro-Beijing parties, implying that Han was the man who called the shots. Whoever leaked the news to Reuters, and regardless of its authenticity, the objective result was to help Han

Zheng to place the blame on somebody else. Han Zheng was said to belong to the Jiang Zemin clique, although, again, there is no proof. Who was behind the leak? Since it is common for different factions to feed selected information to news agencies as a way to fight their battles, it is reasonable to suspect that the same old game of factional fighting was going on in Beijing as much as in Hong Kong.

In January 2020, Wang Zhiwen, head of the Liaison Office, was replaced by Luo Huining. A month after, the head of the State Council's Hong Kong and Macau Affairs Office (HKMAO), Zhang Xiaoming, was replaced by Xia Baolong, the vice-chairperson of the Chinese People's Political Consultative Conference. Besides demoting the two officials, Luo Huining, along with the director of the Liaison Office in Macau, Fu Ziying, were also made deputy directors of the HKMAO, practically putting the Liaison Office under the jurisdiction of the HKMAO, despite both offices being of equal ministerial grade. This implies that Beijing may want to end the previous competition between the two offices through stronger control from the centre. But is it entirely the fault of the Liaison Office cadres that the bill failed? Or were the top Liaison Office officials really plotting to artificially manufacture a Hong Kong independence movement so as to make things difficult for Xi, as reported by *Sing Pao*? Our discussion on the relations between Beijing and the local tycoons may shed further light on the Beijing black hole.

THE LOCAL TYCOONS

The Hong Kong business class is not known for supporting democracy. Indeed, it has always been on the side of Beijing. On 25 July 2014, five main chambers of commerce released a statement condemning the planned Occupy Central protest. On 21 September, a delegation of local tycoons, including Li Ka-shing, were invited to visit Beijing, and were received and lectured by Xi Jinping on how the central government opposes any 'illegal' actions in Hong Kong. What followed was even more interesting. On 25 October, at the height of the Umbrella Movement, the Beijing-controlled Xinhua News Agency released an English-language commentary headlined 'Hong Kong tycoons reluctant to take sides amid Occupy turmoil'. It is worthwhile to quote the *South China Morning Post* report on this commentary at length:

The article – which singled out Li Ka-shing of Cheung Kong [Holdings] and three other magnates – was removed at 7 p.m. The retracted commentary did mention Li calling on the protesters to go home and not to 'let today's passion become tomorrow's regrets'. Yet, it added: 'Asia's wealthiest man did not make it clear whether or not he agrees with the appeals of the protesters' . . . At issue is their failure to take action. It is no secret that many tycoons in Hong Kong campaigned against C. Y. Leung in the 2012 election. It was not a fight about ideology but who got to eat the cake – the old or the new interest groups.[11]

Then, in September 2015, the Chinese official research organisation Outlook Think Tank published an article, 'Don't let Li Ka-shing run away', criticising Li for profiting from China without fulfilling his social responsibilities. The article was quickly removed yet it had already achieved its goal.[12] On 28 September Li struck back at his critics by releasing a statement, denying that he was divesting from China, defending his patriotism, and lastly stating that 'it is with deep regret that the tone of the articles sent chills down people's spines with a distorted view'.[13]

When Carrie Lam tabled the extradition bill in 2019 the local tycoons hesitated to support it even after Lam watered it down, and even after their political representative, the Liberal Party, declared its support. Yet Beijing continued its attack on Li Ka-shing, the tycoon who had long ago lost its favour – his huge influence and his long-time connection to foreign capital, such as HSBC bank, surely did not help when Xi Jinping began to dress himself up as the new nationalist leader fighting a propaganda war against 'foreign aggressors'. What was more alarming to the hard core of the local tycoons, the real estate developers, was that this time it was clear that attacks on Li were meant as an attack on all of them.

On 14 August, Li's Cheung Kong Holdings (although he officially stepped down in 2018) released a statement appealing to protesters to stop using violence. Two days later, Li personally released two short public statements, with the first one echoing Cheung Kong's statement, and the second one quoting an old poem written by the son of Empress Wu Zetian of the Tang dynasty, in which he begged his mother not to kill him after she had killed his brother. The allegory was clear: a veiled warning to Beijing not to go too far. On 8 September, Li told reporters that the government should show leniency towards the young. This time he had really provoked Beijing. On 12 September, the CCDI retorted that 'those who called for leniency were pampering criminals'! The next day the CCDI broadened its targeting of the property developers and said that the root cause of the current protest movement was the high prices in the property market, which were the result of the developers' monopoly on land supply. 'The young people only vented their anger at the government', said the CCDI.[14] The CCDI's singling out of local developers was of dubious legitimacy: Chinese companies had long ago joined the scramble for land in Hong Kong. Carrie Lam soon echoed the CCDI's opinion, however. The developers, sensing danger, announced that they would lend out their land to the government to build public housing. Surely, they were not happy doing this. Shek Lai-him, the legis-lator who represented the real estate functional constituency, retorted to Carrie Lam that she had forgotten that the protest movement was about the five demands, not about the lack of housing.[15] Their grievances did not stop them from continuing to back the government's repression of the protesters however. On 22 November, the twenty biggest companies in Hong Kong, including Cheung Kong and Cathay Pacific, released a joint statement condemning the protest movement.

The tycoons will continue their double game. They are certainly the 'old interest groups'. But who are the 'new interest groups'? At around the same time as the CCDI was attacking Li Ka-shing, the State-Owned Assets Supervision and Administration Commission of the State Council (SASAC) summoned representatives from one hundred Chinese state-owned enterprises, telling them that with the help of the Hong Kong government, they should strive to secure a larger role in Hong Kong. Financial Secretary Paul Chan Mo-po immediately set up a meeting with these representatives of bureaucratic capital.[16]

THE 1997 GENERATION

The Role of the 1997 Generation

Studies on generations help us to understand how each generation develops its own values and expectations, and how this is related to the social context in which it grows up. Roughly speaking, the 'Umbrella

Movement generation' consisted of those who were born before the 1997 handover, while the students who participated in the 2019 revolt were born after 1997. Together they constitute what I call the '1997 generation', and they are most affected by the '1997 blues'. In comparison with other generations, the 1997 generation was the most important component within the revolt.

The CCPOS's August report shows details of protest participants in 2019.[17] The breakdown of participants for the following significant sanctioned public protests (totalling 1 million, 2 million, and 550,000 protesters, respectively) held by the Civil Front are listed below:

Table 2.1   Breakdown of protest participants according to age, June–July 2019

Age group	9 June	16 June	1 July	Age group as % of total pop.[18]
19 or below	10.5%	15.6%	12.9%	3.9%[19]
20–24	20.7%	16.3%	18.6%	5.7%
25–29	11.6%	18.3%	18.3%	6.6%
Sub-total:	42.8%	50.2%	49.8%	16.2%
30–34	8.4%	12.9%	11.0%	7.5%

The first two age groups mostly consist of those who are still at school or college, while the third age group is mainly the Umbrella Movement generation and are likely to have been working in 2019. Broadly speaking, this layer of the youth vanguard was composed of students and young wage-earners. The fact that these three age groups (the 1997 generation) account for half or nearly half of the protesters, and that their participation accounts for several times their share of the total population, is phenomenal – especially if we compare this with the figures for the 30–34 age group.

For the 30–34 age group, their share of participation in the above protests is just slightly higher than their share of the total population. The above table does not show that the participation rate of older protesters tends to decline in relation to their share in the total population, which is normal.

According to the same report, in smaller but more radical actions – involving civil disobedience (both expected and real), clashes with police, or occasional violence – the participation of the 1997 generation was even higher:

Table 2.2 Breakdown of protest participants according to age, June–August 2019

Age	12 June	17 June	21 June	14 July	27 July	4 August[20]
19 or below	6.3%	15.5%	14.6%	7.3%	6.0%	6.8%
20–24	27.9%	33.0%	54.2%	23.9%	26.0%	28.7%
25–29	34.2%	25.8%	16.4%	18.5%	19.6%	21.4%
Sub-total:	68.4%	74.3%	85.2%	49.7%	51.6%	56.9%
30–34	19.0%	11.4%	8.6%	12.3%	18.3%	11.4%

In all cases but one, the percentage of those aged 20–24 who participated was higher than that of the group aged 25–29. A possible explanation is that while most of the former are students or fresh graduates and hence have more free time, the latter are more likely to have stable jobs. Does this also mean that the latter are less ready to fight with the police or support these kinds of actions? It seems that at present there are not yet enough studies to prove this.

A second measurement is the percentage of protesters in the above actions that had also participated in the Umbrella Movement. The above-mentioned report has these figures:

Table 2.3 Percentage of protesters who had also participated in the Umbrella Movement, June–August 2019

12 June	17 June	21 June	14 July	27 July	4 August
76.6%	72.5%	64.0%	59.3%	67.2%	60.2%

Again, this shows that although the Umbrella Movement failed to get what it demanded, it succeeded in giving the youth their first political enlightenment and training, thus empowering them to take the initiative in 2019 to resist one of the most powerful empires in the world.

In Chapter 1 we showed the distribution of different political inclinations among the yellow camp. But how about for the young people? The following table dispels the common impression that young people are predominantly localists:[21]

Table 2.4   Political inclination, 15–29 age group (%)

Period	Localists	Democrats	Pro-establishment centrists	No political inclination/ not responding
June–July 2019	17.9	36.8	3.5	41.8
Oct-19	27.7	53.2	2.1	17

'Post-Materialist' Youth?

Why did the 1997 generation suddenly politicise and radicalise itself in a successful free port where its citizens have long been known to be politically apathetic?

Nearly a decade ago, some Hong Kong scholars began to use Ronald Inglehart's 'silent revolution' theory to analyse the new Hong Kong generation. Inglehart, borrowing heavily from Maslow's hierarchy of needs, opined that with the coming of economic affluence, the welfare state, and long-term peace, the public was now able to meet its basic material needs, resulting in a value shift from prioritising economic materialities towards prioritising lifestyle concerns, individual freedom, and self-actualisation. Inglehart called this a shift from materialism to post-materialism. He devised a simple questionnaire to identify three different sets of values: materialist, post-materialist, and a mixed type. He found that with the replacement of the older generation, who were more materialist in their outlook and values, with the younger generation, who had more post-materialist values, society became more post-materialist. This value shift across generations was further manifested through increased political actions, including mass protests and student revolts – which were not lacking during the great youth revolt in the 1960s and 1970s.[22]

Francis Lee and Joseph Chan applied Inglehart's theory to explain the young generation in Hong Kong. They reported that in 2012, 16.7 percent of their respondents were classified as post-materialist. In 2014 this had risen to 22.8 percent. Among the 18–29 age group the proportion of post-materialists was 34.4 percent and 44.7 percent in 2012 and 2014, respectively, double the overall figure. As such, they concluded, the youth are more likely to harbour post-materialist values.[23]

Chapter 1 described how, since 2007, a thin layer of young people had begun to be attracted by various social movements. By that time a lot of people, including certain older social activists, were puzzled by young people's enthusiasm for the movement to conserve the Queen's Pier in 2007 and to conserve the small village of *Coi jyun cyun* from being dismantled to give way to the high-speed train link with mainland China, in 2010. Wasn't the Queen's Pier a colonial symbol? Shouldn't economic development take priority over a small village? The findings of the above report by Francis Lee and Joseph Chan seem to correspond with what these movements had shown: young people prioritise post-materialist values over materialist ones. Since the rise of the 2019 revolt, Inglehart's theory has been brought up again to explain the motivations of the youth.[24]

Inglehart's theory alone is insufficient to explain the entire Hong Kong situation, however. In 2011, the Hong Kong scholar Ma Ngok found that although the city had already transformed itself into a post-industrial society since the 1980s, 'the 1990s showed only a minimal proportion of respondents who could be classified as "post-materialists" . . . only 0.3% of respondents [were classified] as "post-materialists", with the vast majority as "mixed type"'.[25]

If Hong Kong became a post-industrial society in the 1980s, why would students and young working people remain socially conservative and politically inactive for another thirty years, until 2014, when they came out en masse to demand universal suffrage?

One of the reasons that the worldwide youth radicalisation of the 1960s and 1970s barely affected Hong Kong was that at that time we simply lacked the basic conditions found in the West. One such condition was the latter's rapid development of higher education to meet the requirement for new skills within a capitalist system that was experiencing a third wave of technological revolution.[26] Many children of working families now had access to higher education. It was, however, not only poorly funded, with overcrowded classrooms and authoritarian administration, but first and foremost designed to serve capitalism. Hence not only did the future jobs of students continue to involve alienated labour, their current education was also an alienated education, which continuously oppressed them so as to make them fit for their role as screws – even if they were upgraded 'screws 2.0'.[27] The student revolts in France and elsewhere took place in a global context where the left was in its ascendance in Europe while the third world had great anti-colonial movements. Hence the youth rebellion was left wing from the start.

In contrast, higher education in Hong Kong under colonial rule was always very limited and elitist. At the end of the 1980s, the admission rate for tertiary education was only 8 percent. It is perhaps not accidental that there never was any massive student rebellion because the college graduates by that time were relatively privileged, against the background of a very conservative free port. Only towards the end of colonial rule did the government begin to gradually invest more in universities in order to raise the admission rate, which continued to rise under the Hong Kong government (as a response to the demand for a knowledge economy), to the extent that in 2015 the admission rate reached 30.8 percent – a massive increase.[28] As usual the government is more concerned with quantity than quality, so instead of funding bachelor's degree courses it funds a lot of associate's degree courses. This has drawn criticism from both educational professionals and students.

With the expansion of higher education we have now come close to the West in one aspect: hundreds of thousands of young people who previously had to work after graduation from high school are now able to come together to continue their study for four years, and this time are no longer being seen as teens but as adults, and as such possess more freedom to think and act for the first time. This greatly facilitated the activism of those who chose to take part in the protests. At least some of them had many grievances: poorly funded education, campuses without enough dormitories, poor job prospects, etc. Meanwhile, across the whole of society the mentality and expectations of the public was already changing in the early 2000s as Hong Kong people now faced new challenges: not only Beijing's aggression but also the Hong Kong government, which was increasingly being seen as colluding with tycoons because of the latter's embracing of privatisation since the 1997–8 Asian economic crisis. On these two fronts the people did fight back, reflecting the changed character of a previously submissive people. According to the above-mentioned essay by Ma Ngok, a 2001 survey showed that less than 5 percent of those surveyed thought they had the ability to participate in politics, but this had risen to 10.4 percent by 2007. All these society-wide changes had an impact on the sensitive youth, and they began to act.

It seems that Hong Kong's young generation is finally on a march towards the 'post-materialist' era. During the 2014 Umbrella Movement there was a moment which I will never forget. There was a street forum in Mong Kok, and some middle-aged men and women were talking about how the land monopoly and the hike in real estate prices had crushed young people's dream for living independently. Suddenly a well-dressed young girl stood up and said, 'our movement is not about material interests, it is about our Hong Kongers' core values!'

But young people are never a homogenous group. Their common denominator is their uncertain future, hence they have an uncertain class status beyond that of their parents – which will decide, for the time being at least, their class lifestyle. We shall elaborate more in Chapter 4 how this class dimension was overlooked by Hong Kong scholars. Here it is sufficient to point out that despite a failing higher education system and despite serious youth poverty, the eventual youth revolt did not occur around social and economic issues, not even the broken promises of education. Rather it broke out, as expected, around another kind of broken promise: Hong Kong autonomy and universal suffrage.

Identity Crisis

The young generation is doubly unlucky. It does not enjoy the stability and prosperity of previous generations and the period that this generation has grown up in has also been a period of offensive after offensive from Beijing. The result of this is that they now identify with Hong Kong much more than with China. The term 'Hong Kongers', if interpreted as 'non-Chinese', has only taken root among this generation as it has been unable to find anything positive in China. (Although it must be added that there are still many, from old to young, who think that being Hong Kongers does not exclude their identity as Chinese.) The Hong Kong Public Opinion Research Institute has reported that, since 1997, Hong Konger identity has gradually risen, reaching an all-time high in December 2019: 55.4 percent of the population now identifies as Hong Konger whereas 'Chinese' identity has nearly hit an all-time low of 10.9 percent.[29] Although it must be noted that the same survey also showed that 32.3 percent of respondents considered themselves to be a 'mixed identity' consisting of being both Chinese and Hong Konger.

If we further break down the statistics in accordance with age, young people (18–29 years old) identifying as Hong Kongers reached 81.8 percent in December 2019, up from the lowest point of 22.9 percent in June 2008; while for people over 30, the figure reached 49.2 percent in the same period, up from 16.6 percent.[30] The China specialist Andrew Nathan remarked that, 'in 1997, in a tracking poll of Hong Kong residents regularly conducted by researchers at the University of Hong Kong, 47 percent of respondents identified themselves as "proud" citizens of China'. But by June 2019, 'only 27 percent of respondents described themselves as "proud" to be citizens of China'.[31] No wonder that before the rise of localism, there had already been a very popular slogan, *loi saang bat zou zung gwok jan*, or 'I don't want to be a Chinese anymore in my next life', which expressed many people's sentiments about China. The slogan came from the title of a book by Joe Chung, who argued for Hong Kong independence.

This Hong Konger identity also creates a kind of commitment to Hong Kong among the young people, which the older generation was always lacking – for the latter there was no such commitment: they would either emigrate to the West if things went wrong (and if they had money) or just withdraw to their private life (if they were poor). It is this new generation's anger and pride in being Hong Kongers that gives it the necessary incentive and energy to fight the police and thus elevate the anti-extradition bill movement into a great battle to defend Hong Kong's autonomy.

The 1997 generation is high-minded but, perhaps because of this, they are also more troubled by anxiety and mental disorders. In 2017 the Hong Kong Food and Health Bureau released a report on the mental health of the population which found that 16.4 percent of Hong Kong adolescents were suffering from different kinds of mental disorders. This is higher than the global average of 13.4 percent,[32] despite Hong Kong being a highly developed city equipped with accessible medical care and a low youth-unemployment rate compared to Europe.

The 1997 generation is an angry generation, because they were lied to, the promises made to them were not honoured, and when they asked questions, they were teargassed. It is a desperate generation, because they witnessed catastrophe after catastrophe, yet their calls for action were largely ignored by their parents until very late. Thanks to their formal and informal education, and a society relatively supportive of free speech until recently, it is a generation which refuses to abandon its idealism. It is also a generation that smells death. On 15 June 2019, very early on in the 2019 revolt, Marco Leung jumped to his death after hanging a banner with the words 'anti-China extradition'. The image of him wearing a yellow raincoat became an icon for the young people, an incarnation of the message 'either you fight, or you die'. From then on there have been more suicide cases which might be related to the protests. A related issue concerns suspected cases of the police murdering protesters.

There is one other interesting thing that needs further study: the massive participation of high school teens in protests, participation which included clashing with the police. They were, however, less visible than college students in the media as they were 'schoolboys and girls' and hence accountable to their parents and schools. This made them more prudent in being seen and heard when taking part in actions. One scholar described his impression of high school students after conducting interviews with them:

Their taking to the streets had even more simple and direct reasons. The youngest of them stubbornly upheld their morals . . . When they saw the reality [the government's tolerance of police wrongdoing] not corresponding to these moral values they would then pose a rhetorical question: 'Aren't you [the government and the police] violating these same values?'[33]

One high school protester, Douglas, talked about his story:

Why did I become a protester? It was because we have to fight for the future of Hong Kong, which is also my own future. If I do not safeguard Hong Kong, then when everyone is silenced [by Beijing] it would be too late to stand up. Would my participation affect my study? Possibly, but the problem is that if the social environment becomes increasingly repressive then, even if one performs very well in one's study, he or she may still end up [with nothing]. Just look at how the [mainland] intellectuals were suppressed during the Cultural Revolution. Only when one lives in a society which is both stable and allows freedom of expression can one apply one's knowledge to the best of one's talent. I am scared of a scenario where no one dares to ask any question and where I am the only one who does and so in the end I will be victimised.[34]

In the end, it should not surprise us that it was the students who bore the brunt of the repression. From early June 2019 until 19 January 2020, the police arrested 7,143 protesters, and indicted 1,106 of them. Of those arrested, 2,902, or 40.6 percent, were students. Among the students arrested, 1,372 were high school students. Most of the arrested students were arrested after the semester started again in September, which once again reflected how, when mass participation in the movement began to recede, it was the students who rose up en masse and kept the movement going until December.

THE BRAVES

The *jung mou paai*, or 'braves', also chiefly emerged from the young people, although there were also 'braves' in their mid-thirties. The braves were composed of multiple fragmented groups consisting of one or two dozen activists (usually started with friends, classmates, and so on) heavily relying on social media to coordinate actions.

The Braves Call for an Alliance

Since 2014 there has been discussion online about borrowing European 'Black Bloc' tactics and applying them to Hong Kong. Once the anti-extradition bill movement kicked off in early June, protesters, usually young people, began to mask their faces during actions such as constructing roadblocks and laying siege to target buildings (like police stations). With the cycle of violence going on and on, the braves' attire also evolved, from wearing full face masks to fight the tear gas to wearing 'full gear' (usually in black) with no parts of their bodies ever exposed. Those who had money might also buy expensive gear such as stab-proof vests to protect themselves.

Another kind of evolution took place whereby those who were previously believers in non-violence evolved into braves. Consider the experience of 'B.K.':

I was a believer in non-violence. But then the demonstrations of 100,000, then 1 million, and then even 2 million took to the streets and Carrie Lam simply continued to ignore us . . . so we broke into your legislature building! . . . On 21 July the police colluded with organised crime, . . . who attacked the people while the police just did nothing. Hence us non-violent believers began to escalate [our actions] step by step . . . With the police having lost all credibility, those who believed in non-violence then slowly understood the anger of the braves.[35]

Judging from the braves' slogan, *ji mou zai bou* ('stop violence by violence'), there seems to have been a strong continuity between the 2014 nativists and the braves of 2019. This is partially true and I will discuss this more below, but it is sufficient to say here that, from the beginning of the 2019 movement, the braves – much greater in number than the 2014 nativists – were usually new hands to politics and might not belong to any nativist parties. More importantly, they differed from the 2014 nativists on one very fundamental point: whereas the nativists regularly verbally and physically attacked the students and the pan-democrat camps during the Umbrella Movement and repeatedly tried to dismantle their stages, from the very beginning the braves had already reached a consensus that they wanted to pursue an alliance with the non-violent protestors, in the name of *wo jung jat gaa* ('non-violent democrats and the braves are one family'). The braves' online communities opined that the reason for the failure of the Umbrella Movement was precisely because the localists (or some of the forerunners of the braves) and the 'non-violence advocates' were divided among themselves rather than joining hands to fight the common enemy. They argued that for this 2019 movement to succeed, it had to avoid this kind of sectarian fighting among the opposition and unite to confront Beijing instead. This consensus, while correct in its conclusion, was factually wrong. There never was any sectarian fight between the nativists and the pan-democrats, as the latter never really fought back. Secondly, if the Umbrella Movement failed in achieving its objectives it was not because of any 'in-fighting' but because, fundamentally speaking, Hong Kong was and is unable to succeed on its own. That was why the 2019 revolt also failed. Despite their factual error, however, their advocacy for a united front between the braves and non-violence advocates was itself politically correct, as well as timely, and contributed immensely to the movement by uniting the great masses and the youth vanguard. So even when the braves took over some of the slogans and language from the nativists they acted differently. In this sense they were acting as constructive democrats, not as destructive nativists, even if they were not conscious of it. Without any guidance from any party or political professional it was the masses themselves, after taking matters into their own hands, who thought hard and learnt quickly in relation to the movement. They made many mistakes, but one must give credit to the masses for drawing the correct conclusion in the face of a powerful enemy: 'united front, please!'[36]

The Army of the Braves

Broadly speaking, the braves could be further broken down into those who used force in the resistance to police violence, also called the 'front-liners', and those who played a supportive role, from providing materials for weapons and making roadblocks, to performing first aid, and so on.

The braves gave funny names to different roles, often adopting military titles and terms, or incorporating characters in cartoons and video games. For the frontline 'Black Bloc' protesters these included:

- *teon bing* (shield soldier) – those who would use whatever materials they came across to make shields for themselves to guard their barricades
- *fo mo faat si* (fire magician) – those who threw Molotov cocktails
- *seoi mo faat si* (water magician) – those who poured water on tear gas canisters
- *git gaai si* (roadblock builder)
- *zyu gau ze* (dog killer) – those who confronted the police
- *zong sau si fu* (renovation technician) – those who vandalised shops from the 'blue camp'

And for those who provided backup:

- *saau bing* (sentinel) – those who watched the police for those on the front lines (there were both online sentinels and on-site sentinels)

- *ji liu bing* (corpsman) – those who performed first aid
- *man syun bing* (designer) – designers of campaign literature and pictures
- *waa gaa* (painter) – those who painted murals on the Lennon Walls
- *haau baa si gei* (schoolbus driver) – those car owners who rushed to conflict zones to pick up protesters when they fled from the police
- *gaa zoeng* (parents) – those people who either paid out from their own pockets or raised money among friends to provide all kinds of daily necessities – from masks and gear to food coupons and travel cards – to keep poor (usually young) protesters going
- *gwan fo soeng* (arms dealer) – those who produced and transported Molotov cocktails
- *cing syun si* (liquidator) – those who filed complaints to government departments for the wrongdoings of the blue camp. For instance, a British-born chief superintendent of the Hong Kong Police Force, Rupert Dover, who was well known for cracking down on protesters, was reported for illegally occupying government land.[37] No one knows who the whistleblower was, but this would be the kind of work that the liquidator would do
- volunteer doctors – mostly doctors from public hospitals. Many braves dared not go to public hospitals for treatment for their injuries for fear of being arrested, so they would seek help from these volunteer doctors, who might joke that they were running 'underground hospitals'

This makes it sound as though the braves and their backup were very well organised. But didn't they uphold spontaneity and refuse organisation with command and hierarchy? Something in-between was true. The discussion and decisions over possible future actions and their preparation was always done online and from the bottom up, but the decisions were not binding, and it was impossible to impose discipline. At the protest sites, different groups of braves might get together under lots of umbrellas to discuss how to act and where. They might reach an agreement, if not they might split up and each carry out their own actions. As for different roles in actions these were all spontaneous, each chose his or her own role which therefore could sometimes be chaotic:

too many first aiders treating too few wounded, yet too few supplies, and so on. But on the whole, the braves and their supporters constituted the vanguard of the 2019 revolt and provided the greatest energy to it.

First aid was probably the biggest component among those who did provide backup. They were also an easy target for the police because of the cross on their clothes; the police hated them as much as the braves and assaulted them whenever they got a chance. The braves or other protesters were grateful for their selfless services. One individual wrote about these first aiders on Facebook after he or she was doused in the blue-dyed water coming from the police water cannons:

> 'Oh look, Avatar!', and then they started making fun of you, but soon they started to figure out how to help you to get rid of the blue dye [from your skin]. 'Try this 75 percent sanitiser!' 'Or this soda water!' 'Or this soap in water!' So, six or seven of them rubbed different kinds of things on your skin. They were so fanatical that one could see they were really enjoying it: 'This one works! Next time let's buy this brand! Yes, it works!' Only after a dozen minutes of experimentation did they remember to ask me the question, 'does it hurt when we rub these things on you?' I smiled back. These first aiders were really noisy and mischievous. At the front line they could also become braves and pick up and throw back the tear gas canisters at the police, as if it was just an orange.[38]

It is also worth talking about the 'designers': the artists who rolled out all kinds of posters, graphics, and handbills. They came from multiple small propaganda groups on Telegram, which could connect to five or six hundred designers, editors, reporters, marketing and IT professionals, legal experts, and so on. All those involved used aliases to communicate, discuss, and reach a consensus. The design would then be sent to public Telegram groups for downloading and printing – without ever requiring any of them to meet in person.[39] The communication revolution makes all this possible.

The Braves in Battle

There is one hard fact that needs to be faced as well. Because of the huge asymmetry between the forces of the braves and those of the police, most of the time during confrontation the braves were on the defensive and suffered many injuries: throwing Molotov cocktails was no match for rubber bullets and tear gas canisters fired from afar. Kyun Go is a worker and unionist who was active not as one of the braves but as a supporter – he disagreed with the tactic of physically fighting the police, but he would look out for the teens who needed help. He was arrested twice. He remarked that

the problem with the braves was that they had no training in self-defence, so even when the situation was favourable to the protesters they were still badly beaten up by the 'raptors' [the special riot police]. The real picture is far from the romanticised version of the braves. The raptors had full gear and were armed, although they had a weakness in that they couldn't see clearly below their waist. Yet the braves always targeted their upper bodies, which was exactly where their strength lay, and hence suffered a lot of their blows. That was also why I saw a lot of the braves who were fully geared but actually did very little fighting, or none at all. There was only one case where I witnessed the braves being able to chase the raptors away temporarily. It was at the 24 August protest in Kwun Tong. The MTR closed its station there under pressure from Beijing to discourage protests, hence the protesters had no way to flee when confronted by the assault of the police. So many of them had to fight back as hard as they could and because they outnumbered the police they managed, temporarily, to chase away the latter and then fled. Other than this case, I had never seen the braves able to fight the police; rather most of the time they were badly beaten up.[40]

In the first half of the movement, the braves were still able to build roadblocks which allowed them to hold out for some hours, while throwing Molotov cocktails to stop riot police from charging too soon. While protesters were learning fast, so too were the police, and in the second half of the movement the police changed their tactics and intervened very early on to stop crowds from gathering, even if they had to immediately ban a legal march. Police were then sent out from all corners to surround the braves, giving them very little time to build any proper roadblocks. The Black Bloc tactics began to exhaust their usefulness.

Only the two battles at the two universities in November had proper barricades as these constituted a 'war of position'.

There was a small group of braves who called themselves the 'Dragon Slayers' and claimed to have twenty members. One of them, George, had this to say in the middle of November:

> The mainstream in society is not ready for revolution . . . you can't even overthrow the police, not to mention overthrowing the government. People like us, in the eyes of the police, not to mention those of the CCP, were just like kids playing with sand. What we can achieve, in the most ideal situation – which is actually also the furthest away from being ideal – is to get to a scorched-earth scenario, this is the only thing we can do. We are already in a bottleneck.[41]

Later it was reported that most of the members of the Dragon Slayers were arrested and the group disbanded.

Are the Braves Black Bloc?

The braves learnt a lot from the Black Bloc, but in the end the former outdid the latter in terms of longevity. Most Black Bloc actions only last several days when there are important international meetings. In contrast, the braves in Hong Kong fought for seven months. On the other hand, beyond their superficial similarities in terms of their appearance and secrecy, how similar are they in terms of politics? While European Black Blocs are considered leftist, or even ultra-leftist, this was more complicated for the braves. The Black Blocs have a long history in social movements, in contrast the 'Hong Kong Black Bloc' just sprang up in 2019 and has no previous record in activism, and these young activists can still be very fluid in their politics. Some commentators regard the braves as mostly right wing or even far right. The problem is that by their clandestine nature the braves would not collectively come out to read a political statement. There were 'online braves' who were visible, and some of them exhibited the usual traits of far-right politics: worship of violence, lack of tolerance, xenophobia, misogynism, authoritarianism, and distrust of democracy. Yet these online braves were not necessarily the real braves who fought in the streets.

On the other hand, there was an argument which repeatedly described the braves as 'nihilists' and spoke in favour of their 'scorched-earth' tactics.[42] In terms of their sense of despair the braves may be comparable to nihilists, yet to ascribe to them any 'ism' is not corresponding to reality. The braves and their supporters, mainly in their twenties and thirties, only became politicised in recent years, and are far from having any consolidated political orientation. They mostly acted from their intuition. Uncritically applying European concepts to the Hong Kong case will risk overlooking the specific context there and lead to erroneous conclusions.

The secrecy of the braves confused the police, but it was accompanied by the problem of how to avoid undercover infiltration. If the braves could not deal with possible infiltrators then their members would soon be arrested; if they did something about it then they also sowed the seeds of suspicion and internal division, something which would be suicidal. Towards the end of December quite a few groups of braves disbanded on their own because they could not stand accusations of having undercover agents in their own ranks.

To compensate for their losses, certain braves turned to urban guerrilla warfare: making and planting bombs or buying guns from overseas. Many were arrested because of this. As a rule, this kind of urban guerrilla warfare, although intended to compensate for the decline of mass mobilisation, often symbolised the end of this mobilisation, or at least the end of its first act.

There is one other important group which is worth acknowledgement: the journalists. They were not part of the protesters, but increasingly their efforts in bringing out the truth put them at great risks in the face of police brutality. Most of them had shown their bravery.

'LOCALISM' WITHOUT THE 'LOCALIST' PARTIES?

By early 2019, after the government's repeated attacks, the nativists' three seats in the legislature were down to one. They were already very weak in terms of organisation – a common phenomenon here – and now they were even weaker. Both the old-generation nativists, the xenophobic trio, and those younger ones such as the Hong Kong Indigenous and Youngspiration, all failed to take any leadership role in the movement. If nativists did have some influence it was chiefly not through parties but their online key opinion leaders. They also made use of the popular LIHKG website, comparable to Reddit, to promote their ideas. But they were not necessarily well received. Their call to attack South Asians failed miserably (see below). If 'localism' had been on the rise it was less because of the strength of the nativist parties, but because of one fundamental feature in Hong Kong: the general conservatism.

Barry Sautman and Yan Hairong, professors from Hong Kong University of Science and Technology and Hong Kong Polytechnic University, respectively, wrote a joint paper, 'Localists and "Locusts" in HK: Creating a Yellow Peril/Red Menace Discourse', in 2015, which provided a comprehensive picture of these xenophobic localists. The authors present the localists as entirely locally bred; they found that their roots lay in the sharp inequality in the city, and added that 'if poverty and inequality have not, in themselves, produced nativism, diminished prospects for young people may still play a role'. They then argue that both the pan-democrats and the HKFS share the nativist worldview.[43] Not once do Sautman and Yan mention the role of Beijing's reactionary policies in the growing influence of the nativists. Instead I will argue that Beijing is the major factor which has helped to promote this nativism. Beijing's policy of imposing its Orwellian society on Hong Kong has driven many local people, especially the youth, into being 'localists', although with quite different interpretations among themselves.

Meanwhile, local factors should not be entirely dismissed. The combination of the colonial legacy of the so-called free market and the city's current status as a successful free port has resulted in a deep-rooted conservatism in Hong Kong. The city has never been receptive to the leftist idea of distributive justice and has been moderately tolerant of the rightist ideology of free market capitalism. And when its citizens began to politicise twenty years ago it was about standing up not to some internal class enemy but rather to an 'external' enemy in Beijing. While Sautman and Yan blamed local factors for the rise of nativism, the nativists blamed Beijing for everything that went wrong in Hong Kong. I will argue that the dichotomy of 'local' and 'external' factors is a false one in the first place. Do not forget that the 'local' factors of inequality and the free market were enshrined under the 'one country, two systems' principle stipulated in the Basic Law, and that this law was made by Beijing. It was Beijing who struck a compromise with Britain in 1984 in maintaining Hong Kong's capitalism so as to profit from it; in the course of which it also co-opted the local business class.

There is a great deal of reasonable aspiration in this broadly defined localism. The five demands are all progressive. It is political radicalism combined with social conservatism, however. Equally true is that this conservatism has not consolidated into any sizable far-right party either.

A Wavering Localist?

There were right-wing localists whose politics were still unclear. Ventus Lau Wing-hong was a localist who is worth mentioning. He became known before the 2019 revolt in a way that was different from the older- and younger-generation nativists. He was not kind to mainland immigrants.[44] He once advocated Hong Kong independence, and his following remarks tell us how conservative his vision of an 'independent Hong Kong' was:

> The independence current should begin to think about the blueprint of Hong Kong independence, so as to convince Hong Kong people to support this and trust us. What kind of blueprint is the most supported? To build more houses? To chase away mainland immigrants? All these answers are wrong. My answer is: 'On the second day of Hong Kong independence, all the lifestyles and custom of the Hong Kong people will remain unchanged'.[45]

When our friends in organised labour questioned the kind of capitalism that allowed 'employees to have the longest working hours globally' (see below), Lau believed that the new Hong Kong state would only change its flag, and everything else would stay the same as it was. He explicitly disapproved of 'chasing away Mainland immigrants' to distance himself from far-right xenophobes, yet one still observes a deep conservatism in this 'radical' blueprint of a Hong Kong state.

Ventus Lau ran in the 2018 LegCo by-election. Before this he announced that he had given up on the idea of Hong Kong independence. Yet he was still disqualified from running by the government. He called for several largely peaceful marches and assemblies during the 2019 revolt. Some of them were quite massive. The 7 July march targeted the terminal for the high-speed train which connects Hong

Kong to mainland China, and which triggered opposition nine years prior. The railway halted ticket sales that day as they perceived that the protesters wanted to harass mainland travellers. Yet Lau had made it clear that the purpose of the march was to explain to the mainland travellers the truth about the anti-extradition bill movement, and to try to win them over. To make his point he stressed that the march was going to be conducted in a 'graceful' manner. He expected 2,000 participants but the turn-out was 230,000, and many people, on their own initiative, printed leaflets in simplified Chinese characters (used by mainland Chinese) to explain the five demands. A mainland visitor responded to reporters that she did not like demonstrations as a medium of expression but that she would read the handbill carefully because she wanted to know what was going on.[46] I was at the march, and I would say that it was one of the most delightful marches that I went on during the 2019 revolt. When people saw visitors that looked like mainlanders, they would shout the five demands in Putonghua so as to connect with them. These were spontaneous acts. Towards the end of the march, the lawmaker Au Nok-hin did the same on stage. For ten years, the nativists had never stopped pouring out insults at the mainland Chinese and saying that the latter were all selfish and could never understand the value of democracy, that they were nothing but locusts. Yet this march, with huge support, approached the mainland Chinese in a friendly way and believed it was worthwhile to talk to them. And it was a conservative localist who initiated the event.

To sum up, the broad term of 'localism' contains multiple contradictions which in the future may blow up in various directions: hardcore nativists, soft localists, or even utopian localists who dream that, with the growth of the 'yellow economic circle', a Hong Kong city-state might be able to be self-sufficient. Surely their future development also depends on how the centre-left and left act, and also on regional and global changes.

THE PAN-DEMOCRATS AND THEIR CONSTITUENCY

When, on 12 June, young protesters laid siege to the LegCo building, followed by clashes with police, both the government and most of the pan-democrats expected that public opinion would turn against the radical youth. They were proved wrong. This kind of scenario was repeated many times until both realised that there had been a fundamental change of attitude on the part of the long-time pan-democrat supporters in relation to violence against government repression. What had happened?

Non-Violence with Chinese Characteristics

This brings us back to the term *wo lei fei* (a shortened version of 'being peaceful, rational, and non-violent') and its origins. Being peaceful, rational, and non-violent had characterised the pan-democrats for the past thirty years, and they had copied this slogan ('heping lixing feibaoli' in Putonghua) from the Beijing student leaders back in the 1989 democratic movement. This was how the doctrine *wo lei fei* became implanted in the brains of the Hong Kong liberals, who by that time were at the head of a great solidarity campaign with the mainland democracy movement. The problem with the doctrine does not lie on its insistence on non-violence, rather it lies on the idea that violence is necessarily irrational, something which is simply not true. Violence in self-defence is surely rational, and in dire situations it is the only choice if one wants to live at all. However, the leaders of the pan-democrat parties continue to preach their dogmatic version of non-violence, to the extent that they even attacked the young for their profanity. When the occupation trio called for action in 2014 they also made it clear that not only was the occupation going to be non-violent but also told the participants to tie themselves up to make sure that when they were arrested they would not be able to resist, even if unconsciously. As we now know, not only did the crowd on 28 September 2014 not tie themselves up, they spontaneously occupied the streets and confronted the police with their bare hands and umbrellas while remaining non-violent. From then on, the pan-democrat parties had lost connection with movement from below.

A New Stage Arrives

This was also the moment when the liberal parties began to lose support from some of their constituency. The Hong Kong Institute of Asia-Pacific Studies compared three surveys on the same topic, in 2014, 2016, and 2017, as follows:[47]

Table 2.5   Percentage of respondents agreeing with the need to take radical action, 2014–2017

Age	Nov 2014	March 2016	July 2017
18–30	29.1	25.9	26.2
31–50	9.9	13.8	12.9

It was clear that radicalism was on the rise among people over thirty before 2019. In 2019 this trend was exacerbated. The above-mentioned institution conducted a survey at the height of the 2019 revolt and found the following:[48]

Table 2.6   Percentage of respondents who favoured being 'peaceful, rational, and non-violent' in campaigning for their demands, 2017–2019

	July 2017	August 2019
Agree	73.4	58.8
Half-half	17.1	31.1
Disagree	5.8	8.2
Don't know/hard to say	3.7	1.8

The survey showed a 14.6 percent drop in those supporting non-violent action over the preceding two years, while those who were of two minds about non-violence saw a similar percentage increase.

The political pendulum now began swinging to the other end, after its previous swing to the extreme pacifist position in 1989. After the 12 June clashes, a late-middle-aged football commentator and previous *wo lei fei* believer wrote a widely circulated confession that caught the spirit of this generation:

> As descendants of a refugee generation . . . we just thought that we should avoid trouble as much as possible. People jumping queues, extortion by organised crime, we all responded with 'avoid trouble as much as possible' . . . As part of the post-1970s generation I deeply apologise to those post-1980s, -1990s, and -2000s generations . . .

Today we are going to march with you, and even if we lose, we will, like you, not give up.[49]

Why the change? In the words of the well-known pan-democrat academic Ivan Choy:

When I discussed with students about liberalism and raised doubts about those overly radical actions some students asked the question 'without the braves, or without the 12 June action, would the government listen to us at all?'[50]

Choy tacitly recognised this student's remark as factual even if he might not agree with their position. Many long-time pan-democrat supporters did feel indebted to the radical young. No wonder whenever there was a big march and when groups of the braves suddenly appeared and marched through the crowd the latter would repeatedly applaud.

Perhaps even Beijing or Carrie Lam worried that the popular sympathy for the braves might escalate into more people joining the fight against the police, which might then give rise to a revolutionary situation – perhaps it was this fear that was behind Beijing's concession to withdraw the extradition bill. The revolutionary moment never came, however. Through to the end of 2019, the great majority of the yellow camp was still not ready for such a daunting task, despite the slogan 'revolution of our times' having been echoed in all the corners of the city.

The Strengths and Weaknesses of the Pan-Democrats

Carrie Lam tabled the extradition bill in February. Very soon the pan-democrat legislators came out to oppose the bill. To their credit, they were by then fully aware what was at stake, and began to call for action, first on 31 March, followed by the 28 April demonstration, where 130,000 people took part. However, the pan-democrats were too fragmented, and lacked credibility in terms of leading social action (see Chapter 1), hence they had to rely on the Civil Front to take the lead. The Civil Front was founded in 2002, in a moment when the main pan-democrat parties were afraid to take the lead to mobilise the people in the face of the passing of the national security bill. Precisely because of this history the main pan-democrat parties could not always impose their will on the majority of the member organisations, on top of which there is always tension between member organisations. From February to late May, the pan-democrats chiefly mobilised protests through the Civil Front. The more the movement began to evolve into gigantic protests from early June onwards, the more the pan-democrats, as political parties, became marginalised. Their leading role came to an end after the 12 June action. It is to their credit that, even if they disagreed with the radical action on 12 June, they did not publicly condemn it as Beijing would have liked them to. This laid the groundwork for unity in action against the government and it was this that allowed the movement to become so powerful. Meanwhile the movement's single demand (withdraw the bill) evolved into its five demands, a gradual process from below in which the pan-democrats played no role at all. The pan-democrats at first only dared to call for the resignation of Carrie Lam but it was chiefly with the spontaneous contribution of hundreds of thousands of protesters, especially from the youth, that the movement began to call for universal suffrage, and as such reconnected with the legacy of the Umbrella Movement. The pan-democrats were slightly revived in popularity only when the climax of the movement passed and when District Council elections began.

The pan-democrats' political and organisational weakness was however compensated by their strong connection to the professional middle class: politicians, civil servants, academics, lawyers, accountants, businesspersons, and so on. In addition to this was the support from *Apple Daily*, along with other influential pan-democrat online media such as *Stand News*. Together they also helped the yellow camp in their ideological battle against Beijing, although mostly along liberal or even neoliberal lines of discourse. The strength of the pan-democrats within the media and academic milieu allowed them to set up the 612 Humanitarian Relief Fund, which raised HK$100 million locally, and has been able to provide legal and material support (from medical care to counselling) to those arrested and/or prosecuted. Its half-year report shows that it helped 7,964 applicants with HK$27 million during the 2019 revolt.[51] They also supported those cases where defendants were charged with violence and/or possessing arms and petrol bombs. Without the support of the pan-democrats the protesters would have had a much more difficult time.

Another source of strength for the liberals is their strong connection to the establishment in both the UK and the US. This is one of the legacies of colonialism. Since the early 1980s the colonial government began to embark on its so-called political reform by introducing partial elections, and through this co-opted a whole layer of liberals into the colonial project of guaranteeing a safe and peaceful transition of power for the British government. We will see in Chapter 4 how the pan-democrat parties became what Beijing called 'foreign forces intervening in Hong Kong'.

THE TRADE UNIONS AND LABOUR

The CTU's Response to the Movement

The Confederation of Trade Unions (CTU), with its new chairperson, Carol Ng, who has on-the-ground union-organising experience from when she led the British Airways Hong Kong International Cabin Crew Association, played a larger role than it did in 2014, by helping to organise Hong Kong's first successful political strike on 5 August, targeting Beijing's puppet government in Hong Kong. The CTU's old cadres had lost a great deal of their self-confidence in the past five years – beginning with the complete marginalisation of the CTU during the Umbrella Movement and followed by CTU general secretary Lee Cheuk-yan's second defeat in his by-election campaign in 2018 (the first was in 2016). This was the price to pay for the CTU's long years of following the liberal parties, even after Lee founded the small Labour Party. On the other hand, the younger cadres of the CTU, emboldened by the demoralisation of the old cadres and more importantly by the 2019 revolt, started to argue for more connections to the revolting masses. On 16 June, after the Civil Front announced its decision to call off the strike on the 17th, there was an internal debate in the CTU about whether to follow the Civil Front or not. Those who were for the Front's decision worried about the consequence of a strike call, while those who wanted to continue preparing the strike argued that keeping the movement going was the priority. Eventually the latter's suggestion was endorsed, although the turnout at the CTU's assembly in the Admiralty area was very small, with only a few hundred participants. This proactive position of the CTU at least helped it to reconnect with the growing support for strike action and later for union organising.

Meanwhile two CTU affiliate unions – the Cathy Pacific Airways Flight Attendants' Union and the Social Workers' General Union – because of their longer tradition of being more assertive and better organised, were more high profile in intervening in the movement than many other unions. The former had staged a seventeen-day strike against its management in 1993, while the latter had been very active in the Umbrella Movement.

Medical professionals in the public sector, including doctors, nurses, and other professionals, are another sector of labour which is worth mentioning. They did not go on strike during the seven months of the protests but angered by police violence against protesters (whom they were treating on a daily basis) they made use of their lunch time or off-duty time to stage demonstrations at the hospitals. The medical care community was also a source of information about how bad the police violence was. The strong solidarity with the protesters finally bore fruit: this milieu of medical professionals gave birth to a relatively big new union, the Hospital Authority Employees Alliance (HKEA).

A New Union Movement

The 21 July attack by members of organised crime syndicates on train passengers triggered off a great amount of anger from all walks of life, after which young radicals began a very enthusiastic agitation for a general strike on 5 August. The CTU, the Cathy Pacific Airways Flight Attendants' Union, and the Social Workers' General Union collaborated with the radical youth in organising mass assemblies in seven districts of Hong Kong. Despite the organisational weakness of the unions, the high tide of the movement prompted many working people to stop working that day. Yet this organisational weakness, compounded by Beijing and the employers' retaliation against unions after the 5 August strike, would continue to constrain later attempts to prepare for a strike. To make up for this disadvantage, the radical youth began to agitate for a new tactic; they disrupted traffic by blocking the doors of subway trains, and when this did not work they escalated their actions by obstructing railway tracks or main roads, making it nearly impossible for many employees to get to work. Those who disapproved of this tactic coined the term *bei baa gung*, or 'being forced to go on strike', to describe it. There were passengers who either supported or sympathised with the actions, but there were also those who opposed them and therefore clashes occurred everywhere. Because of its unpopularity, a group of activists who had been involved announced on 14 August that they had stopped the action.[52] Yet this did not stop other radical young people from continuing to resort to this tactic again and again, culminating in the occupation of two universities in November. This controversial tactic also began to divide the yellow camp, and the CTU was reluctant to support it as well, although broadly speaking the division did not develop into a split.

The *bei baa gung* tactic also exposed the weakness of radical youth discourses. Reading through their strike-promoting campaign literature was a bit distasteful. They thought that if a great number of employees did not go on strike it was because they were obsessed with the 'value' of going to work, that they worshipped this value so much that they treated it as sacred. If only they replaced this wrong value with the value of revolting against the government then everything would be fine. Surely if employees desperately needed to work this was because it was the only way to earn a living. No wonder the radical youth found it hard to persuade employees to strike. In a second tactic of persuasion, taking advantage of the widespread guilt among the older generation (for their previous inability to fight back), the radical youth posed the question, 'if we can shield you from bullets, can't you go on strike?' But any sensible employee could easily respond, 'I thank you for shielding us from bullets, but the problem is that we simply cannot go on strike again and again without prior proper preparation. Strikes are not instant noodles, my friend'.

The failure of the *bei baa gung* tactic prompted people to look for an alternative tactic to make the general strike possible. It was at this moment that there emerged a new and quite effective campaign led by a new layer of young workers. Firstly, there was the 'Lunch with You in Central' activity. Beginning from early October and lasting for weeks, every day, and later every Friday noon, more than a thousand white-collar workers would spontaneously gather and then march through the main streets in Central (equivalent to Wall Street) to protest. This always lasted for an hour and then they dispersed and went back to work. Previously white-collar workers were not well known for protesting. (A lot of the white-collar sector did join protests from June onwards, but they joined as individuals, not as a collectives.) Although the 'Lunch with You in Central' action was spontaneous, it had a very clear identity; white-collar workers working in Hong Kong's equivalent of Wall Street now wanted to have a voice of their own. This practice soon spread to other areas.

This was just a symptom of a strong undercurrent now surfacing. A new layer of young employees had started to call for organising new unions to prepare for future strikes. They were mostly in their late twenties and early thirties, worked in white-collar jobs or were professionals, and were outside of the traditional unions. On 7 October these young union activists founded a Telegram channel called 'United front for a two million-strong general strike' whose objective was to found new unions as leverage to strike against the government. Very soon the subscribers to this channel had reached ten thousand, and then in three months nearly eighty thousand, with 42 new unions being founded as a result. The list of these unions showed that they are mostly white collar and professional. Here is part of the list:

Union for New Civil Servants
Hong Kong Testing and Certification Union
Hong Kong Information Technology Workers' Union
The General Union of Hong Kong Speech Therapists
Hong Kong Financial Industry Employees General Union
Hong Kong Alliance of Accounting Professionals
Hospital Authority Employees Alliance
The Union of Hong Kong Occupational Therapists OC
Hong Kong Music Industry Union
Bartenders and Mixologists Union of Hong Kong
Hong Kong General Union of Physical Therapists[53]

The Union for New Civil Servants was initiated by a group of young civil servants, with Michael Ngan as one of the main leaders. He took part in the Umbrella Movement as the vice-chairperson of the CUHK students' union. Similarly, the HAEA's vice-chairperson, Ivan Law, was the chairperson of the HKFS standing committee. Both unions played a great role in later mobilisations and strikes.

Precisely when the 2019 revolt was trapped in a bottleneck, it suddenly burst out with an entirely new union movement. It was ill-prepared, organised in haste, and different people had different agendas. The stronger voices said that 'in order to promote a general strike one has to unionise', but some thought that founding a new union would allow the opposition to have more votes in the Chief Executive Electoral Committee (according to the Basic Law, labour unions have a small number of seats on this committee, which 'elects' Hong Kong's chief executive). The latter opinion might have a very different agenda from the former, especially when they repeatedly emphasised that their enemy was Carrie Lam's government and not the bosses. These two agendas actually were exclusive to each other: building a union which can strike requires strong membership and rank-and-file activism, especially a level of union dues high enough to sustain the union when it goes on strike; while building a union merely to gain a vote in the CE 'election' only requires the union to meet basic legal requirements in terms of membership (seven members) and proper registration – the opposite of building a strong union. Yet within the new union movement there was inadequate serious discussion about the differences over its objective. Anyway, there was a new enthusiasm over union organisation and in the first three months of 2020 there were 1,578 new union registration applications, a one hundred-fold increase from 2019.[54] One wonders if quality will be sacrificed for quantity? Will tiny unions which lack real strength be promoted instead?

Nevertheless, the boost was driven by thousands of activists who were inexperienced but committed. During the 2020 Chinese New Year this new union movement, with the HAEA at its head, was put to a severe test in the midst of the coronavirus pandemic.

The CTU was in danger of being bypassed by this new union movement. A number of older cadres have found it hard to digest the fact that these young unionists largely supported the braves. They also found themselves facing a digital divide. While older cadres were accustomed to meeting face to face, the young generation mainly coordinated their meetings and prepared for strikes through online communication software such as Telegram. Even Facebook was considered outdated. This imposed obstacles for the old cadres connecting with the young activists. Luckily, the younger CTU cadres did a lot of work to bridge both the gaps of division in mentality and the digital divide. With more experience in running trade unions and recruiting, the CTU did provide some necessary labour education to this new generation of labour activists. Eventually even if the new unionists did not see the CTU leadership as their natural leader, a portion of them did work with certain unions affiliated to the CTU.

Whatever its shortcomings, this new wave of unionisation brought with it a dynamic which in the long run may far exceed what the initiators had imagined. One person posted the following message on the 'United front for a two million-strong general strike' Telegram channel:

> If we want to liberate Hong Kong we cannot limit to punishing the black cops or making the high officials accountable . . . we also need to reclaim the economy, to take care of our *sau zuk* [brothers and sisters], to support democracy and justice, get rid of those pro-Beijing merchants who only want to squeeze money as much as they can. We need to reclaim our relationship, no longer care about money . . . There are problems with this extreme capitalist society, but we had chosen to get used to it and to shut our own eyes. The 'white terror' at Cathay Pacific made all of us worry about if we will be the next ones affected . . . For years we are used to being the employees who have the longest working hours globally, we are used to attend to on-call duty even after work . . . How could we tolerate all of these?[55]

DISSIDENT CIVIL SERVANTS

The extradition bill was also highly unpopular among civil servants. In late May, when a second reading of the bill was scheduled, even judges, who usually refrain from commenting on politics or legislative matters, revealed to Reuters their concern that they were 'being put on a collision course with Beijing' because of the bill.[56] One High Court judge, Mr Li, made an unusual move by signing his name on a petition opposing the bill.

'White Police Officers'

The police called anyone who disobeyed them 'cockroaches'. We know what we do to cockroaches. The protesters responded to it by calling the bad cops *hak ging*, literally 'black cops', with the words 'black' meaning 'mafia' or 'being evil'. Good cops were called 'white cops' – not in the sense of skin colour, but in local language meaning dissident or pro-revolt police officers. Testimony from protesters themselves often told stories about how, when chased by police, the first to reach them would leave them untouched, sometimes even with words such as 'run faster, those behind me will really hit you without mercy!' There were also riot police who, in crackdown operations, banged their shields loudly with their batons but did not actually hit anyone.

Some anonymous police officers posted online criticism of their leadership. While some of these posts remain, most vanished. Below is one of the few that still exists. This officer asked why management tolerated its officers refusing to show the public their warrant cards while carrying out duties:

> Why did the police use abusive force against protesters on 12 June? Weren't we taught to stop using force once our goal of controlling suspected persons was attained? How could you, commanders, unlawfully exercise your power?[57]

Another officer described the situation within the police towards the end of July as follows (the post is no longer online):

> At present, thirty general-grade cadets and intern officers from the police college have resigned because the image of police is too bad nowadays. The Yuen Long incident on the 21st made some of them demoralised. Even many 'dark blue' police felt embarrassed over this, because they knew too well that it was really a case of collusion between organised crime and police. Now from top to bottom the police are fully aware that outsiders are 'prejudiced' against them and dare not reveal their occupation when off duty. Last but not the least, the police have been unable to decipher Apple phones.[58]

Still by that time this reminder was very important to those protesters prepared to be arrested. As we shall see, the Yuen Long incident on the 21st was one which antagonised so many civil servants, including the police.

The 'yellow' families of the police openly came out to protest Carrie Lam. A Facebook account called 'Police relatives' connection' was created and they held a rally on 25 August with the theme of 'returning the police to the people'. Around one hundred people took part. Its appeal said:

> As family members we deeply love our police. Deep inside their hearts the police believe in justice. They want to protect the public with the rule of law. However, because of political problems, the police have been forced to confront the public. It is tragic that the police force has been mismanaged. Individual frontline police officers have used methods that have made the police–civilian relationship fall into an abyss.
>
> The only way to save the endgame is to listen to the voice of the public and set up an independent investigation committee to thoroughly look into the improper police management and behaviour, and to also rehabilitate the decent police officers.[59]

A wife of a policeman said that it was hard for them to talk to each other, and if she pushed then it might end up in divorce. She still tried to persuade him not to attack the protesters. 'If you want to hit somebody, hit me', she said.[60]

It was reported later that 'more than 400 police officers quit the force during the anti-fugitive bill [anti-extradition bill] unrest while new recruits fell 40 percent year on year'.[61]

A dramatic case of dissident police officers was revealed on 17 January 2020 (after the movement had entered its decline phase), a 31-year-old off-duty police officer was caught, along with his girlfriend and her mother, posting 'illegal' posters on a Lennon Wall, condemning the new head of the police, Chris Tang, for police violence.[62] He was reportedly doing frontline work and so possibly also faced daily confrontation with the protesters. One may wonder how he managed this double life.

Dissidents in Other Departments

More alarming to Carrie Lam was that a lot more dissident civil servants, from low to high, from many other departments, began to semi-openly criticise her soon after the Yuen Long incident. Dissident civil servants from the Immigration Department, firefighters, and medical professionals openly criticised police inaction when organised criminals attacked common citizens. This was followed by an open letter from more than a hundred civil servants from 23 departments voicing the same concern. Then, in the last week of July, four hundred executive officers from different departments wrote to Lam condemning the police, followed by more than a hundred administrative officers (AOs). Under colonial rule the AOs were the administrative elite. Yet a section of these elite officials now openly disagreed with the head of the government and wanted an independent inquiry into the police. Encouraged by the AOs' move, civil servants from two sensitive departments, the Security Bureau and the Prosecution Division of the Department of Justice, also voiced their disagreement. None of these dissident civil servants revealed their names. Their usual practice was to post their letters online, with photos of the back of their warrant cards showing the name of their departments. Even the Policy Innovation and Co-ordination Office, founded by Carrie Lam in 2017 and seen by her as the brain for policy innovation of the government, had a Lennon Wall in its office with posters calling for independent investigation and for the 'political controversy to be settled by political means'.

This internal rift within the government eventually snowballed into a 40,000-strong rally of civil servants on 2 August. Michael Ngan was one of the main organisers of this protest, which laid the mass base for the Union for New Civil Servants, founded in November. Meanwhile the government responded to the rally by accusing the civil servants there of breaking the occupational requirement to maintain political neutrality. One of the speakers retorted that, 'you can take away my job as a civil servant, but you cannot take away my identity as a Hong Konger'.[63] According to a survey, 93.1 percent of the rally participants demanded an independent investigation into the 21 July Yuen Long incident.[64] Towards the end of August the dissident civil servants at the Department of Justice struck against the police again. The Hong Kong Court Prosecutors Association sent an internal letter to their department head accusing the police of lying.[65] The leaking of this letter was probably deliberate.

Carrie Lam retaliated in November. Ninety firefighters were investigated for allegedly posting the derogative 'black cops' label online. On 11 January 2020, the government announced that a total of 41 civil servants were arrested during protests and 31 had had their duties suspended. After all these events it would not be surprising to see further and bigger purges among civil servants in the coming months and years.

On the other hand, the ICAC (Independent Commission Against Corruption) began its investigation into police conduct during the Yuen Long incident soon after its outbreak.[66] This was not good news for Lam or the police force (for more see Chapter 5).

MAINLANDERS

Mainland Chinese in Support of Hong Kong

Throughout the more than six months of struggle some mainland Chinese in China came out as individuals to support the Hong Kong movement. Very often they were arrested and disappeared. Still, people could get around censorship to speak out. Hu Xijin, the well-known hard-line editor of the *Global Times*, tried to convince the public with the official line explaining the extradition bill. Many netizens posted comments like 'normal Hong Kongers won't demand independence, right?'; 'Hu, why not talk a bit about why us mainlanders cannot receive a single piece of news about the Hong Kongers' demands? Is this normal?'; and, 'Hu, tell us more news about Hong Kong, so that we can criticise it'.[67]

As one mainland scholar said:

My circles have very strong sympathy for the Hong Kong people. Discussions in more than fifty WeChat groups of my association over the past two months show overwhelming sympathy for the Hong Kong people and contempt for the Beijing regime. Neither the state media nor social media under party control reflect public opinion or even the public sentiment of mainland Chinese.[68]

In general, however, it seemed that many mainlanders believed Beijing's messaging about the Hong Kong protests. But even here things were not developing in a linear fashion. After Carrie Lam announced the 'death' of the extradition bill in August, nationalist mainlanders angrily responded:

'So, is this a way to compromise with terrorists?'
'This shows the weakness and compromised nature of the bourgeoisie'
'Can such a rubbish government govern Hong Kong?'
'Only crying babies get milk to drink?'
'Rubbish central government, rubbish Hong Kong government, they
   should all step down!'

Beijing has found itself in a difficult situation for some time now. On
the one hand, it has needed the service of nationalism to legitimise its
one-party dictatorship, yet on the other hand it is concerned about how
this nationalism might grow stronger and become a source of unrest.

Mainland Chinese Immigrants

Over the past twenty years there have been a million immigrants
to Hong Kong from the mainland, amounting to one in seven Hong
Kongers. On top of this, there were seven thousand mainland students
in Hong Kong in 2019. They are of course also stakeholders in Hong
Kong. What were their attitudes towards the revolt? And how did the
yellow camp see them?

Certain liberals and nativists argue that local people are democracy-
lovers while mainland immigrants are not. The following debate about
the extradition bill is interesting. Kevin Lau, a well-known liberal writer
and former editor-in-chief of *Mingpao* (who was later seriously wounded
in a mysterious attack), instead of opposing the bill as a whole, argued
for an amendment to the extradition bill to target only non-permanent
resident mainland Chinese in Hong Kong.[69] This immediately drew
criticism from Li Ming, a lecturer at the Education University of Hong
Kong, who came from the mainland:

> It was the common experiences of being oppressed which constituted
> the base of our aspiration for democracy and which is also where our
> strength lies. If we cut across this universal connection of our fate
> and go so far as to rank people into different grades so as to allocate
> our universal values accordingly . . . we are betraying the very idea of
> universal values.[70]

In less than two weeks Li Ming would help to launch a petition among mainland Chinese immigrants to oppose the bill as well as calling for mainlanders to join the planned march on 9 June.

Reuters commissioned a survey at the end of December 2019 to ask Hong Kong residents to gauge their support for the protest movement. 44 percent of those born outside Hong Kong supported the movement while 20 percent had joined a protest. For those born inside Hong Kong the corresponding figures were 67 and 46 percent. This poll was conducted by telephone in Cantonese.[71] It is reasonable to guess that most of the interviewees born outside Hong Kong were Cantonese-speaking mainland Chinese, as their number is immensely higher than other ethnic minorities who can also speak Cantonese. This rebuts the nativists' argument that mainland immigrants are necessarily pro-Beijing. This is also in line with previous findings. Back in 2015, Ray Kin-man Yep from City University of Hong Kong said that there was no big difference in terms of political position between mainland immigrants and native Hong Kongers. What was noticeable about mainland immigrants was not the supposed inclination towards pro-Beijing parties, rather it was the high percentage – 70 percent – who were neutral. Yet, again, the native Hong Kongers also had a similar proportion of politically neutral people.[72]

In 2016, Ngok Ma and two other scholars conducted a study which claimed that

> Chinese immigrants in Hong Kong are more pro-establishment and supportive of pro-government parties. With China's huge population, this implies a strategic importing of Chinese migrants, whose inflow to other Asian states can significantly skew the politics of neighbouring states in destined directions.[73]

Susanne Yuk-Ping Choi from CUHK debated this conclusion by pointing out the weakness of the study. It had failed to provide the actual share of pro-Beijing Chinese immigrants among the total number of Chinese immigrants, and its conclusion only relied on one year of data, having only asked a single question. Actually, the three scholars admitted that as far as support for democracy was concerned, there was 'no significant difference between the latecomers [Chinese who immigrated after 1997] and the natives'. Choi questioned whether, if only earlier and older immigrants were more pro-Beijing, might this not be more the result of their lived experiences in Hong Kong rather than on the mainland?[74]

Francis Lap Fung Lee showed that if Ngok Ma had used column percentage rather than row percentage for his analysis, it would show that the actual share of pro-Beijing Chinese immigrants among the total number of Chinese immigrants and the picture would be clearer:[75]

Table 2.7   Political inclinations of Hong Kong natives and mainland Chinese immigrants

	Natives	*Mainland immigrants*
Pro-Beijing	8.6%	11.4%
Pro-democrats	51.7%	27.6%
Neutral	24.2%	25.8%
Uncertain	17.6%	32.8%
Total	100%	100%

Again, instead of showing that mainland immigrants were mainly pro-Beijing, the table showed that more than 25 percent of them were pro-democracy, while nearly 60 percent were either neutral or uncertain. The logical conclusion for democrats is to double our efforts in winning neutral immigrants to our side. To say otherwise is most likely to end up with a self-fulfilling prophecy.

Mainland Chinese Students

How did the seven thousand mainland students studying in Hong Kong view the 2019 revolt? A survey showed the following:

Table 2.8   Views of mainland Chinese students in Hong Kong[76]

Attitude towards the anti-extradition bill movement	
Strongly and relatively supportive:	34.7%
Strongly and relatively disagree:	36.2%
Neutral and do not understand:	29.1%
Attitude towards the demand for independent inquiry into police conduct	
Strongly and relatively supportive:	60.4%
Strongly and relatively disagree:	11.6%
Neutral and do not understand:	27.9%

Attitude towards the demand for universal suffrage

Strongly and relatively supportive:	35.1%
Strongly and relatively disagree:	27.7%
Neutral and do not understand:	37.3%

Mainland students' support for the protesters was lower than that of mainland immigrants, but still one-third supported the demand to withdraw the bill and for universal suffrage, while the overwhelming majority supported an independent inquiry into the police. There was also consistently a high percentage of those who said that they were 'neutral or do not understand', which suggests their capacity for doubt, in spite of their supposed loyalty to Beijing.

WOMEN AND MINORITIES' PARTICIPATION

In general, a relatively high proportion of women took part in the seven months of protest. From early June until early August, across twelve protests, women accounted for 45.6 percent of the participants on average.[77]

At first the braves were thought to be nearly all men until it was found that there was also a significant number of women. Some were interviewed by the media. In the period between June 2019 and January 2020, arrested women protesters accounted for 25.4 percent of the total, or 1,816 out of a total of 7,143.[78] One can guess that among the arrested women protesters, a certain proportion of them were braves. This largely dispels the masculine image of the braves, especially after a beautiful painting of a seemingly young girl in full protective gear spread in graffiti and online. This icon was eventually made into a 'Lady Liberty', with one hand holding an umbrella to express her connection to the Umbrella Movement and then another hand holding up a flag with the words *gwong fuk hoeng gong, si doi gaak min*, or 'liberate Hong Kong, revolution of our times', to represent the way forward. On 13 October, a four-metre-high Lady Liberty, weighing 80 kilograms, was carried to the top of the Lion Rock Hill, an endeavour made possible by crowdfunding. A Telegram channel with 1,400 subscribers discussed details of the project and then an online referendum was held in which six thousand citizens voted on nine different designs. Although it only stood for a night and was destroyed the next day, it went down in the memory of the public. The choice of Lion Rock Hill was also deliberate. Originating from an old television program with the same name, Lion Rock Hill symbolises the so called 'Hong Kong Spirit' – hardworking, self-made, optimistic: a happy version of laissez-faire capitalism, one might say.

One tactic that some in the blue camp employed in their propaganda war against the yellow camp was to appeal to misogyny, attacking women protesters as 'sluts' or 'whores'. Law Fan Chiu-fun, the former education secretary, declared that women protesters provided free sex to male protesters, although no evidence was provided. Prince Wong. a former spokesperson for the youth organisation Demosistō, once held up a placard with the words 'HK police are murderers and rapists' at a protest. In the following days her photo was circulated online, with her holding up an edited placard with the words 'HK comfort women reward the cockroaches [i.e. the protesters] by letting them fuck them as many times as they like'. She condemned the act for showing that Beijing supporters only saw women as sexual objects and nothing more.[79]

Some in the yellow camp also made sexist and misogynist comments targeting the blue camp. The private photos of a female police officer were put online after she had some confrontation with protesters. Chapman To, a local celebrity, reposted some of them and mocked her figure and hinted that she was sexually promiscuous. The next day he posted another female police officer's photo, mocking her for being overweight and suggesting that the police sent this policewoman to confront the protesters because they 'wanted to convince the public that not all female police officers are sluts'. A woman activist criticized these yellow camp people for doing exactly what the conservative blue camp had been doing to stigmatise women.[80]

Women protesters twice asserted their roles as mothers in the movement. On 14 June and 5 July some women activists held rallies in the name of mothers, to support the young protesters and condemn police violence. Their big banner said, 'Don't shoot our kids!' Thousands of mothers and fathers attended – they mostly had children involved in the movement. A group of 'housewives' organised many solidarity actions to support the protests as well.

Ethnic Minorities

Hong Kong is not kind to poor 'foreigners' – a term local Chinese often used to describe ethnic minorities even if they are permanent residents here. Jeffrey Andrews, a Hong Kong-born Indian and social worker, looked back on his experiences of being discriminated against when he was young. 'I hate my colour. I don't know who I am: not Indian, not an international citizen, not a Hong Konger, not Chinese, who am I?', he asked himself.[81] After the outbreak of the great resistance, many ethnic minorities joined the protests as individuals. On 16 October, the convener of the Civil Front, Jimmy Sham, was badly attacked by organised criminals, some of whom were allegedly South Asian. Immediately there were online hate speech against South Asians and calls to attack the mosque in Tsim Sha Tsui at the next march on 20 October. The shop owners of nearby Chung King Mansions, famous for their ethnic diversity, were also very nervous about the possible attack. The online response overwhelmingly condemned the racist call, however. On the day of the march, shop owners from Chung King Mansions, mainly South Asians, distributed free water to protesters, while the latter came to greet the ethnic minorities with slogans such as 'we are all Hong Kongers!' Both sides chanted the same slogan, 'five demands, not one less!' That was a moving scene. On the same day, someone left graffiti on the wall with the words, in English, 'HKer is not defined by race'. In the ensuing days, a lot of people came to buy from the shops just to show their solidarity. In the face of a racist attack both sides connected with each other on their own initiative for the first time.

Hong Kong has more than 300,000 foreign domestic workers, mostly from the Philippines and Indonesia. Some of them sympathised with the movement but their status was too vulnerable for them to speak out. The case of Yuli Riswati was alarming. She had been an Indonesian domestic helper for ten years, and also a writer who had written reports on the lives of migrant workers like her. She took part in many marches in 2019, taking photos and reporting for her fellow workers. The government soon detained her and deported her in early December. There was much less solidarity with her case.

In this great revolt many people tried to do something so they mustered up whatever community or identity they could conceive of to support the movement. Both Protestant and Catholic priests, as individuals, gave active support to the protest. There was also the *ngan faat zuk*, or 'senior citizens', who would go between the police and the protesters to slow down the police actions.

The LGBT community held a 6,500-strong pride parade on 16 November to support the movement to defend Hong Kong's autonomy. The rally particularly highlighted the opposition to the government's face mask ban because some in the LGBT community do not feel that it is safe to come out and choose to wear face masks at a public event like this. When the LGBT community posted their campaign literature on LIHKG before their parade it was met with great hostility. LGBT people either retorted back, or patiently explained why it was important for the LGBT community to participate in the movement against Beijing, pointing out that 'most LGBT people are also liberal minded and hence they are part of the present movement'. Some tried to convince the homophobic nativist critics by saying that 'if we have equality of gender and sexual minorities here then it will make the need for a separation between Hong Kong and the mainland even more convincing'.[82] By this the author of this comment meant that if you want to separate Hong Kong from the mainland, then recognising LGBT rights would help to achieve this goal as it is something that the mainland would never do. This argument is questionable though. Instead of demanding the same rights for the mainland LGBT community, this LGBT activist reassured the homophobic critic by appealing to the common goal of separation from the mainland. When it comes to mainlanders, very often the universal values which certain Hong Kongers hold dear are not applied.

SUMMARY

In the first two to three weeks of the 2019 revolt there was a new challenge to foreign reporters: they could not find a protest leader to interview as it was a leaderless movement. It was an intensely spontaneous movement, with the masses themselves taking matters into their own hands. With little experience, without leaders and making a lot of mistakes, they learnt quickly. Young radicals, students, working people, the middle class, women, ethnic minorities, and senior citizens stuck together as much as they could to pose the greatest threat any Hong Kong government has ever faced since the CCP's urban guerrilla warfare against the colonial government in 1967. The protesters were mainly new hands to politics, coming from very different backgrounds and carried with them very different political inclinations – far right, centrist, moderate, leftist, liberal, and pacifist – but which were all far from consolidated. On many occasions, when some protesters went too far in their violence against people from the blue camp, there were always people with a kind heart who tried to stop them. This led many people to believe that there was a mechanism to right the wrongs within this great spontaneity, and no need for organised intervention. To what extent this was true I will leave to the discussion in Chapter 4.

3

Events

THREE CRUCIAL DAYS IN JUNE

The 9th, 16th, and 21st, when the 2019 revolt broke out, were the most important days in June. Before the first great march on Sunday 9 June, even if one felt the discontent of the people in the air, the demoralisation of the past five years made most opposition parties pessimistic about the response of the people to the call. An anonymous pan-democrat politician told the press towards the end of May that he or she wondered 'if there could be hundreds of thousands of people taking to the streets. In 2003 they did because at that time the economy was bad, but currently the economy is okay and people have not yet felt the pain of the extradition bill'.[1]

On 9 June, one million people would take to the streets. They had prioritised politics over the economy, and they felt the pain of the bill. That figure far exceeded the record number of participants in a march in Hong Kong, which was set when 500,000 people marched against the national security bill in 2003. The police figure for the 9 June march was 240,000. Professor Ron S. Y. Hui of Hong Kong University put it at between 810,000 and 1,080,000. The last time that I saw such a big march was in 1989 when local people marched to support the democratic movement on the mainland.

The protesters began marching at 3 p.m. and they did not finish until 10 p.m. Many shop owners along the main road distributed bottled water for free, and those who had their businesses affected by the march said they really did not mind at all. A survey by the *Mingpao* newspaper showed that for one-third of the participants it was the first time that they had ever joined a protest.

On the same day, solidarity rallies and marches were held in 29 cities around the world. Sydney's rally seemed to have been the biggest, with five thousand protesters. The overseas Hong Kong diaspora was not known for its interest in politics, however this time it helped to build these solidarity actions. The Taiwan government's Mainland Affairs Council expressed its admiration for the march and appealed to the Hong Kong government not to ignore the protesters.

The march encouraged everyone. On 10 June, the Social Workers' General Union called for a strike, followed by student unions from seven universities calling for a class boycott. The High School Students Anti-China Extradition Bill Concern Group echoed the call. The Hong Kong Professional Teachers' Union supported the class boycott but not the strike. The Catholic Diocese of Hong Kong announced their respect for those teachers and students who took part in the class boycott – the Catholic Church owns a lot of schools in Hong Kong, as do several Protestant denominations. On top of this, more than a hundred shop owners called for the stopping of business to protest the government.

The pan-democrat parties, after some internal debate, decided not to condemn the protesters' violence after 9 June, as they would have done previously, and instead targeted Carrie Lam's refusal to withdraw the extradition bill.[2] This made the united front between them and the braves possible.

The LegCo was supposed to convene again to have a second reading of the extradition bill on 12 June. Meanwhile, young Hong Kongers were busy joining Telegram channels and debating what to do next. Some of these channels had 40,000 subscribers. In the end a consensus was reached: they were going to assemble at 8 a.m. on 12 June to lay siege to the LegCo building. On that day the action was carried out as planned: they occupied the two main roads, despite the police attacking them with a lot of pepper spray. Several drivers, seemingly deliberately, pulled over in the middle of the road under the pretext that their cars had broken down. The whole area was in chaos. In 2014, on the last day of the occupation at Admiralty, the protesters had hung a big banner from the footbridge across the main road with the words 'we will be back'. They did come back on 12 June 2019. Upon learning of the protest, the speaker of the LegCo announced the postponement of its meeting. The protesters, allegedly numbering 40,000, besieged the building regardless. At 3.30 p.m. they started to charge the LegCo building and the government headquarters. Clashes with the police broke out. Some protesters threw bottled water and possibly bricks at the police. The radical young people wanted to vent their anger at the bill and the government, regardless of whether the legislature was holding meetings or not.

One participant wrote the following account of that day:

> At 2 p.m., a group of Christians sang 'Sing Hallelujah to the Lord' to the police . . . I understand some would not comprehend why they were doing this or might have thought that they were just being silly. But they had already been singing for more than fifteen hours, since the night before . . . Yeah, some people began to do some silly things in a very serious manner, but that would carry with it an element of strength and make it very touching. Even netizens on LIHKG applauded them.
>
> This resistance [the siege of the LegCo building] did not have 'the stage' [meaning organisation or leadership] so whenever the frontliners lacked helmets they would just turn around, face people behind them, raise their two hands above their heads and yell 'helmets!', and then the people behind them would transmit the message to people further behind and soon piles of helmets were passed from the back to the front. The same went for cable ties and umbrellas.[3]

When night fell, the MTR Corporation closed Admiralty station to stop people going to the LegCo building. One female student, when asked why she would risk injury to join the protest, had this to say:

> My parents worry that our protest may affect our future careers. What I want to say is that if one does not see any future for the place one lives in, how would it be possible that I would have a future?[4]

The hard-line crackdown by the police angered a lot of people. One senior civil servant, in a newspaper article, asked Carrie Lam: 'What did the protesters do on 12 June that convinced you to allow [the police] to open fire at people's heads?'[5] There was daily resistance to the police during that week, even inside the hospitals. The police complained to the press that after the crackdown on the 12th, their officers were constantly bullied by hospital nurses and other professionals. During the week following 12 June, police officers stationed in the hospitals were often addressed as 'dogs' by nurses, who took away their seats when they were not present. Hence the police withdrew from their posts there, at least for a while.

The protests continued for the next two days. A lot of young people disrupted transportation by stopping the doors of MTR trains from closing. They called this a 'non-cooperative movement'. At one point the police fired tear gas grenades and rubber bullets at reporters. One foreign reporter, pointing at the police, yelled: 'You shoot the journalists! You shoot the journalists! Hong Kong is not China, not yet!' These words went down in the memory of Hong Kongers. Online debates now called for a general strike with the slogan 'is there any non-cooperative movement more powerful than a general strike?' The next day the police were very much annoyed by the reporters who were present at its press conference as most of them wore helmets to protest the shooting of reporters. The Civil Front, emboldened by the uprising and the fact that public opinion had, instead of turning against the violence of the radical young, turned against Carrie Lam, announced that it would plan another march that coming Sunday (16 June) and appealed to protesters to wear black that day. This was to be followed by 'three suspensions' – a general strike, class boycott, and stoppage of business – on Monday. Disrupting trains, wearing black, protesters fighting police, tension between police and reporters, repeated calls for 'three suspensions', building human chains – all of these defining elements of the 2019 revolt, or at least their prototypes, were already evident in early June.

So too was death. On 15 June, 35-year-old Marco Leung killed himself after hanging an anti-extradition bill banner on the terrace of a mall in Admiralty. He had joined the Umbrella Movement and had been politically active since then. The news shocked and grieved many people, especially the young, at a moment when most of them were in high spirits preparing for the second great march the next day. The image of Leung, wearing a yellow raincoat with his back facing the viewers, immediately became another legacy of the protests, and Hong Kongers felt deeply connected to it. As one young woman said:

[May's shaking hands were covering her face, crying] On 15 June our first martyr, wearing yellow, jumped from a height. This left the deepest impression on me . . . I was not there. On his 'tau cat' [the first week after someone passes away] I [visited the site] with flowers to pay tribute to him. He was compelled to take his life by this government . . . On that day many people there cried.

I don't trust this government, or its police. I don't trust those who only think about money, about their interests, and about themselves alone . . . Previously I didn't care about politics. Yet this movement makes me concerned about these social issues. Just think, if our generation's situation is worsening, how can it be possible that the next generation will fare better? . . . This movement is a revolution by the Hong Kongers! Because people around me look like they are going to give up everything to fight![6]

Carrie Lam, after talking to Beijing, announced on the 15th that she would put a hold on the extradition bill. This at least appeased certain sections of the moderate opposition. People such as Law Wing-chung, a former political assistant to the financial secretary, argued that Lam's putting a hold on the bill meant that it would be withdrawn, and that violence must be avoided. Some pan-democrat parties now wavered and convinced the Civil Front to call off the three suspensions scheduled for the coming Monday. This angered a lot of people, and this time even the CTU was not convinced and announced that they would go on with their three suspensions.

On Sunday 16 June, two million people took to the streets. Before the march there was already online discussion saying 'Marco Leung will march with us'. When the Civil Front announced the number of protesters that evening it said that 'two million plus one took to the streets'. The 'one' referred to Leung, now considered the first martyr of the movement, to whom the Civil Front wanted to pay tribute. The march was so big that it did not finish until midnight. It was and is the biggest march ever held in Hong Kong. On the same day, forty cities around the world also held solidarity marches and rallies. The Taipei rally drew ten thousand people. The newfound bond between Taiwan and Hong Kong was further consolidated. Carrie Lam apologised and this was met with contempt by protesters.

The success of the great mobilisation on the 16th sent most people to a state of euphoria in the following week. A sense of pride, of assertiveness, of being Hong Kongers swept across the city. The radical youth kept their non-cooperative movement going, this time by flocking into the buildings of different government departments and obstructing their work. It became a very risky endeavour when they targeted the police headquarters, however. On the 21st, thousands of young protesters laid siege to the police headquarters for fifteen hours. The police were surprisingly restrained and stayed inside without seriously attacking the protesters. The unprecedented great protest and Carrie Lam's apology had put the police on the defensive. But the siege still created a very tense situation. Three thousand fully armed riot police were already stationed inside the headquarters, while another thousand were stationed not far away at Victoria Park, waiting for the order to surround the protesters from behind. 'What if some radical protesters start breaking into the headquarters?' This was the question which hundreds of thousands of yellow camp members had been asking the whole day, with great anxiety. If this happened, surely the police would retaliate with bloodshed. Late in the night, the crowd had to decide whether they would stay or leave. Joshua Wong was there, and he proposed an online vote to decide. Ten thousand people would join the vote, and 81 percent chose to leave at 11 p.m. However, many refused to accept the vote and said that many who voted had not been present at the protest and therefore had no right to vote in the first place. Some claimed that it was all up to individuals to decide what to do and that a collective will was not a good thing. Some accused Wong of being responsible for the failure of the Umbrella Movement, and now they did not want to listen to his command. Of those who wanted to stay, some might have wanted to try to break into the police headquarters. Luckily, even if there was such an adventurist proposal it was not listened to by the crowd. What's more, the deadlock itself had prompted more people to leave. Eventually the protest dispersed. Nonetheless, that the young people dared to lay siege to the police headquarters showed that even when the movement was still largely defensive in terms of its objectives, its tactics were already on the offensive.

The last week of June was dominated by protesters making use of the G20 summit in Osaka, on the 28th and 29th, to advance their demands. Through online discussion and preparation they managed to use crowdfunding to get advertisements published in many well-known international media outlets a week before the summit, followed by the Civil Front's rally of ten thousand people on the 26th to ask Xi Jinping to respond to the Hong Kong people's demands during the summit. This successful attempt to gain greater international visibility strengthened

Hong Kongers: it was a reminder that Hong Kong is an international city, not a more inward-looking mainland city.

Meanwhile everyone was looking forward to the coming annual 1 July march, another chance to put pressure on Carrie Lam.

1 JULY: THE OCCUPATION OF THE LEGCO BUILDING

The 1 July march was smaller than the two in June, but it still drew 550,000 people, the largest 1 July march since 2003. In recent years the 1 July marches were characterised by huge diversity and pluralism – there were no widely accepted common demands, and civil associations and parties just took the chance to promote themselves. This time was different. All participants, including the Civil Front, would agree to the following four demands:

1. withdraw the extradition bill
2. stop labelling protesters as 'rioters'
3. drop criminal charges against protesters
4. conduct an independent inquiry into police behaviour

It was the fifth demand which still lacked consensus. Before the march there was a lot of online discussion about whether the protesters should just call for the resignation of Carrie Lam, or call for universal suffrage, or both. Certain radical youth immediately understood what was at stake and they mostly opposed the first proposal: 'What is the point of merely replacing Carrie Lam with another Beijing-appointed CE?', they asked. Yet the Civil Front, on its 1 July handbill, merely called for the resignation of Carrie Lam and to 'restart political reform' – which was hollow in substance. My group of friends and I were on the side of the radical youth, but we were not sure how broad the support for universal suffrage would be. Had the people forgotten about what they had demanded in 2014? Instead of joining the march that day, we set up a booth and with loudspeakers we chanted the demand for universal suffrage to see how popular the demand would be. We were delighted to see that a lot of people chanted with us. The people had not forgotten. Quite a lot of liberal politicians had, however, and were soon punished.

On the night of 30 June, a thousand young protesters gathered outside the LegCo building so that they could disrupt the hoisting of the Chinese flag – commemorating the return of sovereignty over Hong Kong to China – scheduled for 8 a.m. the next day. This forced the government to proceed with its ceremony indoors instead. On the morning of 1 July, there were repeated clashes between young people and the police. Several hundred protesters eventually occupied the main streets around the LegCo building. They gathered and discussed what to do next. Five targets for siege were proposed; after some chaotic discussion they managed to vote, and the majority chose the LegCo building. But they could not come to a consensus as to when they should begin. They dispersed and each acted on their own.

From 1.30 p.m. to 5 p.m. several dozen protesters, after working for hours, successfully broke several glass doors to the LegCo building. Several pan-democrat legislators tried to stop them, and one of them took to one knee to beg them, but the protesters ignored them. After the march started at 3 p.m., a lot more people came to join the protesters outside the building and there was soon a big crowd. According to Siu Wan, a citizen reporter, there were about 50,000 people outside the LegCo building. At 6.30 p.m., twenty protesters went into the reception hall of the building through the broken doors but were stopped by another metal door inside. They began to break the metal door, and at 9 p.m. they succeeded in breaking through. By that time there were hundreds of riot police behind the metal door. When a hundred protesters were about to charge through the broken metal doors and everyone was expecting clashes to happen, the intruders were instead able to go inside without a fight because the police suddenly evacuated and disappeared altogether, allowing the protesters to break in. (Three weeks later we would witness this kind of mysterious conduct by the police once again.) Once they were inside of the building, however, the protesters began to smash things and spray graffiti, destroying the photos of old and new speakers and breaking electronic and audio devices. Some painted slogans on the walls, including 'it is you who taught us merely demonstrating is useless' and 'genuine universal suffrage'. Some waved the former colonial flag. They occupied the building for three hours before retreating. One reporter noted that:

Someone tried to touch some objects but was shouted at by others with the words 'please don't touch!' Another person, while walking down the stairs, shouted 'we occupy, not vandalise!' The one who was shouted at defended themselves and said that 'I am just examining this thing which was already broken'. But the guy was once again shouted at: 'because someone has broken it! Please don't do these kinds of things!'[7]

Someone tried to damage the building's library as well, but they were stopped by other protesters. This kind of scenario would repeat itself many times during the brief occupation. One of the protesters was distressed to see so much vandalism and expressed regret that he had not stopped these acts. Another explained:

> I don't know what the purpose of breaking into the LegCo building is, and I don't know what to do, but I will say it is . . . to show the people's determination and ability to confront the government and make them fear the people.[8]

Leung Kai-ping, a localist and postgraduate who once edited *Undergrad*, the student magazine of the University of Hong Kong, appealed for outside support and hoped a thousand more protesters could come into the LegCo building. At that moment, there were thousands of protesters outside watching; many were sympathetic but were not ready to join those inside. On the other hand, Leung Kai-ping and some others, both at the site and online, worried that without a public statement on why they occupied the legislature they would only be seen as 'rioters'. Soon three drafts were prepared; none of them demanded independence. They were sent to those inside the legislature and eventually one was chosen to be read to the public. That was at 11 p.m. 'The Declaration of Hong Kong Protesters' traced the roots of the occupation to the fact that

> The current Government of Hong Kong is no longer making Hong Kongers its priority. To ensure the voice of the Hong Kong people is heard, we, the Hong Kong citizens, are forced to take non-cooperative actions, such as occupying streets and even the Legislative Council today.[9]

Towards the end it reiterated the five demands; once again the fifth demand was about universal suffrage, not just Carrie Lam stepping down. This was the moment when the 2019 revolt finalised its official version of the five demands. Upon hearing that the police might come back at midnight, the occupiers retreated in haste. Yet when everyone was outside someone suddenly realised that four protesters had remained inside, determined to continue their occupation even if it might cost them their lives. According to Siu Wan, at this moment someone in the crowd just outside the legislature suddenly shouted *jat cai zau! jat cai zau!* ('retreat together!'), and soon everyone echoed the same words. A man with a loudspeaker ordered, 'whoever wants to wait for the four brothers step forward!' Everyone did. And so, everyone waited, despite the ticking clock. Several dozen protesters hurried back to the conference hall and dragged the four out against their will. Then the big crowd dispersed towards Central when the police began to advance.[10]

Both the government and certain moderate liberals still expected that the next day public opinion would turn against the 'violent intruders'. That day never came. The government was also disappointed by the pan-democrat's failure in condemning the occupation. A week later, after another great march on 7 July, the Civil Front, in their new statement, quietly replaced their obsolete demand for Carrie Lam to step down and embraced universal suffrage instead. The pan-democrats quietly followed suit sometime later.[11]

The sympathy for the young intruders was huge, to the extent that many insisted that the protesters had only destroyed symbols of the current government, even if this was not exactly true. Nonetheless, some of the damage done was quite meaningless, and as we have seen, there were always protesters coming forward on the spot to stop excesses.

However, if one compares the events of 1 July with the Taiwanese students in 2014, who occupied their legislature for more than three weeks (the Sunflower Movement), then the shortcomings of the Hong Kong case are obvious. Precisely because the latter was organised before they took the action of occupying the legislature, they ran the occupation in a more orderly manner, had their statement properly read out very early on, and organised meetings and actions inside and outside. There was no vandalism. If the occupation was meant to be the people taking back power, surely vandalising the facilities in the legislature did not help at all. But that was what had happened in Hong Kong.

Yet despite its shortcomings, the occupation of the LegCo building helped to consolidate the militant democratic line of the revolt. It practically told everyone, 'we don't want to replace this ruler with that ruler, we want regime change! We want democracy!'

21 JULY: WHEN COPS PAT THE SHOULDER OF ORGANISED CRIME

Three events occurred on 21 July, marking the date as another watershed for the movement. First, the Civil Front held its sixth march on Hong Kong Island, in which 430,000 people took part. Few knew however that a trap was being laid at the Liaison Office, and that another ambush was awaiting protesters who lived in Yuen Long (which is close to the border with mainland China).

With the march drawing to a close on the evening of the 21st, a big crowd of protesters continued to head towards the Liaison Office. I was among them, and I received a message and a photo from my friend, whose friend lived close to the Liaison Office. His message was that the police outside the Liaison Office had suddenly retreated at around 6 p.m. and there were no more officers guarding the building. The attached photo proved it. I arrived at around 7 p.m., along with a big and angry crowd. Indeed, there were no police (later there was a report that four police officers were inside the gate, but I did not see any of them). The Liaison Office has always been heavily guarded, as it is a popular target of protest. If one considers that just across the street there is a big police station, then the scene begins to look like a trap. Soon the youngsters there began to throw anything at hand at the Liaison Office, to spray graffiti with slogans, such as 'fuck *Zi-naa*', on the wall, and to throw paint at the national emblem. Soon rumours spread that the police were coming, and everyone retreated. I went along with them and passed by the police station. Its door was shut. I then tried to go up to a road where the MTR station is but was stopped by a bunch of youngsters telling me that they had found out that a big team of riot police was stationed two blocks away. These police officers had just stood by within a hundred meters, allowing the protesters to humiliate one of the symbols of Chinese authority in Hong Kong.

The protest soon developed into serious clashes between the police and the braves. Those who chose to return home had also begun their journey. Meanwhile, an MTR train heading towards the New Territories West was carrying hundreds of passengers: some were protesters, some were just regular passengers. At 10 p.m., when the train arrived in Yuen Long, some passengers got off and some remained inside. Suddenly a crowd of around one hundred men, wearing white, rushed up and began indiscriminately hitting the passengers, inside and outside the train, with sticks. People screamed for help. Two policemen walked past but simply ignored what they heard. Similar attacks also occurred outside the station. That night, within three hours, 24,000 emergency calls to the New Territories North police call centre were recorded, but the police did nothing. In one typical case, a caller was simply told, 'if you are afraid stay home'. Some went to the nearby police station to report the incident, but it was closed. The police did not arrive until 39 minutes had passed. Their inaction led to a reported 45 injured victims, with five left in serious condition. The victims included a pan-democrat legislator.

The next day the police could not explain why they were 39 minutes late when their police station was so close to the MTR station; especially considering that hours before the incident two pan-democrat District Council members had already warned the police about a possible attack by organised criminals, but were simply ignored. A former senior police officer challenged the commissioner of police, 'will you dare to say that in Yuen Long that night there were only two police officers on duty?' The former officer went into detail about the hierarchy of the police to show that the Yuen Long police station had abundant manpower but had knowingly abandoned its duty.[12]

A spontaneous collective endeavour among reporters, civil servants, scholars, and common citizens immediately began to try to learn the truth. Soon the truth, or at least part of it, was revealed. Back on 11 July, Li Jiyi, head of the New Territories Working Bureau of the Liaison Office, told the members of the Shap Pat Heung Rural Committee that if the rioters ever dared to come to Yuen Long then they as patriots should get rid of these people. One day before the incident there were also signs showing that members of organised crime syndicates were preparing an attack. A post by one anonymous administrative officer warning about the coming demonstration on the 21st began to circulate:

X Waan [the Liaison Office] has already mobilised . . . The authorities concerned have arranged for several thousand unknown persons to replace the police in dealing with the braves' attack, first by making a fuss with demonstrators, and then manufacturing a conflict between the braves and the patriots. The police would emerge after all of this to clear things up, so as to win back public support . . . As for demonstrations in different districts, the power organs ['qiangli bumen'] have already met with local organisations. Yuen Long is one of them.[13]

Most of the protesters had not learnt of this warning before they went to the march.

The public broadcaster Radio Television Hong Kong made a documentary demonstrating that the Yuen Long police had not only been aware of the mobilisation of these organised criminal syndicates hours before the attack but had also chatted with some of them outside the train station when the attack had started inside. A senior officer was seen patting the shoulders of one such individual. Lynette Ong, an associate professor at the University of Toronto, who has written on the Chinese state's collusion with organised crime, commented on the Yuen Long incident and said that it was comparable to the Mong Kok incident during the Umbrella Movement, albeit more organised.[14]

The attack angered a lot of people. But the next day a strange thing happened that stopped the people coming out to protest.

On the morning of the 22nd, warning messages circulated which indicated that organised crime groups were going to attack again in the afternoon, affecting not only Yuen Long but also Tuen Mun and Tsuen Wan (all three are in the New Territories West region of Hong Kong). Fear gripped these areas. At 3 p.m., all the shops closed, and the streets were empty. I walked around Tuen Mun and only saw a few pedestrians. But there was no attack. This became one of the many mysteries in the seven-month revolt. No matter if it was a plot or purely a rumour, the objective effect was to stop the protests from happening, at least for one day.

Beginning from the 23rd, the yellow camp started to fight back. This was the starting point of the high tide of the movement. The whole week saw the mobilisation of protesters from all walks of life. On the 24th and 25th, the radical youth went to the MTR in big crowds to conduct 'non-cooperative actions' and disrupt the transport there. On the 26th, 1,500 medical workers staged a sit-in at the Queen Elizabeth Hospital. On the same day, 15,000 aviation industry employees and other members of the public staged a sit-in at the Hong Kong International Airport to condemn the government and the police. They distributed handbills to visitors to explain why they were there. It was also the first time that the movement came up with the slogan, 'Hong Kong police knowingly break the law!' The protesters also repeatedly sang 'Do you hear the people sing?' This sit-in at the airport was important because it would be the first of a series of subsequent occupations of the airport, about which the government was deeply concerned – it was too important to fall into the hands of the protesters, yet cracking down on the latter before the eyes of foreign visitors was definitely not good for Carrie Lam.

Meanwhile someone applied for a license to march on the 27th in Yuen Long, to protest the actions of the police. Many people had been looking for a big march like this to vent their anger. The police refused to issue a license. It was the first time since the movement began that the police had refused to sanction a demonstration – and this set a precedent for the many more bans that would follow. When the news that the police had denied the applicant a license became known, protesters quickly came up with a brilliant idea for making the march possible. They appealed to people to go to Yuen Long to buy a special kind of cake there, called a 'sweetheart cake', so named because among Cantonese-speaking people it is given to one's relatives and friends when one gets married. There were plenty of reasons to go to Yuen Long to look for the cake – there are several shops there which are famous for making them. As a precaution, the night before the 'sweetheart cake' rush, the police arranged for workers to weld together the metal fences in Yuen Long to discourage the radical youth from breaking them and using them to fight the police. Meanwhile the city was boiling with anger. Some radical youth called for attacking the suspected territory of the organised crime syndicates there, while some seriously disagreed and warned of the consequences.

The next day, I arrived at Yuen Long at 3 p.m., but for a while I only saw a hundred or so protesters. I heard that several blocks away there was a long queue in front of the sweetheart cake shop – but not very many in the streets protesting. Would it be that people were afraid of the legal consequences of joining a banned march? Suddenly I saw hundreds of thousands of protesters coming from different directions. Later we heard that around 280,000 people took part. The street was so crowded with people we could barely move forward, and we all sweated under the sun. It was an angry protest. People laid siege to the police station and put stickers on its walls condemning the police. Suddenly there was commotion ahead. The police shot tear gas at the protesters ahead of us and we all fled to side streets. Meanwhile at the front, serious fighting broke out between the police and the protesters.

This action was a great civil disobedience. Hundreds of thousands of previously moderate democratic supporters, although not ready to join the braves, now dared to defy the police ban and march in the streets. Yes, they were very angry. They believed that the 'mainlandisation of Hong Kong' was occurring in front of their eyes. Many now became believers of the call to 'the revolution of our time'. This laid the groundwork for August.

THE 5 AUGUST GENERAL STRIKE AND ITS AFTERMATH

In the last week of July, the yellow camp was in a highly agitated mood. The radical youth repeatedly campaigned for 'three suspensions' again on Monday 5 August. A consensus was soon reached that on that day there would be strike rallies in seven districts to draw people together. Artists now rolled out eye-catching handbills and cartoons to promote their messages, such as 'triads and police are all alike, Hong Kong People go on strike!'[15] Employees from the catering industry circulated pictures of a chef cooking dishes with the words, 'you still work and cook? . . . we will all soon be cooked in a big hot pot!' They staged flash mobs in the streets and knelt to beg people to go on strike. On Sunday 4 August, 150,000 took to the streets in Tseung Kwan O to protest, and another 20,000 in Central. The next day, the radical youth took the chance to destroy many traffic lights to stop traffic. From then on, pedestrians and car drivers have had to be particularly careful. It is half a miracle that there have not been any serious accidents.

The CTU announced that 96 of its affiliated unions were prepared to join the general strike. Seven aviation industry unions, including the flight attendants' unions from Cathay Pacific, Cathay Dragon, and British Airways, supported their members going on strike (but were unable to join officially as time did not allow them to hold a convention to vote for an official strike). *Apple Daily* also became the main mouthpiece for the general strike. It was able to draw in many small business owners by reporting on yellow camp owners who supported the idea of a strike. These owners are very concerned about collusion between the police and organised crime in Hong Kong, as they know that they will become easy prey to this kind of collusion, as this is what happened before the founding of the ICAC in 1974.

On the morning of 5 August, the youth vanguard, dressed in black, dispersed to different subway stations to block the train doors to stop people from going to work. While some passengers quarrelled with the young protesters there were a lot of others who defended them. The subway transport was half paralysed until 1 p.m., making going to work in the morning nearly impossible for many employees.

Many employees did actively respond to the strike call by voluntarily stopping work. That was also why many employees were happy to cooperate with the radical youth in bringing down the subway. The weakness of the local trades unions in organising official strikes was compensated by the initiatives from below. Many employees simply abstained from work with different excuses, such as sick leave or family affairs. Many employers were tolerant of the first political strike in fifty years. The strike affected a lot of sectors: aviation, transport, finance, retail, catering, and the government. The aviation industry and the airport were the most severely affected. On the night of the 4th, one-third of the airport's air traffic controllers told management they would be taking sick leave the next day. They also released a statement informing the public they were going to carry out a work-to-rule action. On the 5th, a total of two thousand employees from Cathay Pacific, and one thousand from other airlines, went on strike. Two hundred baggage handlers joined the strike as well. According to the CTU, 350,000 workers joined the strike across the city. The Airport Authority Hong Kong (AA) knew they would not be able to fly as many flights as on normal days, and asked Cathay Pacific to cut half of their flights. According to one *South China Morning Post* report, the AA had to cut 250 flights in total on the 5th. Usually 68 flights land or take off each hour at the airport. The AA had to cut that down to 34. On the same day, thousands of protesters held a sit-in at the airport, and many tried to approach visitors to explain why they were on strike. Outside the airport, two hundred drivers for local bus operator Citybus (10 percent of its workforce) went on strike. A lot of bank workers also stopped working, forcing at least 51 branches to close. Less-affected branches had to downsize their services by closing some of their counters. Fifteen main roads and most of the MTR lines were either blocked or stopped running. What was likely to have been even more annoying to Beijing was that the heads of Citibank, HSBC, and the Hong Kong Jockey Club said they would be tolerant of the strikers. Nine important publicly funded theatre companies also expressed understanding over their staff going on strike, and 827 offline shops and 485 online shops also stopped doing business.[16] The impact was relatively small but it laid the ground for the later development of a yellow camp campaign that called for consumers to both boycott 'blue shops' and to encourage buying from 'yellow shops'.

Meanwhile 150,000 protesters (some say 300,000) joined the seven rallies in different districts, which was followed by the radical youth roaming the streets across fourteen districts, destroying traffic lights and building roadblocks. It was reported that a total of two hundred sets of traffic lights were damaged. But online posts from some self-professed traffic light repair workers said that some of the traffic lights were simply turned off by the Transport Department. At night, a total of thirteen police stations were under siege and a lot of clashes followed. In North Point and Tsuen Wan, organised crime syndicates attacked people in black clothes, but unlike during the Yuen Long incident, the latter fought back and chased them away. The ensuing weeks witnessed mobilisations nearly every day. The city seemed to be on the edge of an uprising.

On 9 August, the Civil Aviation Administration of China (CAAC) hit back by publicly warning Cathay Pacific that from the 10th onwards it would ban any staff who had taken part in 'illegal protests' from flying to or from the mainland. The protesters planned another action for the 10th, called 'Ten Thousand People to Pick up Passengers', with the aim of occupying the airport again; the action was supposed to end on the 11th. Hence, they also took the chance to protest the CAAC as well. Their action paralysed half of the flights arriving to and leaving from Hong Kong (some say that the real figure were closer to one-third and one-fourth being cancelled on the 10th and the 11th, respectively: according to one pilot, the AA overstated the number of cancelled flights while in fact it quietly allowed certain 'cancelled' flights to take off).

A self-identified air traffic controller, in response to online comments by certain braves expressing dissatisfaction with the two-day action at the airport, called it a 'once in a lifetime' success:

What you have accomplished today was far more successful than the 5th . . . After the actions the authorities preferred to play down [the effect of] the air traffic controllers' strike, do you know why? It is because the airport is the lifeline of the Hong Kong economy . . . The long-haul flights to Europe need the planes flying to Southeast Asia in the afternoon to fly back to Hong Kong before they can have planes to fly. If you cancel the Southeast Asian flights then it will affect later flights . . . Hong Kong has handled the highest amount of cargo traffic globally for eight years, if the chain [of services] is cut, a lot of couriers will have to pay compensation . . . This is big money. On the other hand, we suffered no loss, nobody bled, nobody got shot, and nobody get arrested, so what is your complaint?[17]

On the night of the 11th a young woman was blinded in her right eye by police fire, although she had done nothing to provoke the police. The image of her bandaged eye became an international emblem of the movement. The protesters now wanted to continue with their airport protest. The concourse, full of protesters, echoed enthusiastically a new slogan: 'black cops, pay back her eye!' The airport had to apply for a court injunction to stop the occupation. At one point, Carrie Lam questioned the intention of the protesters: 'are the rioters making a revolution?'

On the night of the 13th, there was an incident which would be used by Beijing to discredit the Hong Kong movement. The protesters at the airport found two suspicious mainland men, Fu Guohao and Xu Jinyang, and tied them up. Fu loudly claimed that he supported the Hong Kong police and told the crowd they could now beat him. The protesters got very angry and, drawing the conclusion that they were spies, started beating them. Other protesters restrained the violence. One of them was the legislator Kwok Ka-ki, who told the attackers to calm down and asked them, 'you condemned the police for lynching, but aren't you doing the same thing?' Richard Scotford, a British freelance reporter, protected Xu when a hundred protesters surrounded and kept kicking him. Both were eventually saved by paramedics, and Fu, upon his return to mainland China, was hailed as a hero by the media there. The pictures of him being attacked became Beijing's proof for accusing the Hong Kong protesters of being 'rioters'.

In the meantime, Beijing escalated its attack. When the occupation at the airport was at its height, the CAAC summoned Merlin Swire, chairman of Swire Pacific, the main shareholder of Cathay Pacific, and told him that a management change was necessary at the airline.[18] On the 14th, Cathay Pacific fired two of its pilots over their support for the protesters. On the 16th, Cathay Pacific CEO Rupert Hogg resigned, along with his deputy, Paul Loo. In its statement, Cathay Pacific reiterated its full support of 'one country, two systems' principle. Then the company turned against its rank-and-file employees, firing dozens and dozens of them, including Rebecca Sy, the chair of the flight attendants' union of the company's low-cost subsidiary, Cathay Dragon, for her support of the protesters. This did not satisfy Beijing, however, and soon it was time for Cathay's chairman, John Slosar, to resign, on 3 September.

On the 18th, the Civil Front held another big march which 1.7 million people joined. Prior to the march, online discussion showed that a lot of radical youth had decided that this march should remain peaceful, to draw the maximum number of protesters to pressure Carrie Lam. In the late evening, when the march was ending, I witnessed a lot of youths starting to appeal to others not to clash with the police and to go home. In any regular protest scene this would have descended into heated debate and a lot of shouting. This time was different though, and the young people willingly agreed to go home.

The last two weeks of August would see students agitating for another round of 'three suspensions', scheduled for 2 and 3 September when schools started again. One incident would help to promote the protesters' cause. On the night of 31 August, the riot police rushed onto a train in the Prince Edward MTR station and indiscriminately attacked the passengers inside without ever announcing whom they were hunting for and on what charges. Many were seriously hurt. Rumours spread that the police had killed someone inside. This event would add more fuel to the next month of protests.

YOUTH RADICALISM IN SEPTEMBER AND OCTOBER

The first day of September was a Sunday. The radical youth called for an action to block the airport one more time as a prelude to the next two days of 'three suspensions' activity. At noon, hundreds of youths arrived at the airport and nearby MTR stations and began to damage the facilities there, including throwing objects onto the tracks to stop the trains from moving, with the aim of paralysing the airport once again. The riot police clashed with them and a cat-and-mouse game ensued, disrupting the normal functioning in the airport. Soon after, the airport was able to extend the court injunction against protesters, and the MTR station was closed. The AA had to cancel 21 flights, however. More young protesters arrived at the airport on foot regardless. When night fell the protesters were stuck at the airport without transport and were in danger of being rounded up. They decided to leave the airport on foot. Afraid of police vehicles chasing after them, a small band of braves stopped the car traffic on the highway to block the police vehicles behind them from getting them. Meanwhile, upon hearing the radical youth were in danger, five thousand car owners drove to the Tsing Ma Bridge, which connects the airport to the rest of Hong Kong, to save the protesters. When the bird's-eye-view picture of a long and winding queue of vehicles in the night was posted online people nicknamed the action the 'Dunkirk evacuation, Hong Kong version'.

Many more young protesters were not able to go to the airport so they began to vandalise MTR stations wherever they could. A total of twenty stations were burned and their ticket machines damaged. This pattern of protest would repeat itself again and again throughout September, so much so that by 2 October the MTR Corporation had been forced to close a total of 47 stations.

Meanwhile, on 2 September, students' unions from thirteen universities and colleges announced a joint statement calling for a two-week class boycott. The deadline for Carrie Lam to respond was set for 13 September. High school students from 230 schools also prepared to move. On the morning of 2 September, Demosistō and the High School Students Anti-China Extradition Bill Concern Group held a rally of four thousand people in Central to call for the five demands. Many more had assembled briefly in the morning before going to class to build human chains to protest. In the afternoon 30,000 university students rallied at CUHK to demand the same thing.

On 1 September, employees from twenty industries released a joint statement calling for a two-day general strike. On the following two days, the CTU helped to hold a rally in Central which attracted 40,000 employees, who had boycotted work to gather there and protest Carrie Lam. This was followed by the usual clashes between youths and police all over the city. On the 4th, Lam announced the withdrawal of the extradition bill, but this did not convince the protesters to stop protesting.

On 8 September, there was a rally followed by a march to the US consulate to petition for the Hong Kong Human Rights and Democracy Act, which had been sponsored by the Republican senator Marco Rubio. It was promoted as a bill that would protect the Hong Kong people from Beijing's aggression. It was claimed that the rally had 250,000 participants. The police suspended the rally though and clashes followed.

The mysterious death of a fifteen-year-old girl, Chan Yin-lam, on 22 September, further antagonised the yellow camp. Her body was found floating in the sea, naked. She had been a protester. A forensic doctor regarded the case as suspicious and asked the police to investigate, but the latter refused.[19] Her case intensified fears of the arrival of a police state.

Throughout September, large and small protests were held every two or three days in various parts of Hong Kong. On 29 September there was a 'global anti-totalitarianism march', which was banned by the police, but which went ahead regardless. Hundreds of thousands of protesters took to the streets again but the police cracked down on them very quickly, which was followed by clashes across the city. Through the effort of overseas Hong Kongers there were solidarity marches in more than sixty cities in twenty countries on the 28th and 29th. The biggest seemed to be in Taipei, where 100,000 people took to the street.

The National Day march on 1 October was similar to the 29 September march – police cracked down, then protesters dispersed into guerrilla conflict with the police. Seeing her peaceful gesture rejected, Carrie Lam further escalated her attack by invoking, on 4 October, the colonial-era Emergency Regulations Ordinance, to impose a ban on face masks. This was simply treated with contempt by the yellow camp. In order to mock Lam, pictures were posted online by people showing how they would mask their faces without formally using any mask, for instance by painting their faces or combing their hair in a funny way. The next day also saw a lot of protests with people wearing masks to defy the ban. The whole city sank into chaos. The MTR halted all of its trains and closed its stations to avoid being targeted again. A lot of malls were closed as well. People started panic buying in supermarkets. The Education Bureau ordered schools to report the number of students who continued wearing masks in classes. This time even school administrators defied the order. On 20 October, another illegal march in Tsim Sha Tsui drew 350,000 protesters. The proud Hong Kongers continued to be defiant.

THE NOVEMBER BATTLES AT TWO UNIVERSITIES

The Battle at Chinese University

On 8 November, the death of a student from the Hong Kong University of Science and Technology (HKUST), Chow Tsz-lok, was announced, triggering off another round of radical protests. Chow was a fully geared-up 'sentinel' during the protest on the evening of the 4th; he was found unconscious after falling from a height. According to one doctor, instead of having serious wounds to his limbs – the usual result of falling from a height when the victim is conscious – Chow had serious wounds to his pelvic bones, which might suggest that he was unconscious when he fell. Some speculated that he might have been unable to move when he fell. Many people thought that Chow might have been chased by police who made him jump from a height or who had just simply killed him and then dropped the body down to the street. The police denied this. It was then that the slogan of the revolt advanced from 'Hong Kongers, resist!' to 'Hong Kongers, revenge!' The protesters soon reached a consensus on holding a week of 'three suspensions' again, plus big protests, beginning on Monday 11 November. This time the CTU was not active in calling for a strike, however, as they were not confident in doing so after the retaliation from Beijing and from big corporations, such as Cathay Pacific, in August. The radical youth once again resorted to the *bei baa gung* tactic of preventing workers from going to work by disrupting traffic. Eleven universities and colleges announced class suspensions.

The most radical action was taken inside CUHK. The so-called 'no. 2 bridge', just outside the campus, crossed a main road and a railway track. In the early hours of the 11th, young protesters took over the bridge and began to throw things from it to stop traffic. The riot police soon arrived and took back the bridge. The two sides fought each other, either by firing tear gas or throwing Molotov cocktails. At some point, the police broke through the students' defences and invaded the campus temporarily. In the late afternoon, the police stopped their attack. Meanwhile, on the same day, many parts of the city had also experienced big clashes, resulting in 287 arrests, two-thirds of which were of students.

The next day, the confrontation between the CUHK students and the police continued. Around one hundred protesters were guarding the no. 2 bridge. At noon, the vice-president of CUHK tried to mediate between the two sides. According to the *Chinese University Student Press*, there was a scuffle between those who wanted to negotiate and those who wanted to fight. One of the latter suddenly shouted, 'those behind wear your gas masks!', and the rear guards immediately followed orders without knowing the argument at the front. Three big garbage bins were rushed to the front. The police on the other side immediately attacked with tear gas, before charging forward and arresting five protesters. On that day at least eighty students were injured.[20]

At night the university president, Rocky Tuan, tried to mediate between the students and the police but was unsuccessful, as the police ignored the students' demand of releasing the five arrested students. At one point the police shot tear gas in his direction. Soon the police attacked again and escalated the violence by mobilising a vehicle-mounted water cannon.

Now many protesters, inside and outside the campus, feared that the police might eventually take over the campus and massacre the students there, repeating what Deng Xiaoping did to Chinese students in 1989, something which has always been fresh in the memory of Hong Kongers. Seeing pictures of the campus filled with fire and smoke, thousands of outsiders began to pour into the campus to help to safeguard it, or to bring supplies. As all transport was closed already, they had to rely on their feet. Only people who had motorbikes could arrive there relatively easily and they brought as many supplies as they could. At its height, probably several thousand students and supporters were on the campus to protect it from police invasion, although the police said they did not have this intention – they only wanted to secure the no. 2 bridge and stop the protesters from disrupting the main road below.

When asked by the press, the police made it clear that they would not refrain from shooting live ammunition as the university had become an 'arsenal'. According to later police reports, there were 3,900 unused petrol bombs on the campus when they got in after the battle. At the height of the conflict, some students broke into the athletics storage room and took away bows and arrows to fight the police. Some protesters even made their own catapult as well. In general, these weapons did not actually work that well. Since the outbreak of the movement, the university had already been nicknamed the 'Hong Kong Rioters Chinese University'. The origin of the nickname dates to late June, when the university's name on Google Maps was briefly tampered with and changed to this. The students might have been proud of the name though, as it now reappeared in the form of graffiti on the campus.

At about the same time, there were calls to confront the police everywhere in the city, to distract their attention and stop them from reinforcing their attack on CUHK. Fighting broke out in many places between the protesters and the police, organised crime, and blue camp supporters.

The police retreated from the campus late in the night. There were reports about frontline commanders having allegedly requested that headquarters order a retreat to avoid casualties on both sides. There was internal disagreement at the top but eventually the doves had it and ordered the retreat.[21] One student, Wong Hon-tung, who was at the site, was sceptical of this report. He quoted his friend, who overheard one police commander shouting to his men to 'stop shooting, we are running out of ammunition!' 'Could this be the reason that the police retreated?', he speculated.[22]

On the 13th, the campus was quiet because the police had not advanced. But the police siege was still in place. The campus was still tense. Beijing, through the Liaison Office, encouraged mainland students in CUHK to evacuate or even to leave Hong Kong altogether. This was followed by similar calls by other countries.

With campus peace restored, at least temporarily, the students had time to learn how to run certain essential facilities. The restaurant was taken over by volunteer cooks who provided reasonable meals; customers paid whatever amount they found fit. Some people began to learn to drive the campus buses. The braves practiced the art of throwing their petrol bombs. Certain posts were circulating online praising the protesters for self-managing the campus. Behind this nice image, however, tension was already building up between CUHK students and those coming from outside – students from other universities and non-students. Some protesters, not necessarily students from CUHK, imposed a 'border control' and checked everyone who wished to enter, including their bags. This annoyed many who taught or studied there. In online discussion and in two public meetings, the two sides crossed swords. There was also chaos and mis-management: smokers smoking besides stocks of petrol bombs, vandalism, outposts without guards, the taking over and driving of campus buses without a license (resulting in injuries to some people). Some non-CUHK protesters were even dissatisfied with the food that the CUHK students provided and insisted on having 'fish balls' instead. The CUHK students accused non-CUHK protesters of vandalising their campus and treating them with disrespect. The latter hit back accusing the former of treating them like 'condoms'. There was also argument about the very purpose of the battle – was it meant to defend CUHK, or was it meant to lure the police in for an attack? There was also a debate on whether they should stay on campus or leave. Many CUHK students approached the student union to intervene in the chaos on the campus, but the union leadership, afraid to assert a leadership role out of fear of being attacked for 'holding a stage' (to be in command), basically fell into inaction, except for holding one of the above-mentioned public meetings. Both meetings ended without conclusion.

The *Chinese University Student Press* released an interesting brief record of the public discussion on the 13th. On the topic of the purpose of occupying the no. 2 bridge, the exchange of opinions went as follows:

> One student argued that the action was to paralyse the transportation hub to stop people from going to work. Another pointed out that most Hong Kongers were *gong zyu* who would not be moved by [our] emotion, hence the need to force them to strike. This opinion was questioned by yet another student, as [forcing employees to strike] did not have the support of trade unions and public opinion, therefore, was it the right kind of strike? A worker-protester thought that, even if one could stop the MTR from running, . . . the boss would tell you that 'you can still come to work if you go around [the blockade] . . . He then reminded the students that while they did have classmates he [as an employee] did not have colleagues who would join him, therefore he needed organisation.[23]

On the 14th, the campus was still relatively peaceful, and the number of protesters had greatly declined – some argued that they should now go to support the students at Hong Kong Polytechnic University (PolyU), instead. The no. 2 bridge now only had twenty protesters guarding it.

On that day, I visited the campus and saw the walls sprayed with a lot of graffiti and slogans, such as 'we burn, you burn with us' and 'organise unions and prepare for *saam baa*'. We talked to friends there and few looked optimistic. In the late afternoon when my friends and I started to leave we were barred from doing so. Several young protesters said the police were coming and they could not let us go. We decided to climb up a slope and leave; when we were outside, we found that there were no police there after all.

At midnight on the 15th, three protesters – ostensibly of their own accord, but obviously guided by someone from the Independent Police Complaints Council – held a press conference announcing that they would reopen the main road if the government agreed not to postpone the coming District Council elections. This immediately created more division. Even if the police had long stopped attacking the chaotic occupation of the campus, the divisions among protesters were enough to demoralise many. Many had already left before Rocky Tuan, on 15 November, publicly asked outsiders to leave or he would seek help from the government. No protesters came out to protest against Tuan's decision. The next day, all the main roads were reopened. To curb the manufacturing of petrol bombs, the government now suspended the recycling of glass bottles.

During the battle at CUHK, a protester posted the following interesting comment on LIHKG:

Don't repeat the mistakes of the Umbrella [Movement]. Guarding the campus is a war of position, and this necessarily requires control and command. But there are people who do not want any 'stage' or have no desire to set up one! [What follows] is internal division, no one is listening to anyone! Especially in PolyU people shouted the f-word at each other . . . Without discipline how can one fight a battle? Please, for those who are guarding [the campus], I know there are people who are mature enough to know what to do, but there are people who are having a carnival instead . . . if you want a carnival go somewhere else please.

The above post also led readers to another post written by a group of employees/protesters who went to the campus to help guard it from the police:

The revolution has not yet been successful, yet we have already descended into internal chaos. The factors which brought us the event in CUHK and its eventual development [tell us that] one cannot all blame the CUHK brothers and sisters! . . . Certain outside brothers and sisters vandalised the campus without any good reason. Isn't our reason in coming here precisely to safeguard the campus in the first place? . . . Certain brothers and sisters sprayed graffiti everywhere, broke windows without reason, spoke with disrespect, assumed command as if it was entirely natural! This surely puzzled the CUHK brothers and sisters, and puzzled us protesters from outside as well . . . There were too many small teams to be able to hold together, rather each just did its own job! And then [we] lost all our credibility and people just left one after the other and returned the campus to our enemy! We had to pay so high a price to occupy it, for what? We are very unhappy with this! . . . Secondly, the term 'no stage' undermined all of us! 'No stage' does not mean you can't have organisation! There were only small teams . . . and anyone who proposed [something different] would be accused of attempting to build their own stage, this disappointed frontliners from outside.[24]

The Battle at PolyU

After the CUHK battle, it was the turn for PolyU's show (there were protests at other universities, but they were much smaller). PolyU also occupied a very strategic location. It is very close to one of Hong Kong's three cross-harbour tunnels. Stopping the traffic there would cause serious disruption. On top of this, it is also connected to the East Rail line of the MTR. On the morning of the 14th, some protesters threw petrol bombs at the railway to stop it from running. The police arrived and fired tear gas. Soon, the fight between the two sides covered the area around the campus. After leaving CUHK, many protesters went to PolyU to help. Both the protesters and the police were aware that the best of the braves were all now concentrated on this campus. In the afternoon, the protesters shot arrows at the police, and others began to occupy the bridge over the cross-harbour tunnel and began to throw things down to stop the traffic. Some went down to the tunnel road and burnt down the toll booth there. A truck drove through the barricades while the protesters threw petrol bombs at it to stop it, and it fled on fire.

Intensive fighting continued until Sunday 17 November, when the police began a strong frontal attack on the protesters there by mobilising water cannons and armoured vehicles. The walls at the campus were now painted blue because of the chemical water from the water cannons. The protesters responded with more bricks, petrol bombs, and even a giant slingshot. They threw petrol bombs at an armoured vehicle and torched it. Nonetheless, a lot of protesters were injured. Two protesters told a reporter, 'you ask everyone here and they will tell you our fight will never succeed . . . knowing this, we fight regardless because this is what we mean by resistance!', and, 'I am prepared to die, and I have prepared my will'.[25] A big group of parents who had children inside the campus, some with tears in their eyes, came to the road leading to the campus for a sit-in to demand the police let them through to see their children.

On the 18th, the police tightened their grip over the surrounding area of the campus. They now preferred to lay siege to it instead of making a frontal attack to take the campus from the students there. The protesters inside knew they were doomed if they did not flee. From a thousand they were now down to around six hundred, and the numbers kept on declining. From day to night they fought to try to break the siege but were unsuccessful. More than seventy of them gave themselves up. Those who stayed continued their fight. Screams could be heard whenever someone got hit by the chemical water from the water cannon. Their skin hurt, and they shivered because of the cold. The police were not content with physical violence, however. Using a megaphone, the police shouted insults at the protesters inside, such as 'if you die it's none of our business' and 'hey, isn't PolyU famous for physiotherapy? They have a lot of physiotherapists to treat you crippled students'. The protesters played the 'Glory to Hong Kong' song in return – this song was written in August and became very popular, people jokingly said it was their Hong Kong national anthem.

On the same day, 'A Letter to all Hong Kong Citizens from a PolyU Student Guarding the Campus' was released online. It had this to say:

If we retreat only one step, we will die without even a coffin. The black cops have attacked PolyU for eight consecutive days. We were under siege in the campus. Outside our brothers and sisters worry deeply about us. Here we feel peace in our heart and knowingly face [our fate]. We have defended the campus with blood and tears from the aggression of the evil police. What sin do we have? The president and the directors [of the university], who are supposed to protect students, instead reported students to the police so that they could be arrested.[26] We will guard the campus until the last moment . . . Give me liberty or give me death . . . History will absolve me.[27]

Meanwhile, on the 17th, the braves called for a big attack from outside to break the police siege on the campus. Some might have hesitated as they were aware of the absolute asymmetry of forces. On the 18th, more than 10,000 people heeded the call for action, regardless. The police, as usual, closed all the MTR stations leading to the campus. Buses were not running as the streets were mostly occupied by protesters. People had to walk if they wanted to go and support the protesters at the campus. Many did and fought the police just outside the campus. I was only able to arrive halfway through, during the late afternoon, and I stopped at Jordan to watch a great scene. From Mong Kok to Tsim Sha Tsui there was now a 1.5-kilometre-long human chain, built with the single purpose of passing all kinds of supplies from the rear to the front – bricks, goggles, umbrellas, water, anything you can imagine. Small groups of people passed by me pushing trolleys with boxes of bottles on them – probably petrol bombs. Suddenly there was a loud explosion, followed by a strong burning smell which hung in the air for a long time – some young protesters had exploded an electrical transformer on the roadside.

Only after I had returned home did I learn that more than a hundred protesters inside the campus had been able to run away at around 8 p.m. A great rescue network had been mobilised to save the protesters, consisting of 'sentinels', 'schoolbus drivers', 'parents', and professionals who knew well the campus sewerage systems. Some protesters abseiled down from a flyover to another flyover below, while dozens of motorbikes were already waiting. They took their passengers to another flyover to find cars which would take them away from the area. According to one motorbike rider, 90 percent of car drivers opened their doors. And then the motorbike riders hurried back to the campus to save more. Many protesters took great risks to rescue arrested protesters outside the campus as well. In the middle of the night, the police arrested a young injured girl in Jordan. An ambulance came to pick up the girl, but it was soon surrounded by a hundred angry protesters who began shouting and throwing bricks at the three policemen inside the vehicle. The latter drew their guns and fired live ammunition at the crowd, but in the chaos the girl ran away. The police later claimed that they had eventually tracked the girl down and arrested her.

The actions outside the campus on the 18th did not save all those inside, however. Instead, many of the protesters outside were arrested or injured. In total, 354 were hospitalised because of this battle. The next day, knowing that hundreds of high school students were also inside the campus, Ip Kin-yuen, the legislator representing the education functional constituency, together with 53 middle school heads, successfully negotiated a deal with the police to allow high school students to leave the campus after registering. Eventually they saved 320 students. A school headmaster told a reporter that one of the students was happy that he could leave but cried because he felt guilty leaving his 'brothers and sisters' behind. At the same time, the police announced that they had arrested 800 protesters (most of whom were not PolyU students) from the campus, and 450 adults, who were allowed to leave after being registered (not including the high school students). Eventually 242 were charged, nearly all were in their twenties. Meanwhile, less than 100 protesters remained inside, and they used all kinds of methods to escape, including through the sewerage system. They were secretly given maps of the sewerage system on the campus to make this possible. Some were arrested the moment they stuck their heads out from the tunnels, however. In the last few days, those who remained faced mental consequences, becoming paranoid and distrustful of one another: the fear of infiltrators made everyone continue to put on their full masks and worry that if others knew of their own escape plan it would only jeopardise it. Many now stopped talking to one another. Some went into hiding and some might have got out using other escape routes. On the 28th, the police seized the campus and did not find any more protesters there.

The Hong Kong people and its young generation will never be the same after these two battles. A student, Mr Chow, who was shot with a live bullet and lost one of his kidneys because of the injury, had this to say:

> People can be killed by bullets, but faith is bulletproof. Faith can spread from one person to another, to ten persons, and then a hundred. Everyone must keep their own faith dearly.[28]

4

Issues

SLOGANS AND SYMBOLS

The 2014 Umbrella Movement was famous for its slogans, *ming wan zi kyut* ('self-determination for our own fate') and *zi gei hoeng gong zi gei gau* ('our Hong Kong can only be saved by ourselves'). Then came the 2019 revolt. The more it became radical, the more people picked up the localist Edward Leung's slogan, 'reclaim Hong Kong, revolution of our time'. The slogan was empty in content but rich in emotion. It was empty from the very beginning as Leung was never able to explain how his 'revolution' worked – what was the purpose of this revolution apart from overthrowing Beijing's rule over Hong Kong? – let alone lay out his vision for a 'new Hong Kong'. The youths who repeated this slogan interpreted it in whatever way they liked. But there was one interpretation which won the hearts of many – the 'scorched-earth' interpretation. Scorched-earth is the name of an account registered with LIHKG, the real name of those behind it has never been revealed. (Before this account appeared, the term 'scorched-earth current' had already been in use since the Umbrella Movement to describe certain localists who advocated a scorched-earth tactic to fight against Beijing, and who later used the motto 'we burn you burn with us'.) Scorched-earth made its name in early June 2019 by lobbying for foreign governments to nullify the citizenship of Hong Kong high officials and pro-Beijing politicians: a lot of them, or their families, are citizens of Western countries. After scorched-earth's initial success, a team came together called the 'LIHKG Scorched-Earth Team', which became an essential platform in lobbying foreign governments and politicians to support the movement. The team, along with eleven students' unions, held a rally called 'Fight for Freedom. Stand with Hong Kong' on 16 August. Scorched-earth's message was also read out during the rally, which explained as follows:

By 'reclaim Hong Kong', I mean reclaim Hong Kong's liberty, human rights, democracy, autonomy in our resources, and international status. By 'revolution of our time', I mean Hong Kongers, within the era of 'fifty years of no change' [as promised by Beijing in the Basic Law], are to rise up from below to rock the regime, to have regime change.[1]

What is worth noting is not the emptiness of this explanation, but the fact that so many young people welcomed it. For them, the point was not working out any detail of this revolution, rather it was the radical connotation that this term carried; they wanted a complete break with a Hong Kong that had always been overshadowed by Beijing's rule, and they wanted it to happen as fast as possible. They were simply not interested in the question 'what next then?' They projected both their hatred of the CCP and their yearning for a new Hong Kong onto this slogan and its advocate, Edward Leung. This phenomenon of projecting a generation's feelings onto a 'hero' who upholds certain radical slogans had already happened multiple times in the past decade – Raymond Wong, Chin Wan, Alex Chow, Lester Shum, etc. The 2019 revolt was an explosion of a great feeling which had been accumulating for at least twenty years, a yearning to be free.

The repression from Beijing and the resistance from Hong Kongers has created a sharp division and this can be seen in the languages both sides use to describe the other side. The police have described the protesters as 'cockroaches', while the protesters have called the police 'black cops' or 'dogs', and this is always followed by the curse 'may all your family go to hell'. Facing a common enemy which is about to strangle Hong Kong strengthens the bonds within the yellow camp. We already witnessed the beginning of this process during the Umbrella Movement. But it has been the young whose bond became so strong that they very soon began calling one another *sau zuk*, literally 'hands and feet', or brothers and sisters. Those over thirty were at first reluctant to pick this up – forgivable, because they had never developed such bonds among themselves. Their generations have very weak 'common identities'.

The 2019 revolt was thus a movement about reclaiming the common identity of Hong Kongers, their rights as a people. No wonder we also witnessed an outbreak of minor cultural regeneration, where 'Glory to Hong Kong' (the unofficial 'national anthem') was sung and a Hong

Kong-style 'Lady Liberty' was put on the top of the Lion Rock Hill, complete with a stunning amount of campaign literature, murals, paintings, posters, and cartoons expressing a strong aspiration to be free. In the course of this they also invented a kind of symbolism and language for the movement. I call this a 'minor cultural regeneration' because Hong Kong under colonial rule was quite barren in terms of culture, so much so that it was nicknamed 'the cultural desert'. This has improved slowly over time, but it has continued to remain culturally poor and lacking in diversity. Only in the past ten years did things begin to change, reaching a breakthrough in 2019.

Figure 2　'LIHKG pig' in protest

The famous 'LIHKG pig', which was first used on LIHKG as a zodiac sign, is now seen as a symbol of the movement. Its predecessor was the term *gong zyu* ('Hong Kong pigs'), a derogative term describing apolitical people, which began to be fashionable in 2014. In contrast, the LIHKG pig was appropriated by young activists to symbolise a new generation of politically active Hong Kongers. Soon the LIHKG pig would be posted on Lennon Walls and depicted in graffiti. With the growth of a 'yellow economic circle', the LIHKG pig further evolved into the icon of a Hong Kong version of *Le Guide Michelin*, the 'Hong Kongers' LIHKG Pig Guide', a guide to pro-democracy cafés and restaurants for the yellow camp.

The protesters also borrowed the 'alt-right' symbol Pepe the Frog, leading many in the West to believe that the protesters were necessarily from the far right. While such people existed in the million-strong movement, the vast majority of the protesters knew nothing about the use of the symbol by the alt-right. Most of them just thought the frog looked cute. The fact that Hong Kongers used a symbol which had originated across the ocean does not necessarily imply that it had the same meaning in both contexts. People in Hong Kong had been kept in a state of ignorance about local politics, not to mention international politics, for a long time. What's more, the frog was not just appropriated to symbolise the movement, rather it could represent anyone. One could find 'Pepe police' and 'Pepe Carrie Lam' as well.[2]

Figure 3   Carrie Lam as Pepe the Frog

As the protests unfolded, the US and the UK flags were more frequently seen. I will deal with the issue of foreign influence on the protests below, but here let us have a brief discussion on how the protesters saw these symbols. No doubt there was a small number of hardcore fans of the US among the protesters. But many of the young protesters who did this were more likely to be new to politics and had little knowledge of what the US flag represents, except that it represents the US as a country. One must also be aware of the general pro-Western sentiment in Hong Kong, which has a very long history. It is important to acknowledge as well that it was not only the US and UK flags that were waved. In many instances people waved flags of other countries, and for many it was because they wanted to send a message to the world that Hong Kong is an international city, not just a regular mainland Chinese city. One incident reflects the ignorance of international politics among the young. This was when they started an online discussion about preparation for another march and came up with the idea of carrying the Taiwanese flag to show their gratitude for Taiwan's support. Yet when they did this it alienated many

Taiwanese – they were not aware that Taiwan, as in other places in the world, is split over what the national flag represents. Taiwan is split into the blue camp and the green camp. The blue camp are the supporters of Taiwan's conservative Kuomintang (KMT) party, while the green camp are more inclined towards Taiwanese independence and are more likely to support the Hong Kong protests. Crucially, many consider the Taiwanese flag to be symbolic of the KMT, not Taiwan as a nation.

Given the fact that the pan-democrat parties were not able to provide leadership in this great revolt, it was left to the masses themselves, especially the youth, to figure out what to do. Without any serious political experience and training, they had to rely heavily on their instincts and imagination, and they often expressed their views through the medium of metaphor.

- Instead of saying 'mobile protests are better than occupations', they would say 'be like water'.
- Instead of saying 'we don't need leaders, representatives, public discussion, meetings, or democratic decision-making', they would say 'no stage!'
- Instead of explaining why vandalising shops whose owners supported Beijing would be helpful in winning democracy for Hong Kong, they would just respond with the words 'we are the scorched-earth faction, if we burn you burn with us!'
- In view of the need to be tolerant when disagreement occurred between the non-violent supporters and the braves, or between the braves and the other protesters, some began to use the metaphor *hing dai paa saan gok zi nou lik* (literally, 'brothers climbing up the mountain but each in his own way', better understood as 'we fight on, each in his own way').
- Instead of identifying different levels of cooperation (one-off alliances, short-term alliances, united fronts, fusions of different forces into one) and different sources of division (personal problems, tactical differences, differences in principles) the discussion within the movement was always the juxtaposition of 'either come with me or *got zik* (split up)'.[3]

The upside of this metaphorical approach was that it made it easy for common people to participate in politics and protests, but the downside was that on many occasions this blurred public debate over actions rather than clarifying it, hence increasingly it exhausted its usefulness. The 'climbing the mountain' metaphor is one example. The more intense the protests became, the more one person's actions affected the whole group: for instance, when one protester from the middle of the crowd would throw a brick at the police those at the front would be arrested, not those in the middle. This scenario happened multiple times. Climbing up a mountain each in one's own way usually does not have consequences for all of those involved. Yet when protests occur in the public domain this necessarily affects people other than the initiator of the action.

There were also disputes about whether protesters should build just one single demonstration or diversify into separate marches. It goes without saying that the question of 'one single march versus multiple marches' is separate from the question of 'should this action have leaders?', yet those who called for the former were often confronted with questions such as 'you want to be leaders?' and 'you want to re-establish the stage?' But it was not clear what 'the stage' meant in this context – it could mean 'elected leaders', or 'un-elected leaders', or anything one could conceive of. The inability to resolve differences through serious political and democratic discussion often resulted in hair-splitting and fragmentation. With the 1 October march, for instance, instead of a single march it eventually became multiple marches at the last minute, leaving many people feeling confused. This scenario repeated itself many times. Another example was the battle at the two universities. If this movement was supposed to be 'like water', why did the battles at the two campuses suddenly change from a 'war of movement' to a 'war of position'? Which options might have worked better is a matter of debate, unfortunately the debate only started after actions to defend the no. 2 bridge had been taken, and by that time one hundred students were already injured.

The so-called 'no split up' principle was also very problematic. When the movement first began, this might have been good advice for helping the two currents, the non-violent supporters and the braves, to cooperate. Yet before long, this led to a taboo against making any criticism at all, even if it was well-intentioned criticism. One protester wrote:

I hope we all seriously think about what is the purpose . . . of all our sacrifice? Is it for the sake of scorching the earth? Or is it for the sake of a democratic and progressive Hong Kong? Is it for the sake of beating up police, or for the sake of justice? . . . The principle of 'don't split up' does not imply that one should be pardoned for whatever wrongdoings, nor that one can't make criticism, nor that one can't do better.[4]

'SPONTANEITY' VERSUS 'THE STAGE'

In this seven-month struggle there were rallies where people gave speeches, but it was rare to see actions related to democratic deliberation and decision. When the LegCo building was broken into on 1 July, the protesters occupied a place which is perfect for holding a people's meeting or a proper press conference explaining their purpose. However, the protesters only began to worry about how they were going to explain to the public the purpose of their breaking in after they broke in, and after many protesters had vandalised the building. And there was no attempt to convene a people's assembly or hold a protesters' meeting to deliberate on how to implement their revolution – because many protesters were obsessed with venting their anger through vandalism.

The upside of the movement was that it stressed a lot of direct action, but this was always counterposed to democratic deliberation, public debate, collective responsibility, and organisation per se. However, increasingly some protesters found it hard to sustain the movement along this entirely spontaneous track.

To be fair there were some kinds of organisation in the form of small groups, and they would, with the help of new communication technologies, coordinate with one another if necessary. One might say it was a kind of super-decentralised form of organisation. We all could learn something from these new experiences and revise our conceptions about democracy and social movements accordingly. This great revolt also somehow shows the limitation of this kind of super-decentralised form of organisation, however. In terms of organised strength, the masses emerged from this movement without becoming stronger because the participants were now as atomised as they were before the movement. (Although there is a new union movement, its base is relatively small.) At the community level, a few die hard blue camp people were able to stop the Lennon Walls from operating despite the yellow camp being much more numerous. The opposition parties also remained very small. This was even more true for the braves because they all hid their faces and often did not even know one another's names.

One CUHK student, 'C.N.', looked back on the campus battle in November and drew this conclusion about the lack of democratic deliberation in the 2019 revolt:

> Talking about the no. 2 bridge battle, the absence of coordination meant that whoever was the most radical controlled the situation. You couldn't stop it; you could only choose to either leave the battle or to follow. And then you might have done harm which you could have avoided if there was coordination . . . This was a movement where people were masked and very atomised, and its battles were led by small-cell organisations, where there was an absence of coordination, and this resulted in a lot of disasters, big and small . . . We should respect the braves and their sacrifice, but in this movement you couldn't criticise the braves. I am not opposed to violence in principle, it depends on how you use it. But if you used guns I would not agree. Because if you have guns but I don't have one, and then both of us charge forward, in the end the one who dies is me, or both of us, but you took up guns without first consulting us. [But if you criticised them] then you would be rebutted with the question: 'You want to *got zik*?' . . . This kind of radicalisation made rational debate of tactics impossible . . . If people think we are ready for armed revolution we can discuss its tactics but in this movement there was no space for discussion.[5]

Who benefited most from the absence of assemblies or even proper procedures for public debate? The bitter experience of the Umbrella Movement told us that it was precisely those who shouted their 'anti-authoritarian' or 'anti-leader' stance the loudest, namely the nativists, who were always the most strident.

In the 2019 revolt, certain braves, in the name of being 'anti-stage', became the actual leaders, yet they were not accountable to anyone. One protester had this to say to this:

The frontliners were prepared to sacrifice their lives in their fight . . . therefore, we all respect them very much. Yet there was obviously some kind of 'moral abduction' . . . when they criticise people who know less than they do as being cowards. We respect the frontliners very much but that . . . does not mean we should deify them, turn their decisions into doctrines. Those who were at the rear were also brothers and sisters who . . . also contributed [to the struggle] and did play a role. Please don't blame them or angrily shout at them.[6]

Most great resistances carry with them elements of spontaneity – it is the essence of revolt from below and of many epoch-changing events. This may entail a distrust of leaders, but this could be a positive thing – we all know that the masses in social movements are often betrayed by their leaders, hence some dose of scepticism about leaders could guide the people toward a healthy distrust of demagogues and usurpers. But it is not enough to bring leaders to accountability, or to remove illegitimate leaders. The crux of the matter is to strengthen the collective will of the multitude by forming assemblies and implementing democratic decision-making, be it by consensus or by majority vote. Without their own assemblies and democratic decision-making mechanisms, the masses are people without strength and power. The 'Yellow Vests' in France began with very spontaneous actions, but they soon realised that if they wanted to block traffic in their community at the weekend they needed to come together to talk about preparation and coordination, hence they held assemblies at the community level. With the protest spreading across the country, these community assemblies soon convened 'the assembly of the assemblies' in January 2019, representing 75 local assemblies. Even the 2011 Occupy Wall Street movement, which was considered highly autonomous, had its assemblies. In contrast, during both the Umbrella Movement and the 2019 revolt it was rare to see actions related to assemblies where people had exchanged ideas or made democratic decisions about future steps to be taken. Even when this did occur, they often ended up quarrelling or splitting up very soon thereafter. The reason for this was less because of inexperience and more because the mainstream among the radical youth was hostile to any idea of assembly, organisation, or democratic decision-making such as voting, believing that these all jeopardised the movement for democracy. No one ever bothered to explain such a self-contradiction, however.

Meanwhile, in early August, certain centre-right liberals tried to convince the movement to agree to the re-establishment of 'the stage', or an alliance to rebut Beijing's attack. This was coldly received, however, as the previous experiences of the pan-democrats' 'stage' were too bureaucratic to make them look credible today.[7] For instance, the Hong Kong Alliance in Support of Patriotic Democratic Movements in China, an alliance of two hundred member organisations, founded in 1989 to launch solidarity with China's democratic movement, has been de facto controlled by the Democratic Party leaders and has always been seen by the radical young as the example of such a bureaucratic 'stage'. But the radical youth went to the other extreme, which was a hostility against any form of proper procedure, even the most democratic kind. This increasingly undermined the movement's strength – heavy prices were paid because of a lack of basic coordination and democratic deliberation. This benefited the right-wing populists as they were the most vocal. A 'third way', involving a democratic perspective which simultaneously embodies initiatives from below and organised forms of people's power, was painfully absent.

Hence it was not that surprising to see that, in the latter half of the movement, certain nativists and localists began to be more assertive in leading rallies, with proper stages and speeches, after they gained some fame in participating in the protest – although the spontaneous nature of the movement continuously forbade them any claim to be its leaders.

Luckily, the revolt was ultimately a genuine mass movement with multiple diverse tendencies. From a movement originally hostile to organisation and leaders, it gave birth to a new union movement which has been exactly the opposite of this, in that it is organising in a democratic way. *The Nation* had an interesting report on how the new General Union of Hong Kong Speech Therapists was learning fast:

> Union organizing is also an exercise in democracy. Lai describes how she and her committee were voted into office during an extraordinary general meeting, with fair and proper procedures in which every members' vote was counted equally, which enabled them to be legitimate representatives of their union.[8]

VIOLENCE VERSUS NON-VIOLENCE

The police repression of protesters on 12 June was the first round of violence experienced by the movement. It set off cycles of escalating violence between the two sides, although, as argued earlier, it was always the police who first started it, often by using brutal violence, followed by their collusion with organised crime. On the side of the protesters, the braves would go from fighting the police to fighting back against organised criminals, vandalising the subways and the traffic lights, burning down well-known blue camp shops, and finally reaching a stage where individual braves would begin lynching armed and unarmed blue camp supporters who had harassed the yellow camp. On 11 November, a protester set a blue camp supporter alight. The latter had scuffled a bit with some protesters inside of an MTR station, but by the time of the attack he had left and had begun talking to some protesters, unarmed; it was at this moment that he was set alight. He lived but was severely injured.

From the very beginning, lots of people suspected that it was undercover police who were involved in at least some of the excessively violent cases. As a matter of fact, undercover police were caught red-handed on more than one occasion. If Beijing and its puppets in Hong Kong did not do this kind of thing then their secret police would have failed in their duty. But even if a lot of the braves' excesses were carried out by undercover police it is also a reasonable guess that individual braves were involved as well. What is more important is that we need to interpret these excesses by the braves within the bigger picture.

A 16 August survey showed that 68 percent of respondents thought that the police used excessive violence while 40 percent thought the same of the protesters.[9] Three months later, the figure for the police would rise to 83 percent while the figure for the protesters remained the same.[10] A third survey in late October could explain the above findings. It showed that 66 percent of respondents agreed that there was collusion between the police and organised crime on 21 July, and 63 percent agreed that mainland police had infiltrated the Hong Kong police.[11] The pan-democrat parties' hope for a reversal in public support for the braves was mistaken from the start because they had not realised that something fundamental had changed in Hong Kong. Now common people, after being enlightened by the youth and seeing with their own eyes what had happened, had come to a full understanding that Hong

Kong as they knew it was dead, and that revolt against this corrupt regime was necessary, even if they were not prepared to join the braves. In another survey, 93 percent of interviewees regarded themselves as *wo lei fei* (peaceful, rational and non-violent), yet 87 percent of interviewees also said they would not *got zik* (split up) with the braves.[12] There were tensions between the two sides, not only because the former largely remained peaceful, but also a great proportion (40 percent) of the *wo lei fei* did acknowledge certain excesses of the braves. This great revolt seems to give us a good illustration of 'the unification of the opposites'.

This 'unification of the opposites' did not just exist on a theoretical level, it existed in the streets, in fighting. Many times, when excessive violence was about to happen, other people appeared to try to stop it, although they were not always successful. People like Kyun Go (see Chapter 2) would regard this as one of their jobs. The next day, protesters would also take to the internet to heavily criticise those responsible for excesses. When certain braves began to vandalise subways stations and blue camp shops in October there were people who argued back:

> Don't you guys always justify yourselves by mentioning again and again how protesters got hurt and how righteous [your violence] is? They were hurt and killed by black cops, but instead of doing something to the black cops, you guys have been doing something to the blue shops.[13]

What purpose did burning the MTR serve? It was common people, including protesters themselves, who would be most affected. Eventually the MTR Corporation's profits did fall, but it can always recover them by passing the burden to the passengers. The best possible explanation advanced by some of the online braves is that it was merely to vent their anger at the MTR, partly because it had cooperated with the police (for instance in the 31 August incident) and partly because of this 'scorched-earth' mentality.

The torching of a blue camp supporter on 11 November sparked a heated debate on LIHKG. According to a BBC report, more than five thousand online commenters did not think this was excessive violence, while three hundred thought it was.[14]

Since 2014, certain nativists have been advocating a kind of radicalism which could easily lead to excessive violence. They developed their arguments as follows:

- 'Our enemy is evil, and this is enough to justify our principle of *mou dai sin kong zang* ["resistance without any bottom line"]. We can do anything to our enemy.' A slightly more moderate version would be, 'matching police violence with our violence'.
- When they draw the line between enemies and friends, they tend to have a very broad definition of 'enemies'. Instead of 'those who have not opposed us could be potential friends', their philosophy is rather, 'those who are not with us are explicitly against us', or worse still, 'those who don't look or talk the same as us are all our enemies', hence they considered the families of the police to also be responsible for police violence, they could lynch anyone who said something good about Beijing, and they could reject anyone from eating in their restaurant if they could not speak Cantonese. This is essentially their 'scorched-earth/you burn with us' philosophy.
- When someone requests that they provide reasons for what they are doing, or says 'we should discuss this', their usual response is 'come on, we are waging a resistance war against Beijing! No time for chatting! Only "left pricks" do useless chatting!'
- Implicitly, the above principles are all self-evident and hence the absolute truth.

A discussion of the legitimacy of violence necessarily carries with it a certain bottom line – how effective is the smashing of the MTR and the setting alight of an unarmed opponent in relation to achieving our five demands? What would be the political and human cost? Whenever we choose a scorched-earth tactic should we not also ask the question, 'what if they don't burn but we burn instead?' Unfortunately, there was a strong tendency to reject proper public debate altogether.

One certainly cannot find any element of democracy, human rights, instrumental reason, benevolence, or tolerance in the nativists' discourse on violence. On the contrary, one only finds 'violence for the sake of violence', 'collective punishment', intolerance of differences in opinion, denial of rational thinking and debate, extreme subjectivism, and authoritarianism – in every way they mirror the enemy whom they hate.

This is not new. It is an example of what I have called a 'Boxer Uprising mentality'. The CCP often used to praise this violent nativist Chinese uprising, which took place at the turn of the twentieth century, as a 'movement from below', and even as 'patriotic' and 'anti-imperialist'. Yet the party forgot to mention that the movement also carried very reactionary elements – superstition (believing their spells could fight bullets and bombs), unrestricted violence against innocent people, collective punishment (even killing Chinese who worked for foreign missionaries), and support for the Qing dynasty. I always argue that the legacy of the Boxer Uprising has continuously haunted modern China as well. One just needs to look at the so-called Cultural Revolution, and the nativists since 2014. Replacing Chinese identity with a Hong Konger identity does not makes one immune from such a horrible legacy.

This great movement brought the term 'revolution' back into public debate after it had been forgotten both in China and Hong Kong since the late 1970s. For many it means a thorough regime change. And for some, such as the nativists, this must involve a certain level of violence. This view has been influential, even if it can't be said to have won the debate.

THE CLASS ISSUE

The 2019 revolt was surely a popular movement. Rich and poor, Chinese and South Asian, all in unison to oppose the extradition bill. Yet behind this grand image, the spectre of poverty haunted many young people. Middle- or upper-class youths could join the movement full-time, but poor college students might have to work part-time to support themselves. The former could buy expensive gear, from first-class face masks to knife-proof vests, and they did not mind throwing them away when they fled from the police (if found in their bags this equipment could be evidence of 'rioting'). The poor youths could not afford expensive gear, and it was common to see them arrested for having protest equipment in their bag because they could not afford to throw it away so readily, or because they had to travel to hide it somewhere else. Many also had difficulties feeding themselves properly, as they had to eat outside more frequently. It was also common to see conservative parents throwing their rebellious children out of home. The middle-class youth might have been able to hang on for a period on their savings. This option was not available to poor young people, who might become homeless and go hungry. The poverty of the young greatly impaired their ability to participate or to keep themselves safe and well fed in the struggle. One could encounter yellow camp people who believed that 'luckily us Hong Kongers are now a community and we take care of each other'. Hence, there were protester 'parents' who came forward to help in every way. Some of them were so kind that, aware of the pride of the poor young, they constantly changed their method of support to accommodate them. They handed out supermarket coupons instead of cash and they inserted encouraging notes among the coupons to avoid being seen as patronising.

All of this was good. But the inconvenient truth is that the poverty issue was rarely discussed in the revolt. Philanthropy is nice but that cannot replace a proper public debate on poverty. There are 1.4 million people living under the poverty line in Hong Kong. The number of poor young people is huge. The Hong Kong Federation of Youth Groups Youth Research Centre published a report on youth poverty in 2014, showing that of those who possessed bachelor's degrees, 29.8 percent classified themselves as 'working poor', while the figure for those who possessed non-bachelor's diplomas was 35.6 percent.[15]

There were voices of discontent over wealth disparity and poverty in both the 2014 Umbrella Movement and the 2019 revolt. In 2019 there was graffiti in Wong Tai Sin with the English words: '7K for a house like a cell and you really think us out here are scared of jail?' Those who had conversations with common folks in the protests would learn that a lot of people were dissatisfied with the super-rich, but again, this never developed into a conscious aspiration for change, and the liberals never bothered to intervene to make the voices of the poor heard. There were some small leftist efforts to try to make this voice heard. In late August, the Hong Kong tycoons released a statement supporting Beijing, and some big hotel chains began to cut wages to shift the burden of the business downturn onto their employees. By then a small group of leftists posted a short article on LIHKG, 'Counter-Attack the Tycoons who are Selling Out Hong Kong, Time to have a Sixth Demand', which suggested the additional demand of a progressive tax on the big corporations to fund a government-sponsored pension fund. Merely eleven 'likes' for this article were recorded.[16] Even though it only targeted the tycoons, rather than the business class in general, it was still largely ignored. The strong pro-business sentiment in the city made any leftist agitation for redistributive justice in the revolt unpopular. In this situation, it was not surprising to see that, when the CTU endorsed a political strike against the government, it reiterated that it was just targeting Beijing, not the employers.

The 2019 revolt was a cross-class movement, but it was not entirely leaderless – in terms of the movement's fundamental direction it was led, not by any individuals or party, but by the cultural hegemony of the upper-middle class, supported by a big tabloid. They were able to dominate the direction of the movement only because of the deep-rooted conservatism of this place. We can observe this in the 'Yi Jin Diploma joke' that circulated throughout the movement. The Yi Jin Diploma is considered a sub-standard version of the Diploma of Secondary Education Examination received by high school graduates. At the beginning of the protest, certain college student protesters started to mock the police as 'Yi Jin boys', as they thought that low-ranking police officers had at most graduated with Yi Jin Diplomas. This was not true, but the crux of the matter here was that the joke reflected a tendency to judge people according to their education: if the police did bad things it was because of their poor education (compared to college students). The middle-class students made songs and jokes to make fun of these 'Yi Jin boys'. The Chinese University Grass Roots Concern Group reminded these college students that many young people who had less education had enthusiastically joined the movement and been arrested en masse, showing that people with 'inadequate' education could still be our brothers and sisters.[17] Unfortunately this righteous comment was a lone voice in the desert.

In Chapter 2 we mentioned that Hong Kong scholars were using Ronald Inglehart's 'silent revolution' theory to analyse the rising youth movement. Here I further pursue the subject in relation to the class issue in the movement. I find the dichotomy of materialism and post-materialism, or their rigid separation into two stages, a bit arbitrary. Obviously, environmental protection is not just for the sake of aesthetics (or 'post-materialistic values'), it is, no more and no less, about the very existence of human beings and hence is a very materialistic issue as well. Similarly, while industrial relations are seen as 'materialistic', as they are about the distribution of the fruits of an ever-rising productivity, the truth is that they also carry a very strong spiritual and cultural element, as trade unions fight for the shortening of working hours so that workers can pursue their own freedom. Doesn't the labour movement motto 'bread and roses' tell us something about the unification of both material and spiritual betterment? As for the youth, they are also separated by class, gender, and ethnicity: they have very different experiences despite their common ground in being young, hence different youngsters could have very different ideas of 'personal freedom'. While middle-class college students pursued their freedom in jazz, painting, and travelling abroad, their poor classmates had to take up part-time work after classes in order to pay their tuition fees. On the other hand, the latter were surely concerned about material issues such as economic security, but this did not make them less concerned about 'post-materialist' values, rather, when they rose up against this unjust society they may, in one go, push for social transformation at two fronts simultaneously, nullifying the idea of the dichotomy of materialism and post-materialism and the separation of these two sets of values into two distinctive stages. The 1968 global youth rebellion was one such example.

Activist Jaco Chow made an interesting short comment about people who quoted Inglehart to interpret the movement as being unrelated to material interests and purely for the sake of democracy and freedom. He sarcastically reminded readers:

> Many front-line young were fucking poor. The message they received was, however, that all those material issues – like they won't be able to buy an apartment in their lifetime, or that they would soon not even be able to afford to rent one, or that when they got old they would not have a pension . . . would never be as lofty and sweet-smelling and glittery as democracy and liberty.[18]

In saying that the young rebels were only interested in 'post-materialist values', both the liberals and the localists were trying to channel public debate to a place where the very materialistic issues of wealth distribution, long working hours, low wages, and the lack of a decent pension fund would not be asked about. They succeeded. This is also why Shek Lai-him could proudly tell Carrie Lam that she did not need to give houses to the poor because the protest movement was about the five demands, not about the lack of housing (see the section on local tycoons in Chapter 2).

Whatever the validity of Inglehart's theory,[19] when Hong Kong liberals and localists alike made use of it to explain the youth rebellion it objectively helped the upper-middle classes to keep the lower class from understanding the roots of their exploitation. Thus, the former could continue to use the latter as pawns to resist Beijing's encroachment on Hong Kong's status quo, even if the lower class also has a stake in this resistance.

The centre-right liberals wanted universal suffrage, but without ever bothering about the issue of distributive justice, because their idea of 'universal values' was essentially a liberal democracy wedded to an illiberal free market. The labouring class and their children, burdened by poverty, their minds dulled by free market brainwashing, lack the economic, political, and cultural resources to confront this illiberal position with this question: 'what kind of Hong Kong community is it if the majority of the population is getting poorer and poorer while the fat cats are getting richer every day?' That they had not asked this question was, and is, because they believed in this laissez-faire capitalism. The above-mentioned youth poverty study also showed that the young interviewees thought that moving upward depended chiefly on individual effort rather than government policy. The centre-right liberals and the nativists were not very successful in fighting Beijing, but they have been quite successful in fooling the lower classes into believing their motto: 'everyone for himself and God for us all!'

But let us not overestimate their power over the lower classes. In the end, material wellbeing is at least as important a factor as ideological manipulation. If Hong Kong's free market capitalism has the 'tacit consent' of many of the underclass it is first and foremost because of its success. Decades of full employment, a semi-welfare state which houses half of the population in public housing, provides heavily subsidised medical care to all, and a safety net, however miserable, for the poorest. The only problem is, will this situation last? With the Covid-19 pandemic sweeping the globe, the Hong Kong economy is now also hard hit, and big corporations are quickly shifting the burden to the labouring class.

TACTICS AND STRATEGY

The 2019 revolt exhibited a high degree of flexibility in its tactics. Certain radical youth thought that the Umbrella Movement had failed because of the tactic of long-term occupation of strategic sites in the city, so they advocated the 'be like water' tactic. When the protesters became aware that the G20 was soon to be convened in Osaka they immediately grasped the chance to have an international presence. When any tactic seemed not to have immediate results, they switched to another or escalated their actions. The rationale was simple: if one level of action does not work then we must try something more radical. How effective this would be at making the government agree to the five demands was never seriously discussed. As for the question, 'what if this approach does not work either, but rather makes us bear the consequences?', the answer was always 'if we burn, they burn with us!' In the end more than seven thousand people were arrested, many hundreds were crippled, more would be sent to jail, but the police were not burned, beaten, and jailed with us. However radical these actions were, they were not able to make Beijing or its puppets in Hong Kong give in. What next? Get some guns and dynamite? Some did, and many of them ended up in jail as well.

Among young people there was talk of revolution, but how would 'revolution in one city' be possible given the absolute asymmetry of forces between Hong Kong and the CCP regime? Certain nativists would endorse the slogan 'Hong Kong independence', but how this might become practical was never seriously tackled either. Be it 'revolution' or 'independence', they were all just empty slogans. No strategy was offered.

The nativists do have a more popular slogan and in a certain sense it is their version of a 'strategy'. That slogan is *gong zung keoi gaak, bun tou jau sin*, which means 'segregation of Hong Kong from China, locals comes first'. Does it mean stopping all mainland Chinese from visiting or immigrating to Hong Kong? Not necessarily.

Nativists such as Chin Wan have been explicit in their class-based exclusionism. In his book *On the Hong Kong City-State*, Chin explained that, on one hand, the reason that Hong Kongers should oppose certain mainland immigrants coming to Hong Kong is not only on the grounds of their using our public facilities such as hospital beds or our welfare benefits, but also on the grounds of anti-communism, of opposing the Communist Party's attempt to . . . infiltrate Hong Kong.

On the other hand, Chin says,

we do not oppose the mainland magnates or nouveau riche immigrants, as long as they accept liberty and democracy and Hong Kong's customs . . . Fellow Hong Kongers, do not be influenced by the foolish leftist thinking – having a preference for the weak and poor but hating the rich and powerful . . . Hong Kong should welcome them transferring property and money to Hong Kong.[20]

Chin is so welcoming to the rich and powerful of mainland China that, after all his talk about building the 'Hong Kong city-state', he campaigned for 'indefinitely extending the Basic Law' (beyond fifty years) in his 2016 election campaign, along with all its clauses promoting close economic integration with the mainland and those which give Beijing the final say in Hong Kong affairs. Yet this did not stop them from scapegoating common mainland Chinese visitors or poor mainland immigrants under the slogan 'segregation of Hong Kong from China', while blaming the 'left pricks' for being 'Greater China pricks'.

The slogan 'locals first', like Trump's 'America first', is just as empty. A quote from the politician and activist Leung Kwok-hung (also known as 'Long Hair') from a few years ago provides as good response to this: 'if one talks about who comes first, shouldn't we call for "the poor come first"?'.

The nativists' repeated condemnation of Chinese people has had a grave consequence. It misleads the young people into finding allies on the right when they become aware of Hong Kong's vulnerability. On many occasions, when I asked them about their strategy, they answered that 'we need international support'. 'How about the mainland democratic movement? Shouldn't we also ally with them?', I asked. The people would answer:

'Wasn't it crushed thirty years ago?'

'No, the mainland Chinese are hopeless'

'Chinese democratic movement? Not in my lifetime'

'As the localists have taught us, if the mainland Chinese get democracy, they would vote to enslave us'

'I have no idea about what will happen to China'

I do not believe China's democratic movement is dead for good. Moreover, I believe that without a strategy to link up with it, the Hong Kong democratic movement will be killed off for good in the long run. 'Revolution in one city' in a China context is absurd. It would be political suicide if the Hong Kong movement for democracy is increasingly wedded to a Sinophobic course.

THE POLITICAL SPECTRUM, WITH HONG KONG CHARACTERISTICS

In Hong Kong the political spectrum is always 'democracy versus despotism' (or 'Beijing versus Hong Kong'), never 'left versus right'. As Benny Tai explained in 2014:

We also have the labour groups supporting us. We also have the lawyers and professionals who may classify themselves as more on the right, but they are also supporting us. So, you cannot put the thing in such a simple way of either left or right. It's more about the relationship with China. In Hong Kong, we have this very unique situation. The way we draw the line is not the traditional left or right but in our relationship with China.[21]

Both the pan-democrats and the localists share the same opinion, the only previous differences between them were, firstly, while the former accepted the constraints of the Basic Law, the latter seemed not to mind going beyond them, and, secondly, the former wanted to remain as non-violent liberals, whereas the latter did not. With Beijing's plot against Hong Kong now fully revealed, the first two differences between them were either outdated or were becoming less important. This was the basic reason for the collaboration between the two at the start of the revolt in 2019.

But this 'Beijing versus Hong Kong' binary, despite its popularity, is flawed, because it simply does not correspond to Hong Kong's power structure or to actual events. According to this vision, there is only one enemy of Hong Kong autonomy: Beijing, an enemy from outside. This is wrong, however. There are a lot of Hong Kongers who have helped Beijing to undermine Hong Kong's autonomy, or who helped to kill its democratic aspirations. That includes the Hong Kong tycoons, including Li Ka-shing. For four decades, since the 1980s, they have been working with Beijing to block democratic changes in Hong Kong, heavily investing in the mainland even after the June Fourth Massacre in 1989 (which brought to a close the Tiananmen Square student protests) and helping Chinese state-owned companies to evolve into global giants. They have done infinitely more harm to the Hong Kong people than poor mainland immigrants – a quarter of whom, as we learned in Chapter 2, actually support democracy. Yet the nativists continue to attack the latter and happily forget the tycoons' crimes. What was more ironic was that, even after Li Ka-shing's company endorsed the pro-Beijing statement which attacked the protesters, certain localists still consider Li as one of 'our fellow yellow camp people'.

We shall see that all of this did not happen 'naturally' – be it a 'Beijing versus Hong Kong' dichotomy, or a political project of demanding universal suffrage while keeping the so-called free market regime intact, or the effort to keep the class or 'materialistic' issues, and along with it, the words 'capitalism' and 'exploitation', out of sight. This is a conscious choice by upper-middle-class politicians, and now used as leverage by those tycoons who have lost Beijing's favour.

With Beijing's rolling back of Hong Kong's autonomy having reached an alarming stage, even conservative local elites began to turn to more 'radical' solutions. In 2017, Joseph Lian Yi-zheng – the former editor-in-chief of the business daily *Hong Kong Economic Journal* (owned by the son of Li Ka-shing), who was believed to have broad connections with local business and to be a supporter of nativist discourses – proposed a 'cross-class localist united front' to oppose the encroachment of mainland 'red capital'. According to him, 'red capital has become the greatest enemy of democracy', and the fight against this red capital has now become a precondition for demanding universal suffrage.[22] So after the pan-democrats prioritised universal suffrage over labour rights, Lian went one step further to prioritise 'fighting against red capital' over universal suffrage. It is, therefore, not accidental that Lian did not say one word about the role of the working people.

The nativists' version of a 'Hong Kong nation' is thus essentially a nation full of class contradictions, where the upper classes continue to dominate the majority of the working people, even if it promises 'universal suffrage' or even 'labour rights' to the latter. In the seven months of protest the big corporations in the airline, catering, and hotel and tourism industries had already started to force employees to take unpaid leave when business became affected. With the pandemic, this situation is worsening.

What is important for the four million working people of Hong Kong is that in their fight – be it for Hong Kong's autonomy, self-determination, or to free the 'Hong Kong nation' – they should not allow the upper classes to rule them anymore. To achieve this, they need to consciously look for their real allies – small shop owners, the lower-middle class, poor mainland immigrants, and last but not least, working people in mainland China. But this also implies that they have to replace the political spectrum of 'democracy versus autocracy' with a 'right or left' vision. Fundamentally speaking, if Beijing is to be seen as the enemy it should be because its regime is a capitalist one.

This leads us to one final issue: how does one characterise the 2019 revolt, with all its political weaknesses? Was it progressive at all? I believe that it was. The five demands certainly are. And let us not forget that the demand for universal suffrage has always been a labour movement demand. Decades of failure by liberal democracy in many parts of the world do not nullify this conclusion. They do reveal its limitation, but in places where it is still denied by the ruling class, it is both legitimate and politically radical to fight for it. Indeed, the more effort working people put into their fight for universal suffrage and distributive justice while maintaining their political independence through upholding their class line, the more their democratic struggle acquires genuine revolutionary potential. The revolt itself has sparked a new union movement which may not be so easily tamed.

The local tycoons and the upper-middle class continue to be domineering but they are politically impotent. Yet the middle and lower classes have shown their courage and their ability to rebel against all the injustice that Beijing has inflicted on Hong Kong. What they are lacking is further political training through struggle, plus a new direction which enables them to find their real allies. This is the biggest strategic issue they face.

FOREIGN FORCES

Some international commentators have claimed that foreign countries had a hand in the anti-extradition bill movement.[23] A hand, yes, but the problem is, to what extent did this hand manipulate the movement? Did it dominate it and lead it to where it wanted to go? The answer is 'no'. The movement was largely spontaneous. Beijing's propaganda, which alleged that certain foreign forces paid the Hong Kong protesters, is laughable and seriously misleading about where the strength of the Western countries lies.

The truth is that 'foreign forces' have, from the very beginning, been recognised by Beijing as among the stakeholders of Hong Kong. Since the outbreak of the current protests, Rupert Dover, the British-born police chief superintendent, has become famous for leading many ferocious attacks on the protesters (late last year he was reported when it was discovered that his home was illegally occupying government land).[24] In fact, there are hundreds of white police officers holding foreign passports in Hong Kong and cracking down on protesters. Hong Kong is not comparable with Ukraine. The so called 'one country, two systems' principle, enshrined first in the Sino-British Joint Declaration and then in the 1997 Basic Law, was, from the beginning, a historic compromise by Beijing with the West. The Basic Law's solemn promise, that 'the previous capitalist system and way of life shall remain unchanged for fifty years', was first and foremost an attempt to appease the West and its business interests. This is also why the Basic Law recognises English as an official language of Hong Kong, allows the local people to keep their British passports, allows Hong Kong to keep its British colonial law, gives the power of final adjudication to the Court of Final Appeal and allows this court to 'invite judges from other common law jurisdictions to sit on the Court' (Article 82), and allows the recruitment of 'judges from other common law jurisdictions' to all local courts (Article 92). This is why 15 of the 23 judges on the Court of Final Appeal are foreigners. Foreigners are also allowed to be employed as public servants from the lowest to highest grades, except the ministerial and chief executive level (Article 101). It is this article which allows Rupert Dover to smash our skulls.

Article 8 of the Basic Law also stipulates that 'the laws previously in force in Hong Kong . . . shall be maintained', which practically keeps intact most of the repressive colonial laws, for instance the 1922 Emergency Regulation Ordinance, which the Hong Kong government invoked on 4 October 2019 to ban face masks altogether. Ironically, the law was enacted by the British colonial government to repress, unsuccessfully, the general strike led by the Chinese Seamen's Union in 1922 – then under the leadership of the nascent CCP. Nowadays Beijing's agents in Hong Kong talk a lot about 'decolonisation', by this they only mean Hong Kong people should stop being pro-West, or that its streets should not retain their colonial names, etc. As for the repressive colonial laws, Beijing is very keen to keep them. Precisely because of this we can say that Beijing has actually been practicing internal colonisation against the Hong Kong people.

The West, with the US and the UK at its head, has surely been pleased with the recognition of its interests in Beijing's Basic Law, and is surely not eager to destabilise Hong Kong. On the contrary, it has supported the Basic Law remaining valid until 2047. According to one American expert on China, the long-standing policy of the US and the UK towards Hong Kong is that both 'accommodated' those arrangements stipulated in the Basic Law, even when 'China wrote the Basic Law in such a way that vested most local power in the hands of people who would not challenge its interest in control' and 'Washington would have been hard pressed to reverse these fundamental, long-standing decisions'. In fact, he adds, when the Umbrella Movement started, the White House released a statement which reaffirmed its respect for 'both Beijing's right under the Basic Law to set certain electoral parameters and the Hong Kong people's political desires'.[25]

The US Congress, after the crackdown on the Tiananmen Square democracy movement in 1989, passed the Hong Kong Policy Act in 1992, stipulating that the special treatment of Hong Kong by the US, in comparison to its stricter policy towards China, depends on Hong Kong maintaining its autonomy under 'one country, two systems'. The three most important aspects are:

[1.] The United States should respect Hong Kong's status as a separate customs territory . . .

[2.] The United States should continue to allow the United States dollar to be freely exchanged with the Hong Kong dollar . . .

[3.] The United States should continue to support access by Hong Kong to sensitive technologies . . . for so long as the United States is satisfied that such technologies are protected from improper use or export[26]

Maintaining the status quo in Hong Kong has always been essential to US interests.

For more than twenty years, the US Department of State always gave a favourable report on Hong Kong's status. As late as May 2018, it submitted to Congress its annual report on Hong Kong, which said that Hong Kong 'generally maintains a high degree of autonomy under the "one country, two systems" framework in most areas – more than sufficient to justify continued special treatment by the United States for bilateral agreements and programs per the Act'.[27]

In June 2015, the LegCo was set to vote on the government's political reform bill. The pan-democrat legislator Ronny Tong Ka-wah, after meeting the UK and US consulates, disclosed that their advice was to accept Beijing's reform package.[28] In May 2015, Matt Salmon, the head of a US congressional delegation visiting Hong Kong, hinted at a similar position.[29] The US government and its politicians only began to change their attitude with Carrie Lam's tabling of the extradition bill in 2019.

Beijing has become increasingly uncomfortable with this. It hates the Hong Kong courts and especially their foreign judges, even if the courts have sentenced many democracy activists to jail. It especially hates the anti-corruption watchdog ICAC.[30] The pro-Beijing media has repeatedly condemned the British influence within and beyond the ICAC. This might be true, but Britain's influence extends far beyond its spies. If some Hong Kong people miss the colonial government and wave its flag, it is only in comparison to Beijing's mandarins and their lower officials. I do not miss the colonial government, and I have been opposed to colonialism all through my life, but anti-colonialism should not stop us from correctly understanding the real strength of the British and the West in general. Its strength in Hong Kong does not lie in funding protesters or deploying a lot of spies, but in its 'soft power': cultural hegemony, a modern approach in political persuasion, relatively good practises in governance, etc. If a significant portion of public employees in the ICAC or other government departments continue to look to the UK as model of best practices it should not be very surprising to us.

Beijing wants to unilaterally change the Hong Kong status quo as defined in the Basic Law. This status quo is reactionary, as it has upheld a laissez-faire form of capitalism since 1997, and it is intended to continue doing so until 2047, but it is also one that allows Hong Kong citizens certain political liberties which are instrumental in promoting their social movements, something that has never been allowed in mainland China. It is this feature of Hong Kong which increasingly worries Beijing. Since the turn of the century, more and more people in the mainland have begun to imitate Hong Kong's social movements, and have started organising, informally or through NGOs. This is the price Beijing has had to pay for making use of Hong Kong to help build China's new capitalism. Increasingly, Beijing has found the price potentially too high, and since Xi Jinping came to power in 2012, Beijing must have thought that it has become strong enough to tear apart Hong Kong's autonomy, along with its social movements. But the erosion of this autonomy necessarily also undermines Western interests – the West has vested interests in Hong Kong and, through it, in mainland China. The city's press freedom, for instance, is crucial for protecting its interests as well. When Beijing tabled the extradition bill, the UK and the US knew that their fundamental interests in China were at stake. This act amounted to tearing apart the Basic Law (and the Sino-British Joint Declaration) before it expires in 2047, hence it was also a refusal by Beijing to honour its promises towards Western interests. A collision between the West and Beijing is now unavoidable. Eventually it will be proved once again that Beijing has overestimated its own strength.

The US is also using Hong Kong to target Beijing. It has been on a path of containing China since 2012. The Hong Kong Human Rights and Democracy Act (the HKHRD Act), which passed in November 2019, is hailed in Hong Kong as a means to save its freedom. Actually, its name is rather misleading. First, Section 3 of the act is very clear about its aim: it is for the maintenance of US national interests that Hong Kong matters. Section 5.a.6 demands an assessment of whether Hong Kong sufficiently enforces US sanctions on certain nations or individuals. Reasons for sanctions include punishing countries or individuals involved in 'international terrorism, international narcotics trafficking, or the proliferation of weapons of mass destruction, or that otherwise present a threat to the national security, foreign policy, or economy of the United States'. This is clearly aimed at protecting US national interests, not defending human rights and democracy for Hong Kongers. This tying of Hong Kong human rights to US foreign policy is a mockery of human rights. The definition of what constitutes US national interest will always lie with the US government. Accordingly, the bill also mandates that the Hong Kong government sanction North Korea and Iran. Even many countries in Europe are refusing to follow the United States' provocative move to abandon the nuclear agreement with Iran.

Before the passing of the HKHRD Act, twenty Hong Kong, Asian, and US organisations released a public statement pointing out the flaws of the bill. They contrasted it with the 1986 Comprehensive Anti-Apartheid Act:

> The U.S. Congress had demonstrated before that delinking these matters [human rights and US foreign policy] is viable in such legislation: the Comprehensive Anti-Apartheid Act of 1986, for one, stands with the international community to oppose South Africa's apartheid regime without any mention of the U.S.'s own national and economic interests.[31]

Neither the defence of US foreign policy, its trade war against China, nor its global strategy, are our battle. In general, the big contest for global dominance between China and the US is a fight to divide up the spoils. Yet one should not deny that, in terms of the present defence of Hong Kong's autonomy in general, and the extradition bill in particular, there is a narrowly defined common interest between the Hong Kong people and the Western countries, given that Hong Kong is such an internationalised city and the West's interests are to a certain extent institutionalised under the Basic Law. We should not be scared of defending and extending our autonomy, or of making Beijing honour its promise of universal suffrage, just because the US and the UK are rhetorically saying similar things. Although one must add that the Hong Kong movement needs to conduct its struggle independently.

The left should also be aware that the historic interest of the Hong Kong working people lies not in defending the whole status quo as defined by the Basic Law. Ultimately the capitalism that Hong Kong has is substantially the same as the mainland's version. Some coined the phrase 'the divided God' to describe the joint capitalist logic of a Hong Kong under the hegemony of both the US and mainland China.[32] But one must also be aware that there is a difference in degree in terms of the protection of political liberties between these two versions of capitalism, and that the Hong Kong working people right now do have something to defend – not capitalism per se, but what is precious for them. Only through this defensive struggle can one speak of turning it at some later date to an offensive struggle for socialism.

Finally, I would like to discuss briefly how the 2019 revolt unleashed another force from Hong Kong, which hitherto had been largely dormant. There have been large numbers of immigrants from Hong Kong in many parts of the world, but they have generally been apolitical. This political apathy was replaced by activism around the 2019 revolt, however. Overseas Hong Kongers in many places launched solidarity campaigns with the Hong Kong protesters, sometimes in connection with local organisations in their host countries. This sometimes resulted in a situation where overseas Hong Kongers linked up with pro-Trump currents in the US, for instance. But interestingly, this also triggered a response among other overseas Hong Kongers, who were not happy with this, and they founded the Lausan Collective to try to argue for a kind of international solidarity movement which moves along a progressive discourse.[33] Sun Yat-sen once remarked that 'overseas Chinese are the mother of the revolution'. In 2019 we witnessed the coming to the stage of a new type of overseas Chinese – the overseas Hong Kong Chinese along with their strong Hong Konger identity. The overseas Chinese community in every part of the world will never be the same.

5

The Dragon, the Goose, and the Coronavirus

Two events in 2019 marked the turning point for both mainland China and Hong Kong: the 2019 revolt and the Covid-19 pandemic. They lay bare the fundamental contradictions of Greater China accumulated throughout the 'reform and opening' period. The two events also started to change the status quo and put the one-party dictatorship in China to an even greater test.

THE DRAGON AND THE GOOSE

In appearance, the 2019 revolt was a conflict over two Hong Kong visions.[1] One is Beijing's version. The dragon in Beijing has always treated Hong Kong as its goose that lays golden eggs, although it also believed that it treated the goose well. This is not how the goose has seen it, however. The dragon has become increasingly annoyed by this goose as it became more assertive, eventually rebelling against the dragon in 2019. 'But the goose could not be its own master', thought the dragon, therefore the goose must have colluded with 'foreign masters' in an attempt to secede from the dragon's animal farm.

The Hong Kong people had their own vision of Hong Kong. They were at first quite satisfied with their status – a privileged goose which enjoyed some degree of autonomy. Had Beijing continued London's soft authoritarianism, the Hong Kong story would be very different – the revolt would not have happened. The goose just wanted to be able to continue speaking Cantonese, while aspiring for more freedom so that it would never have to worry about being forcefully recruited to Beijing's animal farm. The dragon, however, feared that if it continued to allow its Hong Kong goose to have free range for too long, the animals in Beijing's farm might begin to imitate the goose. Hence the Beijing dragon decided to finish off the Hong Kong goose by caging it. But the goose defied the dragon, hence the 2019 revolt.

Beijing's discourse on the reason for the revolt is essentially wrong, not because there are no 'foreign forces' involved in Hong Kong affairs but because Beijing now feels strong enough to break its promise to both the 'foreign forces' and the Hong Kong people, forcing the latter two to defend themselves. A second discourse, from the yellow camp, considers the revolt a democratic movement aiming at freeing Hong Kong from the despotism of Beijing, as in the goose metaphor above. The second discourse is apparently more correct but previous chapters have shown the limitation of the explanatory power of this 'Beijing versus Hong Kong' dichotomy. Obviously, not all Hong Kongers support democracy. The most powerful local social groups, the tycoons and (most of) the upper class, do not. Nevertheless, the revolt, despite its internal divisions and certain drawbacks, was a popular democratic movement against Beijing and its puppet government in Hong Kong. If Hong Kong identity played a unifying role on top of the five demands then it is legitimate. Certain mainland or international leftists hesitated to support the revolt because of the apparent absence of the class issue. But when two million people, with working people as the majority, took to the streets to fight for universal suffrage, followed by the birth of a new trade union movement, this spoke to some aspect of working-class politics. Secondly, as we have discussed, it is entirely legitimate for Hong Kongers to reclaim their own identity. We have always been denied a voice, and our fate has always been decided outside of Hong Kong.

A few years before the Umbrella Movement, the rising Hong Kong identity began to increasingly mix with a xenophobic discourse which victimised the mainland Chinese and their immigrants. This led the very marginalised leftists to be even more hesitant in supporting the discourse of Hong Kong identity. But localism does not equate to nativism and is not exclusively the remit of the right, there can be both left- and right-wing perspectives. Do not forget that in the past century socialists in many former colonies stood at the forefront of their national liberation movements. That today the US appears to be interested in supporting Hong Kong democracy does not nullify the progressive nature of the Hong Kong democratic movement. In Hong Kong, the more vocal right-wing localists began to attack, and successfully paralysed, the marginal leftists. The latter's inability to respond could partly be explained by the defects of their analysis: many thought that class discourse necessarily excludes Hong Kong identity or all discourses about 'identity politics'. But one can be sensitive to Hong Kong identity without subscribing to 'identity politics'.[2] Further on, among the participants in the new social movement since 2007, there were progressive people who advocated a kind of localism which was not nativist, yet their localism exhibited a kind of inward-looking perspective which forbade them from looking beyond Hong Kong to allies both in mainland China and the international arena. Instead of 'think globally, act locally', they only did the last half, and hence were unable to combat their right-wing xenophobic competitors. In the absence of a left that was able to argue for an open and inclusive Hong Kong identity, a section of young people, in an era of crisis which promotes great anxiety, found in xenophobic localism a common ground of anger against the establishment. This was the base of the xenophobic localists. As described in the previous chapter, this is also a base which is far from consolidated, and both future events and a correct intervention from the marginalised left may still be able to neutralise this base.

The 2019 revolt has shown the great force of this Hong Kong identity. I continue to argue that it is legitimate. Since 1949, the fate of the Hong Kong Chinese was very different from mainland or Taiwanese Chinese. On the one hand, they were luckier; most of them, as refugees from the mainland, found in this colony a stable shelter in the midst of civil war and starvation in the mainland. They continued feeling lucky when they witnessed, from a close distance, the bitter factional struggle at the top in mainland China and the great madness of the Cultural Revolution. On the other hand, most were merely colonial subjects of the British government and were oppressed as such. They were of course also divided within themselves. Supporters of the KMT and CCP bitterly opposed each other, while the silent majority was apolitical. From the 1970s onward, this division increasingly sounded obsolete to the new generation. There was a strong feeling that both the KMT and the CCP had failed them and had left them to rot under British rule. They felt strongly that they were just refugees or visitors in this 'borrowed place at a borrowed time'. This generation called themselves 'a rootless generation'. Chapter 2 quoted Jeffrey Andrews, a Hong Kong-born Indian, as follows: 'I don't know who I am: not Indian, not an international citizen, not a Hong Konger, not Chinese, who am I?'[3] This grievance sounds very familiar to me. In 1974, I went to the Immigration Department when I turned eighteen to apply for an adult identity card. I needed to fill in the blank which was marked 'nationality'. I did not know what to fill in. The officer told me, with some impatience, 'it doesn't matter at all, you can fill in "Chinese" or "British", it doesn't count anyway'. I remember I filled in 'Chinese'. Only when I grew a bit older did I fully understand this official's words – filling in 'British' would not entitle one to any of the rights of British citizens; but in filling in 'Chinese' one had to be aware that whatever Britain did to you, the two Chinese governments did not give a damn. Since then I have always asked myself the same question: 'who am I?' I am a British subject, but never British; I am Chinese, but the Chinese governments don't care about me. I am a person with no homeland.

My identity crisis was eventually resolved when I embraced the ideas of world citizenship and socialism. Most people of my generation resolved it through forgetting it altogether, or moving upwards on the social ladder, usually both. For the first time in the history of Hong Kong there began to develop, slowly and quietly, a 'local' identity. The main sentiment was 'forget about China, we just work hard here and make a living, and if possible, emigrate to the West'.

This narrative of Hong Kong's contemporary history could give us more understanding of the nativist slogans, 'I don't want to be Chinese in my next life' and 'segregation of Hong Kong from China'. I argued against these slogans in the previous chapter. But in order to fight them we need to redouble our efforts to understand why they capture the heart of the people here. Thanks to the practical 'segregation from mainland China' between 1949 and 1997, Hong Kong was spared the madness of the Great Leap Forward and the Cultural Revolution, while also benefitting from the post-war boom in the world financial market. When Deng Xiaoping made a comeback in 1979, and soon after called for learning from Hong Kong, this further boosted the pride of Hong Kongers. After all the unhappy experiences since 1997 it was natural for people to draw a lesson from their history, that 'segregation from mainland China' is best for the Hong Kong people. 'Leave us alone!' was their main concern.

Time and time again reality forced them to remember China, and they had to come to terms with that: sometimes negatively, sometimes positively. Which direction it went always depended on what had happened in the mainland. When things turned out positively then Hong Kongers might remember their Chineseness favourably; if they turned out negatively then they would then want to forget about it. Despite ups and downs, the general trend has turned more negative in the past four decades. Localism existed long before the 2010s, and in a certain sense it was also legitimate. 'China has failed us multiple times and now we just want to be left alone. We don't want to be your goose that lays golden eggs anymore. We want to be human!'

Beijing's policy on Hong Kong has been a kind of internal colonisation from the start. It is less about sending mainland immigrants to Hong Kong and more about Chinese state capital overwhelming the city; and Beijing's continuous disfranchisement of Hong Kongers, while keeping intact the repressive British colonial laws. The 1997 handover of Hong Kong to Beijing was never once consulted about with Hong Kongers. Similarly, the drafting and promulgation of the Basic Law never had their consent.

Hong Kongers do enjoy certain privileges, but at the same time, while mainland people nominally (through the constitution and the electoral law) enjoy universal suffrage, Hong Kongers are not only being denied this right in relation to Hong Kong but also in relation to China as well – they have never seen their ballot to elect their deputies to the China People's Congress (the Hong Kong deputies are hand-picked by Beijing), despite the Basic Law granting them this right. Beijing disenfranchised Hong Kongers by refusing to implement the clause in the Basic Law about passing a law on the election of congressional deputies in Hong Kong. Hong Kongers are as disfranchised under Beijing's rule as they were under British rule.

Hong Kongers were moderate, however. For a long period of time they had not intended a showdown with Beijing over their rights. Yet successive rulers in Beijing keep patronising them day in and day out. Xi Jinping's even stronger version of 'Great Han nationalism' now not only wants Hong Kong to continue to be his priceless goose but wants it to be caged, dressed in traditional Chinese gowns, complete with a tongue which speaks Mandarin. A clash between the two sides was and is unavoidable. The popular saying in Hong Kong, 'those who shit in the streets rule over those who don't', although somewhat exaggerated, shows the contempt of Hong Kongers towards Beijing's rule. It contains a grain of truth: that the CCP has ruled the country with what

Hong Kongers consider to be a partially premodern, medieval political mindset, while most Hong Kongers consider themselves already enlightened by democratic values from the West. This finally culminated in the 2014 Umbrella Movement, which was also the moment when the radical wing of the democrats began to demand self-determination.

There are people who deny that Hong Kongers have the right to self-determination because Hong Kong does not constitute a nation separate from China. Yet whether Hong Kong is or is not a 'nation' has no bearing on whether Hong Kongers enjoy the right to self-determination. When the people of a place are denied the right to elect or recall their government, and when their continuous petition is repeatedly trampled on by the same tyrant, they constitute a political community and are entitled to the right to self-determination. The Canadian Supreme Court, in its 1998 judgment on issue of Quebec's secession from Canada, outlined the situation in which a people enjoy the right to self-determination:

> In summary, the international law right to self-determination only generates, at best, a right to external self-determination in situations of former colonies; where a people is oppressed, as for example under foreign military occupation; or where a definable group is denied meaningful access to government to pursue their political, economic, social, and cultural development. In all three situations, the people in question are entitled to a right to external self-determination because they have been denied the ability to exert internally their right to self-determination.[4]

For the advocates of Quebec's independence this may be too narrow (the court ruled against Quebec's independence), but Hong Kong does satisfy the first and the third condition laid out by this moderate judgement.

A HONG KONG NATION?

Is Hong Kong a nation then? Most nativists may say 'yes' and link it to their demand for Hong Kong independence. I disagree with both positions. The idea that the term 'nation' signifies an objective entity which could be identifiable through checking boxes about whether the community under discussion satisfies all the main characteristics of being a 'nation' is now largely obsolete. There is always a subjective element in the making of nationhood. I do not object to people insisting that Hong Kong is a nation, nor, to some extent, to nationalism. If Hong Kong responds to Beijing with its 'nationalism' then this is the nationalism of the oppressed, and hence this could be progressive to the extent that it constitutes a fight against oppression. The left could critically support it, although with clear boundaries. Yet until now the number of sub-scribers to the 'Hong Kong nation' discourse has been very small, and even smaller for its 'nationalism'. There is strong support for Hong Kong identity, but this is different from a 'Hong Kong nation'. And the voice for independence accounts for just one-tenth of the population. What's more, as Chapter 2 mentioned, one-third of local residents still consider themselves to be both Hong Kongers and Chinese, and it is questionable whether they support the idea of 'Hong Kong nationalism' or 'inde-pendence'. Behind this figure is also the fact that while Taiwan's 'native Chinese' severed their ties with mainland clan members for hundreds of years and there has been little migration flow between the two sides (except when the KMT fled to Taiwan in 1949) in Hong Kong many local residents still have strong family ties with the mainland. That is why only Hong Kongers have the term *faan hoeng haa* ('going back to our home village'), while the Taiwanese do not. Drawing a hard boundary for the 'Hong Kong nation' could be highly divisive and explosive. Hence it is also politically suicidal – it will antagonise the mainland immigrants and push them towards being receptive to CCP propaganda. Any polit-ical solution that aims to free the Hong Kong people while leaving out how those who still consider themselves to be 'Chinese' and do not want outright independence could not be democratic, nor feasible.

I consider that, for Hong Kongers, the best way forward is neither nationalism nor independence; we only need to be assertive in our identity and our vision for Hong Kong's self-determination – these two values are enough (relative to the idea of a 'Hong Kong nation demand-ing independence') to guide our fight for genuine freedom. Whereas, the idea of Hong Kong independence, even if it eventually recruits more fol-lowers, would immediately split Hong Kongers right down the middle, leaving no space and time to settle our differences before being crushed by Beijing. Challenging Beijing's Great Han nationalism with Hong Kong nationalism is both strategically wrong and tactically impractical.

Conversely, our advocacy for Hong Kong identity and self-determination is slightly more moderate, but also more flexible, and therefore more suitable for a small autonomous city standing up to a formidable central government. Also, it could unify the broadest possible alliance in two senses. Firstly, it is innately flexible as it does not reject independence as a political option, therefore those who call for independence are also given a chance to present their case as well. Secondly, while the slogan of independence indicates breaking away from mainland China right away, along with all the grave consequences this entails, the slogan of self-determination has the benefit of connecting with mainland people if we extend this slogan beyond Hong Kong and encourage the mainland people to pursue their own right to self-determination as well – internal or external self-determination, depending on their own wishes. In response to the accusation that this is helping the US empire to break up China as a country, we could reply that we are only breaking up the one-party dictatorship. Instead of breaking up China, we pursue a new democratic, mutually respectful reunion with mainland China through self-determination of the people. This response is also in line with the strategy of Hong Kongers pursuing a democratic alliance with mainland grassroots people, mentioned in Chapter 4.

Further on, Hong Kong independence could only be envisaged with the help of another hegemonic power. Certain right-wing localists already have a Moses at their head, namely the US empire. Yet the idea of Washington risking a fight with Beijing on behalf of a port in China is very unlikely to come true, to say the least. The examples of Singapore and Taiwan could not be copied in Hong Kong because the relationship of forces which made the former two possible does not exist in the situation between mainland China and Hong Kong. Not to mention that in this scenario Hong Kong independence is not that 'independent' after all.

Neither is it desirable. Readers only need to remind themselves of Ventus Lau's answer, cited in Chapter 2:

On the second day of Hong Kong independence, all the lifestyles and customs of the Hong Kong people will remain unchanged.

How would working people benefit if everything remains unchanged after independence? Is it worth spilling their blood for this kind of 'independence'? Most Hong Kong people want to defend their autonomy against Beijing, which is what the second version of the 'Hong Kong vision' is about. Yet, the notion that 'all the lifestyles and customs of the Hong Kong people will remain unchanged' simply does not correspond to the interests of working people at all. Their material and spiritual interests demand the overthrowing of the status quo and its replacement with a more equitable society. Even if Hong Kong's lower and upper classes come together in the common fight against Beijing, the two sides continue to diverge in their basic interests. The Covid-19 pandemic laid that bare. We are witnessing how the big corporations shift the social cost of the pandemic to lower classes by dumping their workers, cutting their wages, forcing them to take unpaid leave for months. The right-wing localists' version is nothing but a dream: to return Hong Kong to the so-called 'free world' of the Cold War period while preserving the status quo of a 'free market'. The working people need their own version of a new Hong Kong, a Hong Kong vision that is guided by not only the values of identity and self-determination, but also two additional values, namely democracy and distributive justice. Therefore, in the longer run, there might not only be two Hong Kong visions, but at least three.

THE ACHILLES' HEEL OF THE CCP

Chapter 1 mentioned how Beijing has been telling Hong Kongers that Hong Kong's importance to Beijing has been diminishing by pointing to the fact that, with China's rise, Hong Kong's GDP has become only a fraction of China's. This is, however, a one-sided view. There are many other aspects where Hong Kong still has its advantage, and in which China is still reliant on Hong Kong. This section makes the following arguments: 1) China's rise is based on its policy of being able to make full use of both its internal market and the world market. Never in China's history has it had such a high degree of reliance on the world market as it has today, both in terms of inflow and outflow of direct invest-ment, of cross-border financial transactions, of imports and exports, and so on. 2) The other side of the coin is that this hyper-authoritarian regime, while effectively controlling everything domestically, also has much less control over its international connections, hence constituting its weakest link. 3) Between its internal market and the international market, Beijing always needs a middleman – Hong Kong. Despite its

increasing control over Hong Kong, its free port characteristic deter-
mines that both 'foreign forces' and the local people still possess a
certain amount of leverage, which may make things difficult for Beijing.
These three factors constitute Beijing's Achilles' heel.

Quite a few Hong Kong scholars have dealt with China's ongoing
economic reliance on Hong Kong. Recently, the British NGO Hong
Kong Watch released a report, 'Why Hong Kong Matters', which con-
cisely sums up this reliance as follows:[5]

- Almost two-thirds of China's direct investment flows are mediated
  through Hong Kong.
- Hong Kong was home of 73 percent of the initial public offerings
  of mainland Chinese companies between 2010 and 2018. Since
  1997, Chinese companies have raised US$335 billion in Hong
  Kong.
- The Hong Kong Stock Connect is increasingly the preferred route
  for Western investors seeking to access the mainland Chinese
  market and US$95 billion flowed into mainland Chinese capital
  markets via Hong Kong between 2016 and September 2019.
- Hong Kong is the largest offshore centre for bond sales by Chinese
  companies, and the largest recipient of foreign direct investment
  from China. It has a vital role in trade finance and is the top hub
  for Renminbi internationalisation.
- Hong Kong plays a key role as a private wealth management centre
  for high net worth individuals from mainland China, including
  many members of the Chinese Communist Party.

These only cover direct reliance. There are also indirect factors or international arrangements which are of no less importance. When the 1992
Hong Kong Policy Act was passed in the US Congress, China accused
the US of 'intervening in its domestic policies'. But the three elements of
the act (see the 'Foreign Forces' section in Chapter 4) are exactly what
have been benefiting Beijing as well. It is here that the interests of Beijing
and the Western elite classes converge. Hong Kong remains an important stopover platform for its overseas investment. In 2017, 58 percent
of China's foreign direct investment (FDI) outflows came through Hong
Kong.[6] A certain proportion of this FDI will then be reinvested into
other parts of the world, sometimes including China itself ('round-trip

investment'). Through Hong Kong, many big Chinese companies, by buying shell companies or founding new ones, have created subsidiaries to help their parent companies to further invest or trade in other parts of the world.

Where do the piles of money which Chinese companies are flooding the world market with come from? A great part comes from Hong Kong. As shown above, Chinese companies, with the stated-owned enterprises at their head, raised a lot of Hong Kong dollars here; and since the currency is pegged to the US dollar at a fixed rate (with the tacit consent of the US under the 1992 Act), Chinese companies that invest or float in Hong Kong always have easy access to US dollars. The mainland companies which do not invest or float in Hong Kong are barred from playing this game, simply because mainland China, unlike the free port Hong Kong, is still exercising capital control and its currency is largely not convertible. Hong Kong, no more and no less, continues to be the US-dollar-laying goose for Beijing.

Using Hong Kong companies as cover for Chinese companies is beneficial to the latter as foreigners are less suspicious towards the former. The Cathy Meng/Huawei incident in December 2018 is a good example of Hong Kong's role as China's connection to the world. Cathy Meng, Huawei's chief financial officer and the daughter of company founder Ren Zhengfei, once served on the board of Hong Kong-based Skycom Tech and was charged by a Canadian court with violating US sanctions on Iran. As early as January 2013, Reuters reported that 'Skycom's office in Tehran offered to sell at least 1.3 million euros worth of HP gear to Mobile Telecommunication Co of Iran, despite U.S. trade sanctions'.[7] The report said that Skycom is a subsidiary of Huawei, although Huawei has always claimed that Skycom is merely one of its 'major local partners'. It is only by making use of Hong Kong that Chinese companies like Huawei could accomplish their global expansion in such a short period of time.

Since Deng Xiaoping, Beijing has always been trying hard to 'build several Hong Kongs in mainland China' by developing a total of eighteen Free Trade Zones (FTZs), beginning with Shanghai in 2013. All of these have been unsuccessful.[8] Beijing thought that a 'free trade' regime alone was enough to make another Hong Kong, without taking into account Hong Kong's better legal system and the hazards of China's own bureaucratic capitalism. Whatever promises officials had made about free trade in these FTZs, in the end they were rarely honoured, for instance the free exchange of the Renminbi. Nothing in China is predictable except one thing: the unpredictable, arbitrary rule of the state bureaucracy. They change their policies at will. No serious companies doing international trade would like to invest in such a place. Hong Kong could succeed as a free port after 1997 only because of its colonial legacy – British laws and courts, tolerance of 'foreign forces', the anti-corruption watchdog ICAC, partial direct elections, relative freedom of the press, opposition parties, an active social movement, etc. – which act as countervailing forces in relation to the arbitrary rule of the government (be it the Hong Kong government or Beijing). In China, no accountancy firm dares to refuse local government officials' pressure to cook their books, whereas in Hong Kong, because of the above-mentioned countervailing forces ('civil society', if you like), accountancy firms that are tempted to do the same thing are also aware that they are taking the risk of being reported in the press, or investigated by the ICAC. Without these countervailing forces, foreign capital knows well that it will easily be crushed by Chinese companies who have the backing of Beijing.

If China continues its attack on Hong Kong's autonomy it will also offend Western interests, until it crosses a point where the US may reverse its previous policy over Hong Kong. If this happens then Chinese companies will be immediately cash poor, and Xi Jinping's Belt and Road Initiative mega-project will be finished off. Hong Kong is Beijing's blessing, but it could also be its Achilles' heel if it tries to eliminate Hong Kong's special status. If Beijing just waits until a later date to settle its accounts with the US, when it has complete control over Hong Kong, when it fully rises up, when the Belt and Road Initiative is mostly finished, when its high-tech is more self-reliant, then things will develop very differently. Xi, however, has opted for an accelerated confrontation with the US, without noticing that this is exposing China's soft belly. Since 2012, Xi's regime has repeatedly overestimated itself and underestimated its opponents, resulting in hasty retreats both in the trade war with the US and in the war against Hong Kong. Within the CCP there is now growing concern about whether the decision-makers in Beijing are acting wisely. Even the hard-line *Global Times* has tried to reason with the top leaders:

Hong Kong's high degree of autonomy must be preserved . . . mainland China does not have the political and legal resources to directly govern Hong Kong. If we nullify Hong Kong's high degree of autonomy this implies rewriting the functioning logic of the whole society. This implies a gigantic risk of governance, including Hong Kong losing its status as an international financial centre. This kind of risk does not correspond to China's national interest.[9]

Ensuing events seemed to prove that the top leaders in China did not listen to the advice of the *Global Times*, hence they suffered a setback. Very soon they would face another, even bigger, challenge.

WHEN THE DRAGON IS INFECTED WITH A VIRUS

China's monolithic party-state could crush any dissident force with ease, yet ironically it is increasingly unable to deal with its own dysfunctions. The previous chapters have shown how, despite having implemented very sophisticated plots in asserting more control over Hong Kong over the years, Beijing's factional fights – its intra-departmental conflicts, its bureaucratic dysfunctions, etc. – have resulted in ugly displays like the 'Causeway Bay Books disappearances', the CE elections, and the failed attempt to table the extradition bill, which have caused a loss of face in front of the whole world. Just as the anti-extradition bill protests began to recede at the end of 2019, the Beijing dragon began to be troubled by the virus which was later to be called Covid-19. For a second time the dragon has exposed its internal weakness in its 'crisis management with Chinese characteristics'.

The pandemic was avoidable from the very beginning. There were several weeks to stop it from spreading to the whole country before the 'chunyun' – the Spring Festival travel rush, which in 2018 constituted some three billion journeys. Yet Beijing acted too late, despite the Wuhan municipal government having known about the spread of the virus early on. We have witnessed similar delays in the UK and the US. In many ways Trump and Xi mirror each other in terms of their arrogance, ignorance, and contempt for specialists. Yet if we look more carefully at how events unfolded in the crucial weeks between December 2019 and January 2020, the Chinese case still displays features that are quite different from the West.

The first confirmed case of 'pneumonia of unknown cause', which later was identified as Covid-19, is understood to have been reported on 1 December 2019 (although a *South China Morning Post* report has claimed, quoting an official source, that the first case was reported on 17 November). By 31 December, the number of confirmed cases had risen to 266, and by 1 January it had jumped to 381.[10] Starting from mid-December, there was 'evidence that human-to-human transmission . . . among close contacts'.[11] Local hospitals sent their samples to Vision Medical in Guangzhou for testing, and on 27 December the genome sequencing results 'showed an alarming similarity to the deadly Sars coronavirus', as reported by Caixin.[12] Vision Medical immediately reported their findings to the Hubei Provincial Health Commission. Yet between 1 and 3 January 2020, they were told by both the Hubei Provincial Health Commission and the National Health Commission that they must destroy their samples, stop doing more tests, and refrain from reporting their findings to the public.

Around the same time, samples were also sent to CapitalBio Medlab in Beijing and it was their findings (mistaking the virus for SARS) that were leaked to Ai Fen, the supervisor at the Emergency Department of the Wuhan Central Hospital, who notified eight of her old classmates, including the doctor and whistleblower Li Wenliang. Li shared the news with a group of doctors on 30 December but was made to confess to spreading fake news by local authorities. He died from the disease a month later.

On the same day as Li shared the news with his friends, two documents from the Wuhan Health Commission, mentioning 'pneumonia of an unknown cause', were posted online, forcing the Wuhan Health Commission to announce, for the first time, that there were 27 cases of 'viral pneumonia', but it toned down the virus by saying that there was no evidence of human-to-human transmission. Both claims were untrue, as the above-mentioned *South China Morning Post* report showed.

On a national level something bigger was going on. On 10 January the Spring Festival travel rush would start. If this went ahead, it would spread the virus all through the country at lightning speed. The clock was ticking.

Instead of the National Health Commission, it was the Chinese Centre for Disease Control and Prevention (CDC) that sounded an internal grade two alert for an emergency on 6 January, and the top party leaders were notified of the newly discovered virus.[13] The next day the Standing Committee of the Politburo convened and discussed, for the first time, the novel coronavirus, albeit as a minor matter. A month later, in the face of mounting discontent with the authorities, Xi Jinping revealed his internal report to show that he had been leading the party's fight against the virus all along. The earliest entry in the report relating to the virus was his remark at a Politburo meeting on 7 January, where it was reported that he 'made requests for the prevention and control work of the coronavirus outbreak'. The fact that he did not explain these requests in detail suggests that they were not substantial. His action – or, more correctly speaking, inaction – also seemed to point to this conclusion, because there was no entry of anything done by him in the period between the 7th and 20th in the published report, the period in which the virus was spreading like fire. He apparently did nothing in these crucial two weeks; merely watched as the travel rush and major public events (see below) went ahead as scheduled. He finally issued a public instruction on the 20th which stated that, 'we must attach great importance to the epidemic and do our best to prevent it'.[14] The 'instruction' on the 20th was slightly more substantial but it was already too late. By that time, tens of millions of passengers were already on their way back to their hometown. Shouldn't Xi have announced this on the 7th if he was fully aware at that time that the virus was able to transmit on a human-to-human basis and that hundreds were already infected? By making his internal speech public soon after it was made, Xi wanted to show that he had been acting on the pandemic early on. In fact, the speech indicated the opposite.

A *Mingpao* report on the Politburo meeting on the 7th suggested that Xi and/or other top leaders might have said something even more catastrophic. According to the report, 'the leader' of the meeting decided that while measures to prevent the outbreak should be undertaken, they 'should not cause panic and affect the festival atmosphere of the coming Lunar New Year'.[15] All the mandarins of the party would immediately understand which message should come first. Hence, they continued to promote the festival while repressing the news about the coming epidemic.

To make sure everything appeared as normal, the authorities of both the Wuhan municipality and Hubei province decided to go ahead with their two scheduled meetings of the People's Congress and People's

Political Consultative Conference during the period of 6–17 January. These were followed by a great feast on 18 January, involving 40,000 families. The feast, which was held by the Baibuting community, has a twenty-year history with local government encouragement.[16] Thanks to these public events the virus now spread even faster. Three days later, Xi Jinping gave his 'instruction' on the 20th. Only when the top leader spoke did his subordinates begin to act, and Wuhan was locked down on the 23rd. Yet five million Wuhan residents had already fled, joining the hundreds of millions of passengers in the travel rush.

According to some experts, if travel bans and contact reductions 'could have been conducted one week, two weeks, or three weeks earlier in China, cases could have been reduced by 66%, 86%, and 95%, respectively, and the number of affected areas would have been significantly reduced'.[17]

Why did the Wuhan authorities act as they did? This leads us to a discussion of certain features of the CCP bureaucracy. One of these is that what the laws say is not as important as what one's superiors may think. Any mainland Chinese, if they can speak freely, will tell you that simultaneously there are two set of rules at work, one is the law, the other is the 'qianguize', or 'hidden rules'.[18] The latter is always more important. We already witnessed this in our narrative about Beijing's policy over Hong Kong, when Beijing suddenly discarded the Basic Law and the laws of Hong Kong and did whatever it liked. Promoting or saving your superiors' 'face' is considered the principal hidden rule. The problem, however, is that your superior is usually too arrogant to tell you what he or she thinks; guessing what your superior thinks is therefore considered an important element of the hidden rules as well. We would witness how this bureaucratic logic fully played out during the pandemic.

According to Article 38 of the Law on Prevention and Treatment of Infectious Diseases, 'the announcement of information concerning infectious diseases should be correct and without delay'. Article 65 stipulates that government departments failing to do so will be liable for administrative penalties or criminal prosecution. Now with the information revolution it is much easier to implement the law to safeguard the wellbeing of the people. The 2003 outbreak of SARS prompted the CDC to develop an automated, web-based infectious-disease alert-and-response system – the China Information System for Disease Control and Prevention (CISDCP) – and this was implemented across China in April 2008.[19] Previously, 'local CDCs would submit a report once a month up the chain to the National CDC. With the CISDCP, hospitals and clinics now immediately and directly reported through the internet'.[20] Yet on 29 December, when the Wuhan hospitals reported cases of pneumonia of unknown cause to the district and municipal health commissions, the latter, instead of telling them to make a direct report through the CISDCP, told them to 'wait for instruction from our superiors'. On 5 January, the Wuhan Health Commission revised the manual for reporting which practically robbed the hospitals of their power to make direct reports altogether and handed it to the Provincial Health Commission. On top of this change, the provincial commission also required the hospitals to report up the chain of district, municipal, and provincial health commissions for double-checks, one by one.[21] In one stroke, the health officials nullified both the law and the CISDCP.

With the pandemic spreading around the globe, the CCP engineered a great self-promoting propaganda campaign by mocking Trump and other Western countries for mishandling the crisis. Trump's administration did act poorly. Yet there is one difference between the US and China. Dr Anthony Fauci of the National Institute of Allergy and Infectious Diseases (NIAID) can openly criticise Trump, while any Chinese expert doing this would not only risk being fired but also being put in jail or simply 'disappeared'. However brilliant a scientist in China is, it is the bureaucrats who have the final say, and who have the power to send scientists to jail for telling the truth. No wonder that when the Politburo founded the nine-member special task force on 25 January to deal with the epidemic, it did not think it was necessary to include any pandemic specialist.

Xi would soon shift the blame to his subordinates by sacking the Wuhan mandarins. This was not enough. According to the law on infectious diseases, they should have been taken to court as well. But let us not place all the blame on them. Xi quietly reminded his party on the 7 January that even when it needed to do something about the coronavirus it should not affect the Spring Festival. Why was he so concerned about the Spring Festival? Bringing joy to the people during the Spring Festival is a state project designed to promote the leadership itself. This is shown in the China Central Television Spring Festival Gala, which has lasted for four decades. Upon watching such a grand show Chinese people would be grateful to the party, again.

We must bear in mind that the 2019 pandemic had its prequel in the 2003 SARS epidemic. The main character in both dramas was the CCP, which acted the same way in 2019 as it did in 2003. It is only the virus that has been different: the 2019 version has been more contagious and deadly. Sixteen years have passed but the party, despite being armed with even more advanced technology, has not only made no progress in overcoming its bureaucratic inertia, it has gotten worse.

I argue that China, as a bureaucratic capitalist country, exhibits both premodern and modern elements; it is deeply connected to global capitalism on the one hand, but also carrys a distinctive logic on the other. But increasingly its premodern features bog down its very functioning. Xi Jinping's personal dictatorship was not consolidated only through the removal of presidential term limits in 2018. At the Nineteenth Party Congress in 2017 he had already told the party that 'we will launch activities under the theme of "passing on *our red genes*; stepping up to the task of making the military strong"'.[22] His linking up of 'our red genes' with 'the military' was intended to legitimise the control of the so-called 'second red generation' over the military. Chinese liberal opinion leaders see these 2017 and 2018 moves as a full restoration of autocracy, and they nicknamed him 'Emperor Xi'. Soon the ambitious Xi would begin his new offensive on Hong Kong, namely the extradition bill. He was defeated, however. He had little idea by then that he would soon be beaten by another enemy, this time the coronavirus. His party bureaucracy has repeatedly exposed its grave weakness in dealing with crises.

To overcome them it is necessary to undertake genuine 'modernisation reforms': the selection of leaders from forces external to the bureaucracy; separation of party from state, creating a peaceful and more efficient method of power succession; the overhauling of the bureaucracy by replacing absolute personal loyalty, personalised management, hidden rules, clientelism, and the tendency of transforming itself into a new aristocracy with a constitutionalist and a Weberian type of modern bureaucracy; rule-based hierarchy; impersonalisation; rationalisation; meritocracy; etc. This is a liberal 'Westernisation' program. Yet even implementing this very moderate program is impossible without gigantic political crises and struggle, simply because the most powerful officials are not going to give up their privileges without a fight, hence their continuous hostility towards the idea of 'Westernisation', even if this is just confined to the political institutions. But clinging to the old 'Chinese' way also necessarily entails all the evils of the senile party-state – succession crises and sharpening struggles between different cliques and factions make such struggles a zero-sum game, hence all players are involved in a life-or-death struggle. Both the extradition bill events and the handling of the coronavirus pandemic point to the degeneration of the state bureaucracy, resulting in a greater and greater dissolution of the social fabric and the emergence of huge centrifugal forces all over China. The remark of the Wuhan resident, quoted in the introduction, has already shown us this.

HOW 'WESTERNISED' ARE HONG KONGERS?

The disease soon spread to Hong Kong. With the 2003 SARS epidemic still in people's minds, they all immediately put on their masks, while demanding that the Hong Kong government temporarily close the border and to provide an adequate supply of masks. The government refused. The newly founded Hospital Authority Employees' Union struck for five days to press for their demands, and at the height of the strike seven thousand nurses and doctors joined the action. Although they only partially succeeded, and at a much later date, the new union had demonstrated their strength.

The coronavirus pandemic has further alienated the Hong Kong people from China and has made the slogan 'segregate Hong Kong from the mainland' even more popular. It also further strengthens the Hong Kong identity, considered to be non-Chinese and pro-Western at the same time. When Hong Kongers stress that Hong Kong is an 'international city' they mean that it should be treated as one of the world's 'modernised and Westernised' cities. This is also precisely what the Chinese nationalists hate most.

In the eyes of many in the yellow camp, a Western lifestyle implies respect for the value of liberty and democracy. Thirty years of electoral politics and a (moderate) democratic movement have allowed local people to develop some kind of citizenship awareness, to begin to concern themselves with politics, and to vote or go to demonstrations. They consider themselves to be more 'civilised' than most mainland Chinese. They do exhibit a less conformist attitude than the mainland Chinese. Yet they should not forget that this is a very recent change. Hong Kongers have made some progress, but in many aspects we are still quite inadequate – we are not as advanced in relation to mainlanders as the nativists argue. For instance, across classes and ages, one can identify the same inadequacy of civil spirit, a lack of ability to run democratic meetings and to resolve differences peacefully, or to be able to join hands with people who have similar ideas and work together. This is not because of a certain endogenous character of being 'Chinese' or 'Hong Kongers', as 'national characteristics studies' or the 'cultural-intellectualistic approach' (which have been quite popular in Hong Kong and mainland China, even among the democratic opposition) may argue.[23] For people who commit to democratic struggle, instead of involving themselves in such broad topics it may be more useful to narrow down the discussion to comparing the *political* culture between China/Hong Kong and the rest of the world, and to learn the best practises. Merely focusing on reforming the political system is far from enough. For whatever reasons, mainland Chinese society is noticeably lacking the political values of tolerance, pluralism, public debate, etc., and Hong Kong is only slightly better. Chapter 3 briefly compared the occupation of the legislature during the Sunflower Movement in Taiwan with the similar action in the 2019 revolt in Hong Kong, and regarded the former as more orderly, constructive, and democratic, which proves that democratic behaviour can be compatible with being Chinese (in this case Taiwanese Chinese), simply because it can be learned, starting from being aware of our own inadequacy. For instance, it was not accidental that when Sun Yat-sen, founder of the Republic of China, agitated for democratic revolution, he found it necessary to first introduce his comrades and compatriots to the parliamentary procedure manual *Robert's Rules of Order*, because the Chinese were not acquainted with resolving their differences through democratic deliberation.

A century later, a Chinese student, Yuan Tianpeng, had a cultural shock while studying in the US. Out of curiosity, he took part in the students' union election at his university. He was given the same book. It was also his first time he had ever encountered proper democratic mechanisms and meeting procedures. After he went back to China, he embarked on a project of teaching Chinese farmers the skill and the art of meeting procedures. He wrote a book summarising his experiences:

For hundreds and thousands of years we were accustomed to only two modes [of decision-making mechanism]. One was a collective with a strongman, and everyone was trampled by him. The other is one which does not have a strongman, and everyone fought each other . . . There must be people like me who neither want to trample upon others nor want to be trampled upon . . . This is what we call 'self-management'. To achieve this, we need to return to the issue proposed by Sun Yat-sen – if the people want to be their own masters, they first must need to learn how to make collective decisions . . . to learn how to run meetings.[24]

By coincidence, I also began trying to introduce meeting procedures to fellow activists in Hong Kong a decade ago and found it quite difficult. It is not just about rules. It is more about political values, habits, and behaviour. One witnessed the same kind of weakness in both the 2014 and 2019 movements. Douglas, the high school student encountered in Chapter 2, shared his experience:

In June, I also joined a high school organisation called 'High School Students Concern Group Against the China Extradition Bill' which was founded in May. Towards the end of August there were differences among us. Some wanted to work with Demosistō and some didn't. On top of this there were people who wanted to be leaders and simply overthrow the rules and take matters into their own hands.

['Wasn't there democratic decision-making?'] Yes, but those leaders would conspire with their cronies and then simply did what they wanted. At this stage one could say that there was only one rule left: *seoi daai seoi ngok seoi zing kok* ['whoever is the big brother or the villain will then always be right', or more simply, 'might makes right', a popular saying during the movement]. Misuse of donations was also a frequent occurrence. The organisation soon split up.[25]

Obviously, changing one's identity from 'Chinese' to 'Hong Konger' is easy, but that alone does not necessary imply that one has transformed oneself inside and out, that one has fully acquired the knowledge and habits of acting democratically. To acquire the ability of self-management requires both Hong Kong and Chinese people to reflect on our inadequacy in relation to democratic culture and behaviours. Unfortunately, in the mainland, the Chinese people are repressed and manipulated so much that it is doubly hard for them to think through things and act accordingly. As for Hong Kong people, their long years of feeling superior and their pride have obstructed many from deeply reflecting on their own weaknesses.

Younger Hong Kongers tend to be proud, as they think that they are more civilised than mainland Chinese, and a great number of them thank British colonialism for this. In some ways, London did treat us slightly better than Beijing does today. At least the colonial government never bothered to make us sing 'God Save the Queen', nor did it penalise those who did not sing it. The Chinese government today is doing exactly this, however. But this does not mean the colonial government ever taught us genuine democracy and human rights. Just the opposite. We never had a law protecting human rights until the last decade of its rule – a bitter drink prepared not for its own consumption, but exclusively for the next ruler, Beijing. Today's young generation thought that the colonial government brought us modernity. This is only half true. If London ever brought 'modernity' to Hong Kong it was a version which was mixed with a heavy dose of colonialism and conservatism. It would never sponsor the importation of British radical thought and radical movements into Hong Kong. Tariq Ali, the well-known British journalist, was a young leftist in the 1970s. In the middle of the 1970s he visited Hong Kong but was ejected right away and sent back to London when he dared to meet up with the local young leftists. The diversity of political thought and culture in the West never had a chance to thrive in this so-called 'cultural desert', leaving the city's deep-rooted authoritarianism unchallenged. When the negotiation with Beijing over Hong Kong's future started in 1982, the British government began to be kinder to Hong Kong. The growing middle class, with encouragement from the colonial government, began to promote liberal values. Yet it was a right-wing version, strongly conservative, and inherited the same kind of authoritarianism no matter whether it came from the West or the East. Hong Kong continued to be a highly monocultural colony. We thought we were already 'Westernised', but we were only spoon-fed with a colonial version. Precisely because we had a mistaken view of democracy, most of us thought that the Basic Law was worth supporting, that the political system it laid down was still somehow quite liberal, and that it upheld a separation of powers and their check and balance – these were all wrong. Yet these mistaken views led Hong Kong's democratic movement to miss its best chance to fight for a better deal, until it suddenly realised that Hong Kong's autonomy was eroding at lightning speed. It was too late. Even when we started seriously fighting back, first in 2014 and then in 2019, we consistently exhibited traits of authoritarianism among ourselves.

We saw how in the 2014 movement the right-wing localists time and again attacked the leading students' organisation, the HKFS, with no justification, while most student protesters kept quiet. In the 2019 revolt participants exhibited great initiatives from below which we should admire but the mainstream of the movement continuously upheld the idea that spontaneity necessarily excluded any kind of organisation, or voting, or holding an assembly, all in the name of *caak daai toi* ('dismantle the stage'). Why is 'the stage' necessarily evil? What is 'the stage' anyway? More importantly, why did so many youth support *caak daai toi?* One may say that this was true of only some of the youths, but why were there no democratic youths who, with equal strength, came out to defend democratic assemblies and organise people from below? As a result, after the 2019 revolt most protesters emerged as atomised as before – although to balance this side of the story we have to remember that the revolt also gave birth to a new union movement as well. In the face of a highly organised and armed-to-the-teeth party-state, who else benefited from this state of atomisation among the people, if not the party-state itself? Why were so many people still hostile to any idea of organisation? Fundamentally speaking, it was because Hong Kong and Chinese people alike have not yet fully acquired the necessary knowledge and habits about democracy and public debate. We will continue to move along this historical trajectory of political inertia if we do not conduct a soul-searching reflection.

In the short run, the yellow camp can continuously resist Beijing through institutional means and social movements. For the former, there are election campaigns, a moderately independent judiciary, human rights laws, and dissident civil servants. For the latter, we have much stronger social support than we did in 2014. But in the medium term it is hard to resist Beijing. Hong Kong is too small to be able to fight alone in the long run. With a divided opposition, Beijing, through its grip over the Hong Kong government and the city's economic lifelines, can easily erode its autonomy in the next five to ten years. Even Hong Kong's water supply is in the hands of Beijing. In search of a way out, both the liberals and the right-wing localists are calling for US intervention. As we have seen, the US treats Hong Kong as a bargaining chip in its striving for its own 'national interest'. If Hong Kong becomes a battlefield for the US–China contest, it will be crushed. As the saying goes, when two elephants fight each other, the grass below them suffers first. On the other hand, most local activists dismiss the mainland people as a potential ally, which may further isolate them in their confrontation with Beijing. For the first time in seventy years Hong Kong is at a crossroads, and also faces a big threat. On the other hand, the coronavirus pandemic has allowed us to see the fact that the party-state is also entering murky waters with great uncertainties. Therefore, we should not imagine that Hong Kong's future will develop in a linear way from the current situation. We have to be prepared for surprises and shocks. The struggles are still ahead of us. In order to grasp future opportunities, we also need to think through all the experiences we have had in both 2014 and 2019, and to draw the correct lessons. So, let us debate.

BEIJING'S NEW OFFENSIVE AGAINST HONG KONG

On 28 May 2020, China's National People's Congress passed the 'Draft Decision on Establishing and Improving the Legal System and Enforcement Mechanisms for HKSAR (Hong Kong Special Administrative Region) to Safeguard National Security'. It 'opposes any form of intervention in the affairs of the HKSAR by any foreign countries or foreign forces' and reminds the Hong Kong government of its responsibility for 'the maintenance of national sovereignty, unity, and territorial integrity'. It also targets actions which may 'endanger national security'. On top of imposing this law on Hong Kong, Beijing is also going to set up a corresponding law enforcement agency in Hong Kong. Meanwhile, pro-Beijing parties in Hong Kong have warned that the draft bill means that anyone in Hong Kong with ties to 'foreign forces', or anyone who calls for Hong Kong independence or self-determination, or calls for 'bringing down the one-party dictatorship', could be prosecuted.

Arbitrary Rule versus Rule of Law

The next day, headlines like 'The End of One Country, Two Systems' filled the pages of the media. The local Bar Association reminded Beijing that Article 18 of the Basic Law requires that laws imposed by Beijing on

Hong Kong be confined to issues relating to defence and foreign affairs. And since Article 23 stipulates that the making of national security law is the responsibility of the Hong Kong government, this implies that Beijing's imposing of national security law on Hong Kong, not to mention setting up a law enforcement agency in the city, is a violation of the Basic Law and therefore an infringement on Hong Kong's autonomy.[26]

Again, Beijing has broken its promise of Hong Kong autonomy as enshrined in the Basic Law. Its officials have done the same to China's own law during the coronavirus pandemic. The party-state has done the same even to their own constitution: although not really democratic, it never stipulates an autocracy, yet this is exactly what Beijing government looks like today. Again, what matters is not the constitution or the laws, it is the hidden rule of the CCP – giving absolute power, unrestrained by laws, to the party leader – which counts.

Ironically, the CCP did admit that China had not yet fully achieved the rule of law, and this was why, at the Nineteenth Party Congress in 2017, Xi Jinping laid out his timetable for achieving that status by 2035, when the country had 'basically modernised' – the party has a timetable for everything, including a timetable for achieving the rule of law. I argue that Xi would never achieve his goal unless his party resolves what I call 'Peng Zhen's puzzle'. Peng was the former head of the Standing Committee of the People's Congress in the 1980s. When asked 'whether the *party or the law* is *superior*' his answer was 'I don't know'. In the end, the puzzle was resolved by Xi, according to a party propagandist. Xi concluded that it was a pseudo-proposition from the start. Instead it was determined that only the question of 'whether power [of the officials] or the law is superior' was a valid proposition.[27] But it is not clear at all why he thought that Peng Zhen's puzzle was a 'pseudo-proposition'. He made a conclusion but gave no proof at all. Raising an additional proposition about 'power and law' was not helpful either. In the end he, just like Peng, avoided the question. Unlike Peng, Xi avoided the question in a very assertive and arrogant way. This is a green light for the party to continuously stand above the constitution and the law. Xi's and his party's contempt for the laws governing the management of infectious diseases was harshly punished by reality – the coronavirus pandemic. But this had not deterred our leader to continuously upholding his autocratic rule.

Beijing stresses again and again that behind the draft bill lies its concern over the threat of 'foreign forces' in Hong Kong. Instead of 'foreign forces', I argue that Beijing's top concern is domestic discontent. The existence of Hong Kong's liberties – the publishing of books which Beijing hates or holding the 4 June memorial assembly non-stop for thirty years – leads Beijing to fear that Hong Kong may one day successfully encourage the rebirth of the mainland democratic movement. Its Orwellian regime simply cannot coexist with Hong Kong's autonomy.

Signs of civil discontent in the mainland during the pandemic are probably additional factors which have led Beijing to launch this round of offensives as well. When the central government sent delegates to Wuhan to investigate the pandemic, local residents shouted 'lies! lies!' to the delegates, telling them that the information released by the local authorities was all fake. All talk about 'foreign forces' is first and foremost an attempt to divert attention from domestic problems.

Beijing's Domestic Concerns

Earlier, I mentioned the premodern political culture of the CCP. This return of imperial China's political tradition tempted Fei-Ling Wang to argue, in *The China Order: Centralia, World Empire, and the Nature of Chinese Power*, that today's China 'is a reincarnated Qin-Han polity', which aims at global expansion and hence necessarily comes into conflict with the US.[28] 'Qin' refers to the first unified Chinese dynasty founded by Qin Shihuang in 221BC. 'Han' refers to the Han dynasty, which succeeded the Qin. The advantage of Wang's term is that it captures the premodern political culture of the Beijing regime, however it misses another facet of the regime, namely that it has been crazily committed to mobilising the people for China's industrialisation and modernisation. Its modern features stand side by side with its premodern features.

The party bureaucracies also enrich themselves in the modern way, the way of capitalism, not through the old imperial way of direct appropriation of agricultural surpluses. They can enrich themselves much more quickly than their counterparts around the world because they have invented a new capitalist means of exploitation (what I have called 'bureaucratic capitalism') that is able to combine both the power of the coercive state and capital in its hands, and hence devours an ever bigger share of social surplus at the expense of the people. The inconvenient truth is that the people have also noticed this through their mobile phones and their internet, all products of modernisation.

The party's industrialisation drive has had another unintended consequence. The party has turned China into a country with a highly educated people, an urbanised society, a large working class and middle class – which certain political scientists regard as democratic classes.[29] No one knows this better than the CCP. It is also one of the main reasons for its constant paranoia over the slightest signs of dissent and unrest.

Even the party has not unilaterally glorified the great leader Xi. Since Xi came to power in 2012, dissident views over his diplomacy (known today as 'Warrior Wolf diplomacy' in China) still occasionally make their voices heard. There has been a 'dove' current, dressed up as academic debate. Recently this voice has been heard again. For years it has been widely believed that it is Hu Angang, an economics professor at Tsinghua University, who has been advising Xi on how great China is today. Hu is well known for 'arguing that China has already overtaken the United States as a world leader in terms of economic and technological power'.[30] We do not know the top secrets of the CCP. Still, lots of clues have been pointing to internal disagreement. In an interview with Phoenix TV's affiliated online news outlet in February 2018, Long Yongtu, a former trade negotiator who played an instrumental role in China's accession to the World Trade Organization (WTO), said that Hu's views were misguided and would not only harm China's foreign relations but also mislead the public.[31] This seems not to be a one-off thing. In August 2018, Hu was further criticised in an open letter written by Tsinghua University alumni that called for the university to fire him. The letter accused him of using 'self-serving criteria' in his research to exaggerate claims of China's greatness.

The China–US Global Contest

In response to Beijing's draft bill, Trump took a very important step by declaring the beginning of the end of the US's special treatment of Hong Kong. In the days following this, a wave of panic buying of US dollars swept across Hong Kong. People feared that Trump could do something at any time to undermine the linked exchange rate system which pegs the Hong Kong dollar to the US dollar. The Hong Kong government tried to calm people down by saying that the territory's trade with the

US is now too small to impact Hong Kong, even if Trump expands his trade war against China to include Hong Kong. This is only a half truth. The crux of the matter is Hong Kong's financial markets, and Hong Kong no longer being able to import high-tech products from the US.

The US also has entrenched interests in Hong Kong. When the American Chamber of Commerce in Hong Kong expressed concern over the draft bill, the Hong Kong government reminded it that Hong Kong is the place where the US enjoys its highest amount of trade surplus – US$297 billion between 2009 and 2018, and that Hong Kong's trade with the US provided more than 210,000 jobs for US workers.[32]

On top of this is the trade interdependence between China and the US. Both countries are among the top three trading partners of each other. Decoupling will be painful for both sides, although the pain will be asymmetrical, as the US trade dependency is less intensive than China's.[33]

But now both sides seem to think that their global contest is more important than the economic pain of their respective countries.

Ironically, the rise of China's 'socialism with Chinese characteristics' was only possible with the help of the West. The well-known Hungarian economist Janos Kornai wrote an article in the *Financial Times* last July with the title 'Economists Share Blame for China's "Monstrous" turn'. He confessed to having advised top CCP officials in 1985 to introduce market reform to China 'by the electric shock of marketisation and private property', but admitted that eventually the endeavour only became 'the modern version of Mary Shelley's Frankenstein'.[34]

In terms of their China policy, the mood among the Western ruling elites in the 1980s was a 'change through trade' doctrine. Bill Clinton had this to say in his 2000 speech, when he tried to explain why allowing Beijing to join the WTO was so important:

> By joining the WTO, China is not simply agreeing to import more of our products; it is agreeing to import one of democracy's most cherished values: economic freedom.[35]

The EU by then shared the same 'change through trade' policy.[36] But history has proved that the CCP's recognition of 'economic freedom' did not result in any democratic change. Making profit (which was the most important incentive behind the West's support of Beijing at that time) and market competition is the 'categorical imperative' of capital, but democracy is not.

Why did the honeymoon between China and the US end so abruptly? At the risk of oversimplification, the background of the present China–US rivalry is like this: when Beijing signed the Sino-British Joint Declaration in 1984, in the words of Deng Xiaoping, it expected that it would take at least fifty years to modernise China and transform it into a middle-income country. It did not know that it eventually only needed half that time. A rising China has become more assertive and increasingly impatient with Hong Kong's delay in kowtowing to Beijing. On top of this, it is concerned about its position in the world. Washington will not give up its hegemony, but neither will Beijing indefinitely accept the status of a second-rate power, hence this latest contest which has been ongoing since 2012. The first stage of this contest has mainly featured three battles – the South China Sea dispute, the trade war, and Hong Kong.

Beijing's present global perspective is to a great extent shaped by two historical lessons that it believes it has fully learnt. The first one is drawn from the collapse of the USSR. Beijing deeply believes that its brutal crackdown on the 1989 democratic movement saved its party-state from meeting the same fate as the Soviet Union. 'No political reform!' is the essence of this understanding of the 'historical lesson'. The more the US lectures Beijing about the advantage of liberal capitalism, the more Beijing believes that the US is aiming at regime change in Beijing, symbolised by the term 'heping yanbian' ('peaceful evolution from socialism to capitalism').

The second 'lesson' was drawn from the US trade war against Japan in the 1980s. By that time, Japan had become the second-largest economy in the world, and a section of the elite class now became more ambitious and called for greater autonomy from the US (see the book *Japan Can Say No*, authored by Sony co-founder and chairman, Akio Morita, and the then minister of transport, Shintaro Ishihara). Their ambition was largely ended after the US successfully concluded the Plaza Accord, which forced the Japanese yen to appreciate significantly, followed by instituting a 100 percent tariff against Japan's imports. Japan's economy was dealt a big blow, and the US continues to dominate Japan, militarily above all. Since the late 1980s, the Japan case has always been the subject of debate among Chinese economists, strategists, and nationalists, and the nationalists' argument has always been the strongest: China as a developing country cannot afford a Japanese-style defeat at the hands of the US, and China must resist the US if the latter begins to show its teeth.

On top of this, there is also a third 'lesson from history' as understood by Beijing hardliners: the only way forward is for a former semi-colonial country, one which was repeatedly invaded in the period of 1840 to 1945, to strive to become the top hegemonic power. While there is a grain of legitimacy in a former semi-colonial country guarding against its former imperialist invaders, the CCP overdid the job when it began to use China's tragic colonial legacy to pursue its expansionism. Unlike Japan, the CCP under Xi is not going to accept a second-rate position. Unlike the Japanese rulers, Xi does want to replace the 'Western' version of globalisation with his 'Chinese' version, right here and now.

On the other side of the Pacific Ocean, confronting an assertive China has also become a consensus among both Democrats and Republicans. Whereas the previous US administration described China as a 'strategic partner', the 2018 US National Defence Strategy Report labelled China as a 'strategic competitor'. Last October, at the height of the 2019 revolt, Mike Pence made a speech targeting Beijing, which some consider to be a pronouncement of a new Cold War. Trump may make more tactical twists and turns in the near future, but the general trend of the US–China rivalry may not be changed easily.

I am hesitant to use the term 'new Cold War', however. During the 'old' Cold War, Taiwan under the KMT allied with the US in their bitter confrontation with Beijing. Meanwhile, the British colonial government kept oppressing the Hong Kong people. Their so-called 'free world' was not that free after all. On the other hand, the CCP in 1949 was never a genuine socialist force, and its contempt towards basic democratic rights was already present. Yet it was also a government leading a former semi-colonial country to achieve national independence, and which had launched land reform and other reforms, such as a new law on marriage which liberated women from half-feudalistic oppression. So, the regime carried both progressive and regressive elements, and could not be treated as equally reactionary as the US.

In contrast, the renewed confrontation between the US and China nowadays is very different. It is different because both the US empire and Beijing's regime have changed a lot, although the latter has changed more. Today's CCP, with its fusion of both political and economic power, its plundering of national wealth through holding such power, its hostility towards people enjoying basic rights of association and free speech, its xenophobia, nationalism, social Darwinism, cult of a corporate state, 'unification' of thought, etc., is so reactionary that it is hard to find anything which is politically progressive. Socially speaking, its labour laws are quite progressive, but since the state has banned any form of worker self-organising and party officials have little incentive to enforce the laws, the legal protection is largely on paper. It is an Orwellian regime through and through. On the other hand, its old rival Taiwan has a liberal democracy, pluralistic party politics, a space for a growing labour movement, thanks to its people's decades-long democratic struggle against the KMT. Hong Kong also enjoys a wide range of political liberties. As for the US, it has surely not evolved into a progressive regime, but its power in the region of 'Greater China' (mainland China, Taiwan, and Hong Kong) is much weaker now. The US no longer has armies stationed in Taiwan, and Hong Kong's handover to China was completed in 1997. We must treat the US and the UK's rhetoric about supporting Hong Kong and Taiwanese democracy with a dose of scepticism, and their agenda with suspicion, but they are not our direct oppressors.

As for the present CCP regime, it is now the direct oppressor of mainland and Hong Kong people. It openly declares its intention to conquer Taiwan by force. Therefore, in the present contest, while the US empire is weaker and therefore more on the defensive, Beijing has been more on the offensive in pursuing its hegemonic ambitions, which can only be satisfied by sacrificing the welfare of the people. Therefore, the relationship of forces and the nature of this new global rivalry between two great powers is very different from the 'old' Cold War.

Where Should the International Left Stand?

The international left is divided over the 2019 revolt. When the term 'new Cold War' began to appear in 2020, it surely made certain leftists even more reluctant to support the Hong Kong protest, if not inciting them to outright condemn it as a tool of 'foreign forces'.

For the past ten years, during international meetings, I have often encountered leftists who wanted to defend Beijing, but they rarely notice that their defence has been eroding and eroding until it has become absurd. At first, their defence was that Beijing was socialist and Washington was imperialist. China's rise at the expense of its working people had become so obvious that some of these international leftists have now quietly dropped their 'Beijing is socialist' argument. However, they then retreated to a second line of defence, arguing that China's rise has turned the unipolar world dominated by the US into a multipolar world, which is a good thing. I do not quite understand why this is necessarily good. And then, more recently when the 2019 revolt broke out, they only focused on the right wing or Trump's supporters in Hong Kong, but largely ignored the fact this was a movement with two million supporters, unified not by being 'pro-US' or 'pro-independence' or 'anti-Chinese', but by the famous 'five demands', with universal suffrage as its core demand. This perspective had led them to the conclusion that the movement is not progressive at all.

There is legitimate concern about the Basic Law's institutionalising of the presence of 'foreign forces' in Hong Kong. Surely it is one of our colonial legacies. Beijing's supporters often accuse the Hong Kong people of resisting its 'decolonisation' efforts. The problem with its version of 'decolonisation' is that while it treats the legitimate local aspiration for democracy as a kind of 'nostalgia for the colonial past', it does not mind keeping all the repressive colonial laws, the very laws that it made Carrie Lam use against the people during the 2019 revolt. This version of 'decolonisation' is fake. I do not think that Hong Kong working people would mind if decolonisation means the replacement of repressive elements of our colonial legacy with something that is really better and nicer. This is not the case, however.

Some of the leftists' concern is that they do not want to be seen as aligning with the US government. But why is the US government's rhetorical support of Hong Kong's democratic struggle enough to make certain leftists give up their own support for this righteous cause? Why is conducting a solidarity campaign with Hong Kong, independently and at a distance from the Trump government, something inconceivable? The more the international left is absent from the solidarity campaign with the Hong Kongers' defence of their autonomy and demand for universal suffrage, the more it makes Trump the only visible force supporting these struggles, and thus gives undue credit to him and reinforces the right-wing localist discourses in Hong Kong.

The Japanese Communist Party (JCP) has proved itself to be truer to the values of the left. On 28 May 2020, it released a statement condemning Beijing for its national security law draft bill. It reminded Beijing that the latter's position of 'no intervention by foreign forces over China's domestic policies' is flawed because 'every country, through signing international treaties, has the duty to respect human rights, therefore infringing human rights is not just a domestic issue, it is also a significant international issue'. It further reminded Beijing that it has endorsed the Universal Declaration of Human Rights and has made an international commitment to safeguard the 'high level of autonomy for Hong Kong'.[37]

Or perhaps there are still people who think that China is a 'socialist country'? The JCP's recent evolution in its position is relevant to our current discussion. Prior to the JCP's swift response to Beijing's move, it had already called for Beijing to stop repressing the Hong Kong protesters last November.[38] In February 2020, the JCP, during its party congress, decided to delete from its programme a reference to China as 'beginning a new quest for socialism, including the effort to achieve socialism through a market economy'. JCP leader Kazuo Shii had this to say about the CCP in his speech:

> The Chinese party calls itself 'socialist' and 'communist', but its great-power chauvinism, hegemonism, and violations of human rights have nothing to do with 'socialism' and are not worthy of the term 'communism'.[39]

A Hong Kong 2020 Revolt?

After reports emerged about Beijing's move to impose its national security law on Hong Kong, protesters took the street again on 24 and 27 May. These protests were much smaller than those in 2019, and the turnout of middle-aged and older protesters was also much smaller. The CTU called for a strike on 27 May. Nothing happened. Maybe the momentum will rise later this year, maybe not. When and if the new national security law is put in place, many people will be afraid of dire consequences. The young people are braver but have rejected party politics or any idea of organisation, it is hard to see how they could confront a state machinery which is armed to the teeth.

Trump has declared the beginning of the end of the US special treatment of Hong Kong. This led US supporters here to claim victory for their 'scorched-earth/we burn you burn with us!' tactic. They expect that the US move will hurt both Hong Kong's and the mainland's economy, and that it may then bring down the CCP regime. My response has been this: no foreign sanction alone, nor an economic crisis on its own, could bring down the regime if no democratic movement is able to grow in the mainland and the counterpart in Hong Kong remains so fragmented and disorganised. On top of this, without the growth of our own democratic forces, we are forever dependent on a great power, be it Beijing or Washington, and are absolutely at their mercy. We will be worse than the 'banana republics' because we will be caught in the middle between two great powers in conflict with each other. Hong Kongers should conduct their struggle against Beijing independently from the US government, although it is not going to be easy.

It is interesting to read that among the voices for securing US support there arises, for the first time, some disagreement. On Facebook, Joshua Wong criticised the leading pro-Trump tabloid's use of the hashtag 'TrumpSavesHK' on its front page, as violating the principle of bipartisanship. Wong asked the question, 'what would the members of Congress of the American Democratic Party think about this?' He went on to comment that, 'if the assistant of Nancy Pelosi emails me asking me about this I think it would not be that easy to give a comprehensive explanation'.[40] This triggered some online debate on the issue, allowing those who are more thoughtful to finally realise that 'America' is not a homogenous entity, and that not any kind of 'support of Hong Kong' is a blessing. America, just like Hong Kong or anywhere else, is a society riven with deep class divisions. Bipartisanship is not enough to help Hong Kongers to navigate an international solidarity campaign. After asking 'what would the Democratic Party think about this', logically it will lead to more questions like 'what would the left wing of the Democratic party think of this? What would the progressive Americans think of this? Who are the genuine democratic forces in the US?' In the end, Hong Kongers will need to answer a final question that they have been trying to avoid: 'whom should we link up with in the US? Rightists, leftists, or centrists? But who are we in the first place? Are we rightists, leftists, or centrists?'

With hundreds of US cities in flames after George Floyd was killed by the police, for the first time the right-wing localists and friends of the US empire in Hong Kong now face an embarrassing situation. They have repeatedly sung choruses for Trump's rhetorical support of Hong Kong democracy, yet his reactionary attitude to the protests across the country, his call for sending armies to crush the protests, has not only exposed his deep conservatism, but also reminds Hong Kong people of the CCP's suppression of both the 1989 democratic movement and those in Hong Kong in 2019. In online debates, people are asking the right-wing localists the question, how can we not support the solidarity protest with George Floyd when we Hong Kongers have just been oppressed by the same kind of police state last year? Thanks to the struggle in the US there are signs that more Hong Kong people are rethinking their political perspective.

Timeline of the 2019
Hong Kong Revolt

Background

1842   China cedes Hong Kong Island to Britain after the First Opium War.

1949   Founding of the People's Republic of China.

1984   Britain and China sign the Joint Declaration, under which Hong Kong will be returned to China in 1997 on the condition of the maintenance of the 'one country, two systems' principle for a further fifty years.

1989   China's democratic movement; crushed on June 4.

2003   The Hong Kong government tables a bill on national security but is forced to withdraw it after 500,000 protesters take to the streets.

2014   On 28 September, thousands occupy the area outside the Hong Kong government headquarters to demand universal suffrage, triggering off what is later called the 'Umbrella Movement'. This soon spreads to four main shopping areas. The occupation lasts for 79 days.

2019 HONG KONG REVOLT

February

12   The Hong Kong government tables the extradition bill.

March

31   The Civil Human Rights Front leads a march of 12,000 people against the extradition bill.

April

28   130,000 respond to the call by the Civil Human Rights Front to protest the bill.

June

6   Several thousand lawyers march on the streets.

9   One million protesters march to protest the bill.

12 The first civil disobedience actions take place, followed by clashes with police outside of the Legislative Council.

14 The first 'Mothers' Sit-In' is held, with six thousand participants.

15 Carrie Lam announces the suspension of the extradition bill. Marco Leung commits suicide after hanging an anti-extradition bill banner near the Hong Kong government headquarters.

16 Two million people march.

21 Protesters put the Hong Kong Police Force headquarters under siege.

July

1   550,000 take to the streets in response to the call of the Civil Human Rights Front. At night, protesters break into the Legislative Council.

7   230,000 protesters march in Kowloon to approach mainland visitors for support.

9   Carrie Lam announces that the extradition bill is dead.

14 115,000 protesters march in Shatin; riot police beat up protesters inside a mall.

21 430,000 protesters march on Hong Kong Island, followed by young protesters gathering outside the Liaison Office and spraying graffiti there. At night, members of organised crime syndicates attack passengers in Yuen Long.

26 Thousands of protesters occupy the airport.

27 280,000 defy a ban and march in Yuen Long to protest the 21 July Yuen Long incident. The march is forcefully disbanded by the police.

August

1   Employees from the finance sector assemble in Central to protest.

2   40,000 civil servants and 10,000 doctors and nurses assemble to protest.

4   Protesters put police stations under siege around the city to protest police violence the previous day.

5   The first successful general strike. Strike assemblies are held in seven districts. At night, members of organised crime syndicates attack protesters.

9–11   Planned occupation of the airport for three days goes ahead.

12   10,000 protesters go to the airport again to protest after the police blind a young woman in one eye the previous day. At night, organised crime strikes again.

18   1.7 million join an assembly.

22   Thousands of high school students and their teachers and parents hold a sit-in in Central.

23   Human chains are assembled all around Hong Kong.

26   The birth of the song 'Glory to Hong Kong'.

28   Two thousand Cathy Pacific employees assemble to protest the firing of dozens of their colleagues. Thousands of women take part in a 'Me Too' assembly to condemn police sexual violence against women.

31   Police crack down on protesters and chase them into the Prince Edward MTR station. Rumours of police killing protesters spread.

September

1   Several thousand people occupy the airport but police soon cut off all transport. Thousands of cars are driven to the airport to pick up protesters.

2   Class boycott by college and high school students.

4   Carrie Lam withdraws the extradition bill.

8   Assembly in Central to petition the US Congress to pass the Hong Kong Human Rights and Democracy Act.

15   100,000 march on Hong Kong Island, followed by attacks and counter-attacks between Beijing supporters and protesters.

22   The naked body of Chan Yin-lam, a 15-year-old girl and supporter of the protest movement, is found.

29   Hundreds of thousands of protesters march on Hong Kong Island; 65 cities around the world hold solidarity marches or assemblies.

October

1 National Day of the PRC. 100,000 protesters defy bans and march on Hong Kong Island and other parts of the city. Clashes with police follow.

2 Carrie Lam invokes the Emergency Regulations Ordinance to impose a ban on wearing face masks at public gatherings. This is immediately met with protests that continue into the next few days.

10 National Day of Taiwan. Thousands of protesters march to express solidarity with Taiwan.

12 Over 10,000 protesters march in defiance of the ban on marches and on face masks.

14 130,000 protesters gather to ask the US Congress to pass the Hong Kong Human Rights and Democracy Act.

20 350,000 demonstrators march in Kowloon in defiance of the ban.

24 Three thousand protesters assemble in Central to express solidarity with the Catalonia independence movement.

November

3 Assemblies and marches in many parts of the city end in chaos after police crackdown. Alex Chow Tsz-lok, a 22-year-old student, is found unconscious; he dies from his wounds on the 8th.

11–15 *The Battle at the Chinese University of Hong Kong*

11–12 Students block a nearby bridge and successfully halt traffic on the railway and highways beneath. Riot police fire numerous rounds of tear gas and rubber bullets at the campus, while students hit back with bricks and petrol bombs.

13 The confrontation is halted and the university announces the end of the semester. The campus is occupied by protesting students and citizens.

15 Rocky Tuan, president of the university, asks all outsiders to leave the campus.

13–28 *The Battle at Hong Kong Polytechnic University*

13 The campus is occupied by students.

16–17 On the evening of the 16th, outside protesters joined the students on the campus and began to protest outside the campus. Clashes with police follow. The next day the police lay siege to the campus and attack the defences of the students.

18   While the students hold their line inside the campus, more than 10,000 outside protesters occupy the streets nearby and the busiest part of Kowloon to try to rescue the students.

18   The High Court rules that the ban on face masks is unconstitutional.

19   More than one thousand protesters inside the campus give themselves up to the police. Meanwhile hundreds of protesters escape.

20   The US Congress and Senate pass the Hong Kong Human Rights and Democracy Act.

23   The university campus is deserted.

24   The opposition wins 389 seats out of 452 in the District Council elections.

28   The police enter the university.

December

1   380,000 march in Tsim Sha Tsui but this legal demonstration is soon forcefully disbanded by police.

8   800,000 protesters respond to the Civil Human Rights Front call for a march on Human Rights Day.

29   Several thousand protesters gather in Central to reaffirm their five demands.

January 2020

1   One million heed the call from the Civil Human Rights Front to march. Forty newly founded trade unions set up booths along the route to recruit members. The police disband the march halfway through.

References

INTRODUCTION

1. 'Wuhan fengcheng, mianlin rendao zainan' (Wuhan Lockdown, Facing Humanity Crisis), *Radio France Internationale* (Chinese edition), 25 January 2020. Translated by the author.

CHAPTER 1

1. This section is adapted from the author's essay on the 2014 Umbrella Movement for Europe Solidaire Sans Frontières, available at www.europe-solidaire.org/spip.php?article53314.
2. 'Deng Xiaoping: Xianggang 50 nian bubian zhu hua xiandaihua' (Deng Xiaoping: Hong Kong Capitalism to Remain Unchanged for Fifty Years to Help China's Modernisation), *Mingpao Canada*, 31 December 2014, www.mingpaocanada.com/tor/htm/News/20141231/HK-gaa1h_r.htm.
3. 'GDP (current US$)', The World Bank, http://data.worldbank.org/indicator/NY.GDP.MKTP.CD.
4. '2010 nian Guangzhou wanren shangjie cheng yueyu' (Ten Thousand Took to the Street in Guangzhou to Support Cantonese in 2010), *Apple Daily*, 25 July 2014.
5. The former chairperson of the Democratic Party mentioned this figure in a 2015 Hong Kong and Taiwan Exchange Conference.
6. 'Chen Jianmin zibian yishu wu Lin Zheng liu jianghua: Minjian gongtou baogao guanyuan liu shuhua' (Chan Kin-man Self-Defence Recalling Meeting with Carrie Lam: The Officials Left the Report on the Civil Referendum on the Sofa), *Mingpao*, 30 November 2018.
7. 'Fandui renda cubao luozha jiyao zhenpuxuan yeyao gaishan minsheng' (Oppose the NPC's Rough Decision, Demand Genuine Universal Suffrage and Improvements to People's Livelihoods), *Inmediahk.net*, www.inmediahk.net/20140923b.
8. 'Prosecutions Hong Kong 2017', Hong Kong Department of Justice, www.doj.gov.hk/eng/public/pdf/pd2017/statistics.pdf.
9. 'Xiangxin tequ zhengfu nuli gongzuo he shehui gejie lixing taolun, yiding neng xiaochu yilü, dacheng gongshi' (We Believe the SAR Government can Eliminate Doubts and Reach Consensus through Hard Work and Rational Discussion with Every Social Sector), *Ta Kung Pao*, 23 May 2019.

10. 'Fu tiaoli xianzhi, guojingke ke yijiao, hangai renhe zaigangzhe' (It is in Accordance with the Restriction of the Bill to Include Visitors for Extradition, as the Bill Said 'Anyone in Hong Kong'), *Mingpao*, 2 June 2019.

11. 'Germany Looking at Current Extradition Law with HK', *RTHK.hk*, https://news.rthk.hk/rthk/en/component/k2/1462720-20190613.htm

12. 'Shangjie pa yijiao, Li Jiachao pao shanghui ji jiehua' (Business Sector in Fear of Extradition, Lee Ka-chiu Hurries to Explain to Chamber of Commerce), *Mingpao*, 7 March 2019.

13. 'Onsite Survey Findings in Hong Kong's Anti-Extradition Bill Protests: Research Report', Centre for Communication and Public Opinion Survey, The Chinese University of Hong Kong, August 2019, www.com.cuhk.edu.hk/ccpos/en/pdf/ENG_antielab%20survey%20public%20report%20vf.pdf.

14. 'Civic Society Sponsorship Scheme: Survey Report', Hong Kong Public Opinion Program of Hong Kong Public Opinion Research Institute, 29 October 2019, https://static1.squarespace.com/static/5cfd1ba6a7117c000170d7aa/t/5db991cae7e33d565bee670a/1572442590417/sp_rpt_special_poll_2019oct29_v4_final.pdf.

15. 'Cong mindiao shuzi, kan butong zhengjian he nianqingren de xinsheng' (Looking at Diverse Political Opinions and Listening to the Youths' Voice through Polling), *Mingpao*, 27 September 2019.

16. 'Anti-Extradition Bill Movement People's Public Sentiment: Report (First Edition)', Hong Kong Public Opinion Research Institute and Project Citizens Foundation, 13 December 2019, https://tinyurl.com/ycntj3ll.

17. Interview with Ho, 29 January 2020. Translation by the author.

18. 'Survey on "We HongKongers"', Hong Kong Public Opinion Institute and Project Citizens Foundation, December 2019, https://tinyurl.com/y9rzl5lr.

19. 'Cong mindiao shuzi, kan butong zhengjian he nianqingren de xinsheng'. The three main demands included in the survey were: 1. to withdraw the extradition bill; 2. to conduct an independent inquiry into police behaviour; 3. to implement universal suffrage.

20. 'Public Opinion & Political Development in Hong Kong: Survey Results', Centre for Communication and Public Opinion Survey, The Chinese University of Hong Kong, 18 December 2014, www.com.cuhk.edu.hk/ccpos/images/news/TaskForce_PressRelease_141218_English.pdf.

21. 'Mingpao mindiao: Yuban youxingzhe ji xingdong shengji, yicheng cheng hui "zhuangxiu" "siliao" xuezhe: Jushi zhuanjing rengcun yinyou' (*Mingpao* Survey: More than Half of Demonstrators Hope to Escalate their Actions, 10 percent Said they Would Resort to 'Renovation' and 'Lynching': Scholar Says Situation Turns Quiet but Still Poses Potential Problems), *Mingpao*, 2 January 2020.

22. 'Xianggang zhengzhi qunti de quxiang yitong he bankuai piaoyi' (Differences over Political Orientation among Hong Kong Political Groups and their Tectonic Shift), *Mingpao*, 31 October 2019. In this survey, there

were three other categories: 'pro-business', 'pro-establishment', and 'pro-Beijing', together they only accounted for 6.1 percent.

23. 'Kangzheng yundong ruhe gaibian Xianggangren de zhengzhi qingxiang' (How the Resistance Movement Changed Hong Kongers' Political Inclination), *Stand News*, 27 October 2019, https://tinyurl.com/y7zuoc7u.

24. 'Onsite Survey Findings in Hong Kong's Anti Extradition Bill Protests: Research Report'.

CHAPTER 2

1. 'Zhonglianban Liang Zhenying huogang, peng qingnian xinzheng ban gangdu' (The Liaison Office and C.Y. Leung Favour Youngspiration and the Latter are Pretending to be Hong Kong Independence Advocates), *Sing Pao*, 3 September 2016.

2. 'Zhang Dejiang cehua "weigangdu" yinmou, quanguo renda lun dianfu zhengquan gongju' (Zhang Dejiang Plots the 'Fake Hong Kong Independence Campaign' Conspiracy, the National People's Congress Becomes Tools of Subversion of the Government), *Sing Pao*, 6 November 2016.

3. See also the following report: 'The Role of Beijing's "Invisible Hand" in the Chief Executive Elections', *Hong Kong Free Press*, 2 April 2017, www.hongkongfp.com/2017/04/02/role-beijings-invisible-hand-chief-executive-elections.

4. 'Exclusive: Amid Crisis, China Rejected Hong Kong Plan to Appease Protesters', Reuters, 30 August 2019, www.reuters.com/article/us-hong kong-protests-china-exclusive/exclusive-amid-crisis-china-rejected-hong-kong-plan-to-appease-protesters-sources-idUSKCN1VK0H6.

5. 'Hong Kong Leader Carrie Lam Challenged: "Have your Hands Been Tied by Beijing?"', *The Straits Times*, www.youtube.com/watch?v=v-gX0d5U1A4.

6. Martin Purbrick, 'A Report of the 2019 Hong Kong Protests', *Asian Affairs* 50:4 (2019): 465–487, www.tandfonline.com/doi/full/10.1080/03068374.2019.1672397.

7. 'Beijing Accused of Sneaking Police into HK', *Asia Times*, 9 August 2019, www.asiatimes.com/2019/08/article/beijing-accused-of-sneaking-police-into-hong-kong.

8. 'Exclusive: China's Internal Security Force on Frontlines of Hong Kong Protests', Reuters, 18 March 2020, www.reuters.com/article/us-hongkong-protests-military-exclusive/exclusive-chinas-internal-security-force-on-frontlines-of-hong-kong-protests-idUSKBN2150JZ.

9. 'Guanyu dangqian jushi de xuanchuan yaoze' (On the Principle of Propaganda under the Current Situation), *Matters.news*, 22 August 2019, https://tinyurl.com/y9u28g07. Translation by the author.

10. 'How Murder, Kidnappings and Miscalculation Set Off Hong Kong's Revolt', Reuters, 20 December 2019, www.reuters.com/article/us-hong

kong-protests-extradition-narrati/special-report-how-murder-kidnappings-and-miscalculation-set-off-hong-kongs-revolt-idUSK BN1YO18Q.

11. 'Beijing Wants Tycoons to Take Action, Not Just Pay Lip Service', *South China Morning Post*, 1 November 2014, www.scmp.com/business/article/1629442/beijing-wants-tycoons-take-action-not-just-pay-lip-service.

12. 'Hong Kong Business Magnate Li Ka Shing "runs away". Chinese Netizens Ask, Why Shouldn't He?', *Hong Kong Free Press*, 17 September 2017, www.hongkongfp.com/2015/09/17/a-hong-kong-business-magnate-runs-away-chinese-netizens-ask-why-shouldnt-he.

13. 'Li's Empire Strikes Back: Hong Kong's Richest Man Slams Mainland Chinese Media for "Totally Unfounded" Reports he is Divesting from Country', *South China Morning Post*, 29 September 2015, www.scmp.com/news/hong-kong/economy/article/1862453/lis-empire-strikes-back-hong-kongs-richest-man-slams-mainland.

14. 'Lun gang binggen, Xinhuashe chi dichanshang tuandi, dijianhui cheng wuhui' (Xinhua News Agency on the Root Cause of Hong Kong Illness, Criticises Developers' Hoarding Land, Developers' Association Says it is Misunderstanding), *Mingpao*, 14 September 2019.

15. 'Shek Lai-him: Wuda suqiu wuhua yao wu' (Shek Lai-him: Five Demands Do Not Include Housing), *Apple Daily*, 31 October 2019.

16. 'Lun gang binggen, Xinhuashe chi dichanshang tuandi, dijianhui cheng wuhui'.

17. 'Onsite Survey Findings in Hong Kong's Anti-Extradition Bill Protests: Research Report'.

18. As of end of 2018. See 'Population Estimates', Census and Statistics Department of the Hong Kong Government, www.censtatd.gov.hk/hkstat/sub/sp150.jsp?tableID=002&ID=0&productType=8.

19. This only includes those between 15 and 19 years old, whereas the parameter in CUHK's report is '19 or below'. But it is reasonable to speculate that the number of protestors below the age of 15 is fewer and therefore the above comparison is still useful.

20. On that date there were two locations where protests broke out, namely Tseung Kwan O and Western District. We choose the latter because it is where the Liaison Office is located and hence clashes are often expected whenever there are planned protests there.

21. 'Kangzheng yundong xia shimin zhengzhi qingxiang de zhuanbian' (The Changes in Citizens' Political Inclination Under the Resistance Movement), *Mingpao*, 24 October 2019.

22. Anamarija Musa, 'Was There a Silent Revolution? A Comparative Analysis of Party Manifestos in Ten European Countries', www.semanticscholar.org/paper/Was-There-a-Silent-Revolution-A-Comparative-of-in-Musa/e0b6611a7f6084d5e1bf2640097521dafe865b55.

23. Francis Lee and Joseph Chan, *Media and Protest Logics in the Digital Era: The Umbrella Movement in Hong Kong*, Oxford: Oxford University Press, 2018, 45.

24. For instance, see local scholar Simon Shen's blog post at https://tinyurl.com/y63hzq4f.

25. Ma Ngok, 'Value and Legitimacy Crisis in Post-Industrial Hong Kong', *Asian Survey* 51:4 (2011): 683–712, https://as.ucpress.edu/content/51/4/683.full.pdf+html.

26. William J. Duiker and Jackson Spielvogel, *The Essential World History*, Belmont, CA: Thomson/Wadsworth, 2008, 619.

27. Daniel Cohn-Bendit and Gabriel Cohn-Bendit, *Obsolete Communism: The Left-Wing Alternative*, trans. Arnold Pomerans, New York: McGraw-Hill, 1968, 41–3.

28. Wu Siu Wai, 'Xianggang gaodeng jiaoyu de fazhan ji guojihua de xiankuang' (The Development and Internationalisation of Higher Education in Hong Kong), *Hong Kong Teachers' Centre Journal* 6 (2017): 55–69, www.edb.org.hk/HKTC/download/journal/j16/A04.pdf.

29. Public Opinion Research Institute poll, available at www.pori.hk/pop-poll/ethnic-identity/q001.

30. Public Opinion Research Institute poll, available at www.pori.hk/hongkonger.

31. Andrew J. Nathan, 'How China Sees the Hong Kong Crisis: The Real Reasons Behind Beijing's Restraint', *Foreign Affairs*, 30 September 2019, www.foreignaffairs.com/articles/china/2019-09-30/how-china-sees-hong-kong-crisis.

32. 'Mental Health Review Report', Food and Health Bureau of the Hong Kong Government, www.fhb.gov.hk/download/press_and_publications/otherinfo/180500_mhr/e_mhr_full_report.pdf.

33. 'Lingda xuezhe fang 1.5 wan jihuizhe, cheng nianqingren pan hanwei daode' (Lingnan University Scholar Surveyed 15,000 Assembly Participants and Said that Youth Wish to Defend Morals), *Mingpao*, 29 November 2019. Translation by the author.

34. Interview by the author, 11 January 2020. Translation by the author.

35. Qiqingshangmian: He/yong fennu hutong, efa gaoya, chouhen gengshen' (Both Non-Violent Believers and the Braves are Furious and the Evil Laws Only Deepen their Hatred and All These are Written on their Faces), *Mingpao*, 6 October 2019. Translation by the author.

36. The original LIHKG post is no longer active, but it was reposted at https://autumnson-nwo.blogspot.com/2019/06/620-5pm-621.html.

37. 'Tao Hui zhifa fanfa' (Rupert Dover Knowingly Breaks the Law), *Apple Daily*, 30 April 2020.

38. 'Wo bu yuedu' (I Do Not Read), anonymous Facebook post, www.facebook.com/186269348933364/photos/a.186274605599505/410005619893068/?type=3&theater. Translation by the author.

39. '600 zhuancai xiaoshuidi huicheng wenxuan gonghai' (600 Specialists: Although Just Small Drops on their own When Converged they Turned into an Ocean of Campaign Literature), *Mingpao*, 9 September 2019.

40. Interview with Kyun Go, 20 January 2020. Translation by the author.

41. 'Xianggang "yongwupai" tan kangzheng kunjing: ziyuan haojin, weiyongwu taiduo, zhuliu shehui ye meiyou zuohao geming zhunbei' (Hong Kong 'Brave' Speaks About the Dilemma of Struggle: Lack of Resources, Too Many Fake Braves, and a Mainstream Society that is Not Yet Ready for Revolution), *The Storm Media*, 12 November 2019, www.storm.mg/article/1937595. Translation by the author.

42. 'The Divided God: A Letter to Hong Kong', *Chuang*, January 2020, http://chuangcn.org/2020/01/the-divided-god.

43. Barry Sautman and Hairong Yan, 'Localists and "Locusts" in Hong Kong: Creating a Yellow-Red Peril Discourse', *Maryland Series in Contemporary Asian Studies*, 2015:2, https://digitalcommons.law.umaryland.edu/mscas/vol2015/iss2/1/.

44. 'Jiudang shi zuihou yici zhengqu minzhu – Ventus Lau' (Take this as the Last Time Fighting for Democracy – Ventus Lau), *Apple Daily*, 30 October 2019.

45. Ventus Lau's Facebook account, publicly available until it was deleted. Hard copy available from the author. Translation by the author.

46. 'Dalu luke jie fansongzhong chuandan, "xiang liaojie Xianggang fasheng shenme shi"' (Mainland Visitors Took Anti-China Extradition Bill Leaflet, 'Want to Know What is Happening to Hong Kong'), *Stand News*, 7 July 2019.

47. 'Qingnian dui jilie kangzheng de taidu yousuo zhuanbian' (The Youth's Attitude Towards Radical Resistance has Changed), Hong Kong Institute of Asia-Pacific Studies, The Chinese University of Hong Kong, 1 September 2017, www.hkiaps.cuhk.edu.hk/eng/news.asp?details=1&ItemID=N20170901.

48. 'Jinban shimin zhuzhang shiweizhe yu zhengfu tong rangbu, yue qichengren liao laiyue chongtu chixu shenhuo genghuai' (Nearly Half of Respondents Advocate for both Protesters and Government to Concede, 70 percent Think Clashes in Coming Months Might Continue or Worsen), Hong Kong Institute of Asia-Pacific Studies, The Chinese University of Hong Kong, 6 September 2019, www.hkiaps.cuhk.edu.hk/wd/ni/20190906-164955_1.pdf.

49. 'Qishi hou canhui: Wo leizuo xiayidai' (The Post-Seventies Generation: We Failed the Next Generation), *Apple Daily*, 15 June 2019. Translation by the author.

50. 'Women yiwang xinshou de zongzhi yi wufa huiying zhege rijian benghuai de shijie?' (Is the Mission We Safeguarded in the Past No Longer Able to Respond to this Collapsing World?), *Mingpao*, 23 October 2019. Translation by the author.

51. '612 jijn bannian zhiyuan 7,964 ren' (612 Humanitarian Relief Fund Supported 7,964 People in Half a Year), *Apple Daily*, 7 January 2020.

52. 'Gangtie buhezuo yundong "shouzhongzhengqin"' (The Non-Cooperative Campaign against the MTR Officially Dies), *Mingpao*, 15 August 2019.

53. See the HK On Strike website at www.hkonstrike.com.

54. 'Xingonghui dengji sheng baibei, shouji 1578 zong' (New Union Registrations Rose One Hundred-Fold, Reaching 1578 Applications in the First Quarter), *Mingpao*, 13 April 2020.

55. 'Qishi wo haojing beiren qingsuan' (Actually I Fear Being Attacked), HK On Strike Telegram group, available online at www.hottg.com/hkonstrike/b644.html. Translation by the author.

56. 'Exclusive: Hong Kong Judges See Risks in Proposed Extradition Changes', Reuters, www.reuters.com/article/us-hongkong-politics-extradition-judges/exclusive-hong-kong-judges-see-risks-in-proposed-extradition-changes-idUSKCN1SZ09U.

57. 'Yiming yi lizhi de ducha: Baixushan, yao duidezhu ge botou' (Former Police Officer: White Shirt Colleagues, You Have to Live up to Your Oath), *Stand News*, 20 June 2019. Translation by the author.

58. Posted on Facebook but already vanished. Concerning Apple phones, later reports suggested that the police were now able to do just that.

59. See this post on the Police Relatives Connection Facebook group: www.facebook.com/PoliceRelativesConnection/photos/a.111212383545519/118728919460532. Translation by the author.

60. 'Jingyuan qinshu shou jihui cu duli diaocha, quanfu wu da shiweizhe' (Families of Police Officers Assemble for the First Time and Demand Independent Investigation, Tell Husbands Not to Hit Protesters), *Mingpao*, 26 August 2019. Translation by the author.

61. 'Unrest takes toll on police recruitment', *The Standard*, 9 April 2020, www.thestandard.com.hk/section-news/section/4/218047/Unrest-takes-toll-on-police-recruitment.

62. 'Sheyu nüyou weilai waimu tie feng Deng Bingqiang wenxuan yundong yilai shouzong xiuban fangbaojing beibu' (Off-Duty Riot Policeman Arrested Along with His Girlfriend and His Future Mother-in-Law for Putting Up Posters Making Fun of Police Head Deng Bingqiang), *Apple Daily*, 18 January 2020.

63. '4 wan gongpu wuju daya bibao zhonghuan "*nei mit dak zau ngo gung mou jyun zik wai, mit m lat ngo hoeng gong jan san fan*"' (Fearless of Retaliation, Forty Thousand Civil Servants Assemble in Central 'You Can Take Away my Post but You Cannot Take Away my Hong Kong Identity'), *Apple Daily*, 3 August 2019.

64. '8.2 gongwuyuan jihui diaocha – jiucheng gongpu cu cha Yuanlang shijian jing chuli shiwei shouduan' (Survey at the 8.2 Civil Servants Assembly – 90 percent Demand Investigation of Yuen Long Event and Police Handling of the Demonstration), *Mingpao*, 10 September 2019.

65. 'Jiankong zhuren hui: Jinghuang sun sifa' (Hong Kong Court Prosecutors Association: Police Lies Damage Legal System), *Apple Daily*, 3 September 2019.

66. 'Lianshu zhudong diaocha youwu jingyuan she gongzhi renyuan xingwei shidang' (ICAC Took the Initiative to Investigate Whether Police Officers Suspected of Misconduct in Public Office), *HK01*, 30 July 2019.

67. See Hu Xijin's Weibo post: www.weibo.com/1989660417/HygGLk46Y.

68. Quoting private discussion among friends.

69. 'Ba kaisa de gui kaisa, songzhong zhi song neidike' (Render unto Caesar that which is Caesar's, Only Extradite Mainland Visitors), *Mingpao*, 21 May 2019.

70. 'Meiyouren keyi chengwei gudao – huiying Liu Jintu xiansheng de "songzhong zhi song neidike"' (Nobody Can be an Isolated Island – a Response to Kevin Lau's 'Only Extradite Mainland Visitors' Remarks), *Mingpao*, 28 May 2019. Translation by the author.

71. 'Factbox: One City, Two Views: Hong Kong Residents Split by Age, Education on Support for Protests', Reuters, www.reuters.com/article/us-hongkong-protests-poll-factbox/factbox-one-city-two-views-hong-kong-residents-split-by-age-education-on-support-for-protests-idUSKBN1YZ0W0.

72. 'Fanmin meiyou fangqi xinyimin de yudi' (Pan-Democrats Cannot Afford Losing New Immigrants), *Mingpao*, 8 January 2016.

73. Stan Hok-Wui Wong, Ngok Ma, and Wai-man Lam, 'Migrants and Democratization: The Political Economy of Chinese Immigrants in Hong Kong', *Contemporary Chinese Political Economy and Strategic Relations: An International Journal* 2:2 (Aug–Sept 2016): 909–940, https://pdfs.semanticscholar.org/e150/f2c42837b5e855f6948fe72c66003159f497.pdf.

74. 'Yimin yu minzhuhua' (Immigrants and Democratisation), *Mingpao*, 29 August 2016.

75. 'Yimin bushi zhende tebie xihuan jianzhi' (Immigrants Do Not Particularly Like the Establishment Parties), *Stand News*, 24 August 2016.

76. 'Xianggang zhongwen daxue neidisheng dui fanxiuli yundong taidu wenjuan jieguo baogao' (Report on Questionnaire on HKCU Mainland Students' Attitude Towards Anti-Extradition Bill Movement), *Matters.news*, 14 October 2019, https://tinyurl.com/y4x5tzmn.

77. 'Onsite Survey Findings in Hong Kong's Anti-Extradition Bill Protests Research Report'.

78. 'O ji: Lida an zhongzhongzhizhong, jizhi wuqizhe' (Organised Crime and Triad Bureau: The PolyU Case is of Utmost Important, it is Tracking Down Weapons Makers) *Mingpao*, 29 January 2020.

79. 'Luo Fan Jiaofen: Shaonü bei wudao, wei "yongwupai" tigong mianfei xingfuwu' (Law Fan Chiu-fun: Young Girls were Misled into Providing Free Sex to 'the Braves'), *HK01*, 9 September 2019.

80. 'Fansongzhong yundong li de nüxing' (Discrimination against Women in the Anti-Extradition Bill Movement), Borderless Movement, Hong Kong, https://tinyurl.com/ybnpr3mh.

81. 'Nanya heyong chongqi connect "*ngo dei lau zyu gong jan hyut*"' (South Asian, Non-Violent Believers and 'the Braves' Connect – 'We all have Hong Kongers' Blood'), *Apple Daily*, 13 January 2020.

82. 'Mingtian shi he ni gay deyouxing' (Tomorrow is the Date of the Hong Kong Pride Parade), LIHKG, https://lihkg.com/thread/1724028/page/1.

CHAPTER 3

1. 'Wang Zhimin xia yingzhishi, you jianzhi shangjie koufu xin bufu' (Wang Zhimin Gives Strong Instructions, Certain Establishment Parties and Business Sectors Comply Unwillingly), *Mingpao*, 20 May 2019.

2. 'Yu wuli chongji bu qiege, minzhupai liao bu yingxiang jihui' (Pan-Democrats Had Not Distanced from Violent Conflict and Expected that this Would Not Affect the Assembly), *Mingpao*, 11 June 2019.

3. '612 jinzhong xing zaji' (Diary of the 12 June Action at Admiralty), *Stand News*, 12 June 2019. Translation by the author.

4. 'Bushui daxuesheng: Ziji qiantu ziji zhengqu' (College Students: We Fight for Our Future), *Apple Daily*, 13 June 2019. Translation by the author.

5. 'Yu Lin Zheng gexi – yige gaoji gongwuyuan' (High-Ranking Civil Servant – I Broke with Carrie Lam), *Apple Daily*, 4 July 2019.

6. 'Ren neng ba women zenmeyang ne?' (What Else Can they Do to Us?), *Mingpao*, 3 November 2019. Translation by the author.

7. 'Zheshi yige chi haizi de zhengquan – 7.1 wanshang wo zai lifahui nei kandao de nianqingren' (This is a Regime that Devours Children – my Observations of the Youth in the Legislature on the Night of 1 July), *Stand News*, 3 July 2019. Translation by the author.

8. 'Shiweizhe: Chuang lihui wei zhan duikang zhengfu juexin' (Protesters: Breaking into the Legislature is to Show our Determination to Confront the Government), *Mingpao*, 3 July 2019. Translation by the author.

9. 'Xianggangren kangzheng xuanyan' (Declaration of the Hong Kong Protesters), Medium, 2 July 2019, https://tinyurl.com/y62gudnv. Translation by the author.

10. Facebook account of Siu Yan, 5 July 2019.

11. 'Wuda suqiu "zhen puxuan" jian dai "Lin Zheng xiatai"', (Five Demands – Demand for 'Genuine Universal Suffrage' Gradually Replaces 'Carrie Lam Steps Down'), *Headline Daily*, 10 July 2019.

12. 'Qian ducha zai zhuanwen: Jiuji fuwei jinge chengjian, Xianggang jingcha hai jide ma?' (Former Police Officer: Do the Hong Kong Police Still Remember Saving Lives and Punishing Criminals?), *Stand News*, 29 July 2019.

13. 'Yiban AO de fenxiang' (Sharing by AO Group), Gold Water Hong Kong Facebook group, www.facebook.com/178965725523592/posts/233 6638383089638.

14. 'Guyuan baotu fei xinshi, cong sanyun shuoqi' (Hiring Rioters is Not New, it Began with the Umbrella Movement), *Mingpao*, 28 July 2019.

15. 'Liandeng wangmin huyu 8 yue 5 ri samba, quangang qiqu jihui' (LIHKG Netizens Appeal for Three Suspensions and Holding Assemblies in Seven Districts on 5 August), *Citizen News*, 30 July 2019.

16. '0805 Quangang dabagong dianpu ji tuanti yilanbiao' (Numbers of Striking Shops and Organisations in Different Parts of Hong Kong on August 5), https://docs.google.com/spreadsheets/d/1XudNUiaZdQ3p5lbveM6r9kyy LrAtttNZhovrIb_jalQ/edit#gid=1075505997.

17. 'Wo shi kongguan zhuren' (I Am an Air Traffic Controller), LIHKG, https://lihkg.com/thread/1458355/page/1. Translation by the author.

18. Danny Lee, 'Hong Kong Protests Have Caused Severe Turbulence at Cathay Pacific but has the Airline Done Enough to Appease Beijing after Heads Rolled at the Top?', *South China Morning Post*, www.scmp.com/news/hong-kong/transport/article/3023273/hong-kong-protests-have-caused-severe-turbulence-cathay.

19. 'Chen Yanlin fushi quanluo you keyi jing ying gongkai gengduo diaocha ziliao' (Chan Yin-lam's Naked and Floating Corpse is Suspicious, the Police Should Make Public More Investigative Information), *Apple Daily*, 15 October 2019.

20. 'Zhongda zhizhan' (The Battle of CUHK), *CUSP.hk*, http://cusp.hk/?page_id=8565. The author would like to thank Wong Hon Tung for giving advice on the first draft of this section.

21. 'Jing cuileidan shezhong zhongda, xuesheng qiyoudan wankang, gongfangzhan shushiren shang, xiaofang yu jing xieyi houtui zan pingxi' (Police Fire Tear Gas at CUHK, Students Respond with Petrol Bombs, Several Dozens Injured after Battle and Police Retreat After Negotiating with the University), *Mingpao*, 13 November 2019.

22. Author's interview, 4 April 2020.

23. '11.13 Zhongda qiantu taolunhui zhenghe' (Notes on the 13 November Meeting on the Future of CUHK), Facebook, www.facebook.com/cuspcusp/posts/2616595291734532. Translation by the author.

24. 'Gei zhendizhan shouzu de hua' (Words for the Comrades in War of Movement), LIHKG, https://lihkg.com/thread/1726362/page/1. Translation by the author.

25. 'Shoushang shi shili, xuesheng zhazhushang' (Student Lost Vision After Injury but Fought Again After Bandaged), *Apple Daily*, 18 November 2019.

26. This accusation might not be precise enough as technically speaking the president only appealed to students to give themselves up to the police. The management of PolyU did at one point report to the police but it concerned the theft of chemical materials from the laboratories.

27. 'Lida liushou xuesheng zhi quangang shimin shu' (PolyU Stay Behind Students' Letter to Citizens of Hong Kong), LIHKG, https://lihkg.com/thread/1732478/page/1.

28. 'Ceng xiangguo huisi, zimian huoxiaqu jianzheng minzhu, zhongqiang qingnian: Zidan dabusi xinnian' (The Youth Who Got Shot: I Thought of Dying but Encouraged Myself to Live to Witness Democracy – Bullets Can't Kill One's Belief), *Mingpao*, 24 November 2019.

CHAPTER 4

1. 'Dazhuan xuejie ji "wo yao lanchao" tuandui xinwengao quanwen' (Press Release from University Students and Scorched-Earth Team), LIHKG, https://lihkg.com/thread/1427184/page/1. Translation by the author.

2. 'How Pepe the Frog Became the Face of the Hong Kong Protests – Despite Cartoon Being a Symbol of Hate in US', *South China Morning Post*, www.scmp.com/lifestyle/arts-culture/article/3023060/how-pepe-frog-became-face-hong-kong-protests-despite-cartoon.

3. At an earlier stage the whole sentence read *bat duk fui bat got zik bat zi zaak*, or 'no to snitching, no to splitting up, no to finger-pointing'.

4. 'Dang dajia shengyin yulaiyuluan de shihou, dajia shi shihou fansi xia' (When Everyone's Opinion is Getting More Chaotic It is the Time to Reflect), LIHKG, https://lihkg.com/thread/1465463/page/1. Translation by the author.

5. Interview with C.N., 29 January 2019. Translation by the author.

6. 'Zhechang kangzheng yundong chuxian le yige haoda liekou, butu bukuai' (I Must Say a Big Breach has Arisen in this Struggle), LIHKG, https://lihkg.com/thread/1373488/page/1. Translation by the author. For more on the concept of 'moral abduction' see https://en.everybodywiki.com/Moral_Abduction.

7. See for instance Simon Lau Sai-leung's video at www.youtube.com/watch?v=az5RaUZ7nnY. Lau was a former full-time consultant of the Central Policy Unit of the Hong Kong government when Donald Tsang was the chief executive.

8. Jun Pang and Nickolas Tang, 'I Am Willing to Take a Bullet for You. Are You Willing to Go on Strike for Me?', *The Nation*, 12 March 2020, www.thenation.com/article/world/hong-kong-unions-strike.

9. '68% ren cheng jing guofen yongwu' (68 percent of Respondents Say Police Abuse Use of Violence), *Mingpao*, 16 August 2019.

10. 'Survey on "We HongKongers"'.

11. 'Mindiao: 66% ren xin 7.21 she "jing hei hezuo"' (Survey: 66 percent of Respondents Believe the 21 July Event Involved Collusion Between Police and Organised Crime), *Mingpao*, 23 October 2019.

12. 'Helifei wangshang diaocha: 95% zhi she duli diaocha weiyuanhui wei dixian, 87% bu gexi' (Survey of Non-Violence Believers: 95 percent Regards

Founding an Independent Investigation Committee as Bottom Line, 87 percent Refuse to Condemn "the Braves"), *HK01*, 17 August 2019.

13. 'Dalan shangpu haoshuang, shiji shang "*laai saai je*"' (Vandalising Shops Makes One Feel Good but Practically this is 'Disastrous'), LIHKG, https://lihkg.com/thread/1624117. Translation by author.

14. 'Jingfang kaiqiang yu shiweizhe shaoren zonghuo, gefang fanying tuxian de butong jiduan' (While Police Opened Fire Protesters Torched a Person, Different Responses Show Extremes), *BBC News* (Chinese Edition), www.bbc.com/zhongwen/trad/chinese-news-50387234.

15. 'Qingnian qiongmangzu neng tuoli kunjing ma?' (Can Young Working Poor Get Out from Dilemma?), The Hong Kong Federation of Youth Groups Youth Research Centre, 18 November 2014, https://tinyurl.com/y9stdtc8.

16. 'Fanji maigang caituan, yaoyou diliu suqiu!' (Counter-Attack Traitorous Tycoons, We Need a Sixth Demand), LIHKG, https://lihkg.com/thread/1498391/page/1.

17. 'Buxiao yijin, buyu diceng shouzu gexi' (Don't Laugh at Yi-Jin, Don't Spilt Up with Poor Comrades), Facebook, 14 January 2020, www.facebook.com/grassrootconcern/photos/a.628651940513607/3034664606578983.

18. See Jaco Chow's Facebook post at www.facebook.com/jaco.hendrix/posts/10206514743103691. Translation by the author.

19. 'Inglehart's theory was subsequently challenged and debated', see Musa, 'Was There a Silent Revolution?'.

20. Chin Wan, *Xianggang chengbang lun* (On the Hong Kong City-State), Hong Kong: Enrich Publishing, 2011, 152 and 158. Translation by the author.

21. 'Interview: Occupy Central Founder Benny Tai Yiu-ting', *Red Pepper*, 11 September 2014, www.redpepper.org.uk/the-spirit-of-civil-disobedience.

22. 'Lun bentu ziben he "kanghong baogang lianhe zhenxian"' (On Local Capital and a 'United Front for Fighting against Red Capital and Saving Hong Kong'), *Next Magazine*, 26 April 2017, https://hk.nextmgz.com/article/2_504059_0.

23. '"No doubt" UK meddling in Hong Kong – Galloway', www.youtube.com/watch?v=zF10WX3C8X4. Parts of the content of this section were originally written for the German website LUXEMBURG, see www.zeitschrift-luxemburg.de/weder-washington-noch-peking-selbstbestimmung-fuer-die-menschen-in-hongkong.

24. 'Tao Hui zhifa fanfa'.

25. Richard C. Bush, 'Political reform: Implications for U.S. policy', Brookings Institute, www.brookings.edu/research/hong-kong-political-reform-implications-for-u-s-policy.

26. 'United States-Hong Kong Policy Act of 1992', www.govtrack.us/congress/bills/102/s1731/summary.

27. 'Hong Kong Policy Act Report', US Department of State, www.state.gov/p/eap/rls/reports/2018/282787.htm.

28. 'Zhenggai fangfeng: Ke lieming 2022 xiugai, xiaoxi zhi tiwei houxuanrenshu keqing, fanmin cu gongkai chengnuo' (Breaking News on Political Reform Package: The Package could be Revised in 2022, Source Said, the Numbers of Members of Nomination Committee also Negotiable, Pan-Democrats Demand an Open Commitment), *Mingpao*, 28 January 2015.

29. 'Mei yiyuan: Zhengzhi xingyibu shi haoshi' (US Congressman: It is Good to See Political Reform Advancing Even Just One Step Further), *Mingpao*, 9 May 2015.

30. 'ICAC "a secret service"', *South China Morning Post*, 26 April 1994, www. scmp.com/article/71813/icac-secret-service. See also 'Zhimindi youling canrao jinri Xianggang' (The Colonial Ghost Still Haunting Today's Hong Kong), *Yazhou zhoukan*, 2 June 2013, www.yzzk.com/cfm/content_archive. cfm?id=1369280457919&docissue=2013-21.

31. 'Hong Kong Human Rights and Democracy Act (HKHRDA): A Progressive Critique', *The Owl*, 21 November 2019, https://tinyurl.com/yaj4keys.

32. 'The Divided God: A Letter to Hong Kong'.

33. See the Lausan Collective site at https://lausan.hk.

CHAPTER 5

1. The Chinese word 'long' (in Putonghua), or 'dragon' when translated into English, has very different connotations from the European origin of 'dragon', which signifies an evil beast. The Chinese 'lung' has a positive meaning, hence in later periods it came to symbolise the emperors.

2. In 2012, in a debate amongst young leftists the author argued for a left wing which simultaneously based itself on class solidarity, internationalism, and also being sensitive to the local identity discourse. But that thin layer of young leftists chose to be silent in the public debate.

3. 'Nanya heyong chongqi connect, "*ngo dei lau zyu gong jan hyut*"'.

4. 'Reference re Secession of Quebec', Supreme Court of Canada, 20 August 1998, https://scc-csc.lexum.com/scc-csc/scc-csc/en/item/1643/index.do.

5. See the Hong Kong Watch website at www.hongkongwatch.org/spotlight.

6. '2017 China Overseas Direct Investment Statistics Bulletin', The Ministry of Commerce of the People's Republic of China, et al., http://img.project. fdi.gov.cn//21/1800000121/File/201810/201810301102234656885.pdf.

7. 'Exclusive: Huawei CFO Linked to Firm that Offered HP gear to Iran', Reuters, 31 January 2013, https://uk.reuters.com/article/us-huawei-skycom/ exclusive-huawei-cfo-linked-to-firm-that-offered-hp-gear-to-iran-idUSBRE90U0CC20130131.

8. 'Bankers' Exits and Zombie Accounts: China's Shanghai Free Trade Zone Sputters', Reuters, 2 September 2019, www.reuters.com/article/ us-china-shanghai-ftz/banker-exits-zombie-accounts-chinas-shanghai-free-trade-zone-sputters-idUSKCN1VN01V.

9. 'Jiu weihu Xianggang gaodu zizhi shuoxie dashihua' (Let's Be Frank About Hong Kong's High Degree of Autonomy), *Huanqiu* (Global Times), 27 August 2019, https://opinion.huanqiu.com/article/9CaKrnKmtV3. Translation by the author.

10. 'Coronavirus: China's First Confirmed Covid-19 Case Traced Back to November 17', *South China Morning Post*, 13 March 2020, www.scmp.com/news/china/society/article/3074991/coronavirus-chinas-first-confirmed-covid-19-case-traced-back.

11. Qun Li, Xuhua Guan, et al., 'Early Transmission Dynamics in Wuhan, China, of Novel Coronavirus-Infected Pneumonia', *The New England Journal of Medicine* 382 (2020): 1199–1207, www.nejm.org/doi/full/10.1056/NEJMoa2001316.

12. 'How Early Signs of the Coronavirus Were Spotted, Spread and Throttled in China', *The Straits Times*, 28 February 2020, www.straitstimes.com/asia/east-asia/how-early-signs-of-the-coronavirus-were-spotted-spread-and-throttled-in-china.

13. 'Jikong zaoshang bao, zhongyang weibao jieri qifen shi liangji' (CDC Reported in the Morning, the Central Government a Prioritised Festival Atmosphere, Resulting in the Missing of Opportunity), *Mingpao*, 17 February 2020.

14. 'Highlights: China's Xi Recounts Early Role in Coronavirus Battle', Reuters, 17 February 2020, www.reuters.com/article/us-china-health-xi-highlights/highlights-chinas-xi-recounts-early-role-in-coronavirus-battle-idUSKBN20B1MC.

15. 'Jikong zaoshang bao, zhongyang weibao jieri qifen shi liangji'.

16. 'Who Says the New Year Has No Flavor? More Than 40,000 Families in Wuhan's Baibuting Community Dine Together', *Australia51.com*, 19 January 2020, https://en.australia51.com/article/87FD1ED5-1166-90E8-B8DC-AB55E0DBF2D5.

17. Shengjie Lai, Nick W. Ruktanonchai, et al., 'Effect of Non-Pharmaceutical Interventions for Containing the COVID-19 Outbreak in China', MEDRXIV, no date, www.medrxiv.org/content/10.1101/2020.03.03.20029843v3.full.pdf.

18. The term was first coined by the writer Wu Si in his book *Qian guize – Zhongguo lishi zhong de zhenshi youxi* (Hidden Rules – The Real Game in Chinese History), Kunming: Yunnan People's Press, 2001.

19. Zhongjie Li, Shengjie Lai, et al., 'Hand, Foot and Mouth Disease in China: Evaluating an Automated System for the Detection of Outbreaks', Bulletin of the World Health Organization 2014:92 (2014): 656–663, www.who.int/bulletin/volumes/92/9/13-130666.pdf.

20. Wang Longde, 'Internet-Based China Information System for Disease Control and Prevention', paper presented at the Twelfth World Congress on Public Health, World Health Organization, www.researchgate.net/

publication/268103880_Internet-based_China_information_system_for_disease_control_and_prevention.

21. 'Yiqing chu zhibao xitong shixiao, wu yujing shiji' (The Direct Report System Failed in the Early Stage of the Epidemic, Missing the Chance for Early Alarm), *Mingpao*, 16 March 2020.

22. 'Secure a Decisive Victory in Building a Moderately Prosperous Society in All Respects and Strive for the Great Success of Socialism with Chinese Characteristics for a New Era', transcript of speech delivered by Xi Jinping at the Nineteenth National Congress of the Communist Party of China, *China Daily*, 18 October 2017, www.chinadaily.com.cn/interface/flipboard/1142846/2017-11-06/cd_34188086.html. Italics added.

23. The renowned scholar Lin Yu-Sheng considered 'national characteristics studies' or 'cultural-intellectualistic approach' as unviable categories of analysis. See *Zhongguo jijin sichao de qiyuan yu houguo* (The Origins of Chinese Radicalism and its Consequences), Taipei: Linking Publishing, 2019, 179.

24. Kou Yanding and Yuan Tianpeng, *Kecaozuo de minzhu—Luobote yishi guize xiaxiang quanjilu* (A Workable Democracy – *Robert's Rules of Order* Going Rural), Hangzhou: Zhejiang University Press, 2012, 39. Translation by the author.

25. Interview by the author, 11 January 2020. Translation by the author.

26. 'Statement of Hong Kong Bar Association on proposal of National People's Congress to enact National Security Law in Hong Kong', Hong Kong Bar Association, 25 May 2020, www.hkba.org/sites/default/files/20200525%20-%20Proposal%20of%20National%20People%27s%20Congress%20to%20enact%20National%20Security%20Law%20in%20Hong%20Kong%20%28E%29.pdf

27. 'Xi Jinping lun fazhi: "Dangda haishi fada shi weimingti, shi zhengzhi xianjing"' (Xi Jinping on Rule of Law: "Which is Superior to the Other, the Party or the Law" is a Pseudo Proposition and a Political Trap), *CPC News*, 11 May 2015, http://cpc.people.com.cn/xuexi/n/2015/0511/c385475-26978527.html.

28. Wang Feiling, *Zhonghua zhixu: Zhongyuan, shijie diguo yu Zhongguo liliang de benzhi* (The China Order: Centralia, World Empire, and the Nature of Chinese Power), Taipei: Gusa Publishing, 2018, 16.

29. Dietrich Rueschemeyer, Evelyne Huber Stephens, Evelyne Huber, and John D. Stephens, *Capitalist Development and Democracy*, Chicago, University of Chicago Press, 1992.

30. 'China's Social Media Users Call for Sacking of "Triumphalist" Academic, as Anti-Hype Movement Grows', *South China Morning Post*, 3 August 2018, www.scmp.com/news/china/policies-politics/article/2158054/chinas-social-media-users-call-sacking-triumphalist.

31. 'Zhongmei jingji shili haiyou henda chaju, yaoyou jipogan weijigan' (The Economic Strength Gap between China and US Remains Huge, an

Awareness of Urgency and of Crisis are Necessary), *ifeng.com*, 22 February 2020.

32. 'Zhengfu shenye fa 1900 zi gao, ji meishanghui cu huafu xiaojian dui renda gongji' (At Midnight the Government Released a 1900-Word Statement Hoping that the American Chamber of Commerce Could Persuade Washington to Tone Down the Latter's Attack on the National People's Congress), *Citizen News*, 28 May 2020.

33. Lawrence J. Lau, *Tianta bu xialai – Zhongmei maoyi zhan ji weilai jingji guanxi* (Heaven Won't Fall – the China–US Trade War and their Future Economic Relation), Hong Kong: Chinese University of Hong Kong Press, 2019, 70, 85.

34. Janos Kornai, 'Economists Share Blame for China's "Monstrous" Turn', *Financial Times*, 10 July 2019, www.ft.com/content/f10ccb26-a16f-11e9-a282-2df48f366f7d.

35. 'Full Text of Clinton's Speech on China Trade Bill', Institute for Agriculture and Trade Policy (US), 9 March 2000, www.iatp.org/sites/default/files/Full_Text_of_Clintons_Speech_on_China_Trade_Bi.htm.

36. 'Report on Trade and Economic Relations with China', Committee on International Trade, EU Parliament, 27 January 2009, www.europarl.europa.eu/sides/getDoc.do?type=REPORT&reference=A6-2009-0021&language=GA.

37. 'Honkon e no "kokka anzen-hō" dōnyū ni tsuyoku kōgi suru', Japanese Communist Party, 28 May 2020, www.jcp.or.jp/web_policy/2020/05/post-839.html. Translation by author with the help of 'Z.W.'

38. Kazuo Shii, 'JCP Calls for Immediate Cessation of Suppression in Hong Kong', Japanese Communist Party, 14 November 2019, www.jcp.or.jp/english/jcpcc/blog/2019/11/20191114-immediate-cessation-of-suppression-in-hong-kong.html.

39. 'Japanese Communist Party's Long Goodbye to its China Comrades', *Nikkei Asian Review*, 19 February 2020, https://asia.nikkei.com/Politics/Inside-Japanese-politics/Japanese-Communist-Party-s-long-goodbye-to-its-China-comrades.

40. Facebook post by Joshua Wong, available at www.facebook.com/1023721804/posts/10218804618959572/?d=n. Translation by the author.

Index

Thanks to our Patreon Subscribers:

Abdul Alkalimat
Andrew Perry

Who have shown their generosity and comradeship in difficult times.

The Pluto Press Newsletter

Hello friend of Pluto!

Want to stay on top of the best radical books
we publish?

Then sign up to be the first to hear about our
new books, as well as special events,
podcasts and videos.

You'll also get 50% off your first order with us
when you sign up.

Come and join us!

Go to bit.ly/PlutoNewsletter